THE END OF THE JEWISH PEOPLE?

THE END OF
THE JEWISH PEOPLE?

GEORGES FRIEDMANN

TRANSLATED FROM THE FRENCH

BY ERIC MOSBACHER

1967

DOUBLEDAY & COMPANY, INC.

GARDEN CITY, NEW YORK

Contents

Preface

This book, the result of two visits to Israel in 1963 and 1964, is a reflection on the Israeli experience and hence also on the past, present and future of the Jews. It is an attempt at an objective survey, and also, by the very nature of the subject, an act of personal testimony, the statement of a personal attitude toward Judaism. In these circumstances I must begin by placing it against a personal background and explaining briefly how and why it came to be written.

I received a first shock in October 1940, when I discovered the shattering importance that the fact of being labeled a Jew could have for me. I still have the official notification under the letter-heading of the Vichy Ministry of Education informing me that henceforth I was subject to special laws. Unless I appealed for special treatment, I should be unable to remain in the teaching profession.

Hitherto I had been one of those who are called "marginal" or "peripheral" Jews by their religious fellows. Having been born in Paris into a family in which the traditional observances had been given up and "mixed" marriage was no problem, and being deeply identified with France, her culture and her way of life, and with a circle of friends and colleagues in which no one asked questions about my "racial" origins or religious beliefs, I had never suffered from anti-Semitism, though my name indicated that I was a Jew, and I had never felt discriminated against in French society, even at school. I had never attended a synagogue service, or, I believe, met a rabbi. During several visits to Poland between 1932 and 1939 I had observed virulent forms of anti-Semitism, both inside and outside the ghettos. These disgusted me, just as the brutalities of the Ku Klux Klan in Alabama disgusted me, but not more or differently. At that time I believed (and my visits to the Soviet Union still allowed me to hope) that the "Jewish question" would be solved by proletarian revolutions all over the world. Those bearded, ringleted Jews, with their dietary laws and religious taboos, seemed to me to be utterly different from "us," the "lost," assimilated Jews of France. Memories of the Dreyfus case, which my father had told me about, blended poorly in my mind and sensibilities with the Jewish crowds in Warsaw or Lodz. I did not then have the sense of "interdependence" with those men and women of the Polish ghettos that, after cruel experiences and reflections, I have with the handful of their survivors today.

In October 1940, it was different. I was thrown out of my profession as if I were unworthy to exercise it and condemned to unemployment with other similarly placed members of the French community to whom I had not felt myself bound by any particular tie. Both intellectually and emotionally this was a shattering blow. For some weeks, in spite of the support of my friends, I was shaken to the core; the very foundations of my being trembled. I had hastily to face up to this brutal assault and build new defenses to meet it. What did it mean? The Nazis were in occupation of France, imposing racialism on my country with their boot-heels. It was not France that imposed this outrage on me, excluding me from her schools, but Hitler and Goebbels. France had nothing to do with it. I tried to see her, and indeed did see her, still intact in the person of my friends (all of whom I should like to mention here, both the living and the dead). Did they not behave toward me as if nothing had changed? Thanks to them, and to my masters Lucien Febvre and Marc Bloch—the latter a symbol of the French Judaism that was willing to sacrifice life itself rather than suffer exclusion from France—it did not take me long to put these events in their historical perspective. I made myself a motto for my private use—*civis gallicus sum*, I am a French citizen. No matter what happened, that was what I was and would remain. Never having made any concealment of my origins in a France that was still free, in the darkness of the winter of 1940 I pondered the question of what being a Jew meant to me. I was neither a believer in the Jewish religion nor was I a Zionist, believing in the existence of a Jewish nation, and, of course, I knew that the work of modern anthropologists had reduced the idea of a Jewish "race" to nothing.

The self-questioning forced on me by the laws of Vichy did not last long. In January 1941, I joined a French Resistance network, and that restored me to a community in which discrimination was non-existent. A paradoxical effect of that unhappy time was that, in the course of the modest underground missions I undertook, my roots in French soil were reinforced. "Gaston Fromentin," and some other personages who used the same initials, had the unforgettable experience of comradeship with men and women coming from many provinces and many occupations who, over and above all their differences, were united by determination and hope. Thanks to them, in the course of those black years I had some of the most stimulating revelations I have had in my life of nobility of character, charity and fraternity.

In short, the French resistance demonstrated the soundness of my motto *civis gallicus sum*. Hence, as soon as the invader was driven out, and with him his infamous laws, I confess that the "Jewish problem" again ceased to be living and immediate to me. There were so many other problems that absorbed our energies and exercised our hopes in a France faced with the tasks of reconstruction. In August 1944, I rejoiced in her restored liberty, the liberty that had returned to the soil of the France I had not left.

Early in 1963, when I first set foot in the Promised Land, I was ill-prepared for the living experience of Judaism. The problems that I had been interested in, both in France and abroad, had nothing whatever to do with Israel. All my work, whether concerned with the Americas or in Europe, with this side of the Iron Curtain or the other, centered round the same questions: The human race has been plunged into the adventure of technology, today on a world, tomorrow perhaps on a cosmological, scale; man is at grips with the products of his

genius. Which nations, understanding what is at stake, will,
thanks to their institutions, their characteristics and traditions,
and their inhabitants' art of living, be able to keep this phenomenon under control, and to what extent? How will the
economically most advanced societies "manage" in the face of
the endless proliferation of new stimuli resulting from the development of the applied sciences, revolutionizing men's work
and leisure, rich in exhilarating and fearful promises and monstrous threats to their liberties, their mental balance, their happiness, and their very life? In the Promised Land a few hundred
thousand Jews, having defeated their enemies and reclaimed land
that had been neglected since time immemorial, had re-estab-
lished a state and opened its gates to all other Jews willing and
able to join them. How would these heirs to one of the most
ancient wisdoms, that of Moses and the prophets, further enriched by their scholars through the ages, "manage" in the face
of technical progress? Would they discover how to put it fully
in the service of man, both mentally and physically, and master
it? Or would they, too, like the men of the great cities and
societies of the West, be threatened by its mastering them?
Such were the questions in my mind at the beginning of February 1963, when I took off for Jerusalem from Lydda airport,
which was in the center of an area scattered with tents, currently
being used as pasture for goats, sheep and camels by Bedouin
tribesmen who had been driven from the Negev by months of
drought.

During my two stays in Israel these questions remained in
my mind, but they were submerged and transformed in a maze
of problems, a sometimes inextricable tangle of economic cal-
culations, exhausting political controversies, social programs,
pioneering institutions, spiritual and religious anxieties. I went
to Israel to observe a sociological experiment in a particular
setting, but I found something quite different. Coming to
grips with Judaism, discussing its role and the mission it attributes to itself in the world, I became personally involved in
a special way. True, the possible contribution of the Israelis to
the humanization of technical civilization remained a central

preoccupation. But on top of it were grafted questions about the "Jewish people" and the Jewish religion, the relations between Jewish messianism and technical progress, the future of the state of Israel and that of the Third World, the destiny of Judaism as written in its 3000-year history, and the universal recognition of man by man.

My encounter with Israel was, in fact, my first encounter with Judaism. With its multiple repercussions it was infinitely more disturbing than the shock of October 1940.

To a Jew, studying Israel means more than observing it. Faced with the efforts and the difficulties, the greatnesses and the weaknesses, the successes and failures (which I have not concealed) of a community that is a kaleidoscope of men of all colors from five continents and one hundred and two countries, who have drained marshes, irrigated deserts, caused new towns to rise from rock and sand and created out of nothing new ports and urban landscapes often as ugly as our own, why could I not be a mere observer? Why, in the crowded bus that took me from the hostel at Rehavia to the hills of Beit Hakerem, in the midst of that relaxed throng whose dominant note was provided by gay, free, confident, athletic young people dressed in bright colors, did I feel as happy as if their freedom and gaiety and confidence were my own? Or why did I feel I was among close relatives when I saw boys and girls lying about on the grass of the campus of the Hebrew University, their books at their feet, talking in the sunshine of a precocious spring, their eyes sometimes exchanging the message of an approaching idyll?

Visiting Israel is certainly a disturbing experience to any Jew, however peripheral or marginal a Jew he may be. It may rouse his enthusiasm or irritate him, but it will certainly shake him. If the most "assimilated" visitor stays there long enough, and particularly if he acquires deeper contacts by working with people, it will establish itself irrevocably in his heart and mind. Israel raises questions, forces him to see where he stands. There are some in whom it stimulates only interest and curiosity. In others it arouses the "temptation of Israel," the desire to share in the experience, or regret at being too old for it. Even if one is not "Israel-centered," has not considered taking part in an *aliya* and is neither a mystic nor an ordinary believer, one has a sense of interdependence (which is analyzed in the course of this book) with the fate of all who are known as Jews and are considered by the world to be the descendants of that minority of a minority that nearly twenty centuries ago refused to recognize Jesus as the Messiah. Again, it is this sense of interdependence that gives a special interest to the possibility of an Israeli society, which would not be "just another": this means a society in which the spirit of the *kibbutzim* might open up a new way to socialism, or, alternatively, in which the aspiration to be a "prophetic nation" would fulfill the promise of scripture, confirming the vocation of a chosen people of priests and right-eous men.

Israel also forces the Jewish observer, in spite of all his ret-icence, to ask himself what his Jewishness is and what it means to him. Does the resurrection of a state of Israel demonstrate the eternity of the Jewish people and their mission, which is the cornerstone of the faith of religious Jews? Or are the two million Jews gathered in Palestine today creating a new nation, a new nationality, endowed with physical and mental character-istics that increasingly differentiate them from Jews brought up in the communities and ghettos of the Diaspora? To what extent do young *sabras* born in Israel identify themselves as Jews, and to what extent can they still be regarded as such? Are we reduced to the choice between an almost mystical conception of Jewishness and another based on history, sociology and social psychology? Or are we to admit that the survival of the Jews is to be explained largely by anti-Semitism, as observers com-ing from many different horizons hold?

The visitor to Israel cannot avoid thinking about anti-Sem-itism. Every day he meets reminders of its existence—above all, the grim monument of Yad Vashem, erected on the outskirts of Jerusalem, in memory of the six million Jews exterminated by the Nazis. How was that massacre possible in the twentieth century? The establishment of an independent state on this strip of Palestine, conquered but still bitterly disputed, sends one back to the imperatives that explain it without, in the eyes of many people, justifying it. How can such a visitor, after spending several months there, fail to discern among political leaders, teachers and the religious a paradoxical but increasing anxiety at seeing the sources and very substance of Jewish life vanishing with the decline of anti-Semitism?

A consideration of anti-Semitism could not be omitted from this book, which is an attempt to observe and understand, undertaken by an agnostic Jew who, in tackling these problems in which so many affective elements are involved, hopes not to offend religious susceptibilities, whether Jewish or Christian. As its concluding words emphasize, this book is steeped in an anxiety to which I felt acutely indebted while writing it and wished to pay off in part.

Vallangoujard, December 1st, 1964.

For the American edition, a certain number of statistical data among the most important, have been brought up to date by the author.

I greatly regret being unable to mention all those in Israel who helped me with their courtesy, knowledge and advice. I alone am responsible for mistakes of omission or commission. But I must at least express my gratitude to the Hebrew University of Jerusalem (and in particular to E. Poznansky, its academic secretary), whose guest I was on two occasions, and to the Technion at Haifa; to Professors Gershom Sholem, Jacob Katz, S. N. Eisenstadt, Louis Guttman, J. Ben David, and S. N. Herman; to Yonina Talmon, Rivka Bar-Josef, and Judith Shuval; to Claude Vigée; to Menahem Rosner, and Jochanan Omri, who permitted me to live in their communities and to discuss their admirable experiment with them and with other leaders of the *kibbutz* federations; to Marc Jarblum and his comrades of the Histadrut; and to J. Rash, the representative of Hashomer Hatzair in France.

Doris Donath, research assistant at the National Centre for

Scientific Research (Paris), who has been engaged in Israel for several years on an important study of the immigrants from North Africa, was an able and loyal assistant during both my visits. In Paris, the collaboration of Marie-Thérèse Basse was, as always, extremely helpful.

THE END OF THE JEWISH PEOPLE?

1

A First Approach

Israel is a remarkable state in many respects. In the first place it is a crucible without parallel anywhere in the world. We shall see later that application of the term "crucible" to Israel is questionable; it suggests the American "melting pot," and must be accompanied by specific qualifications and reservations. We shall nevertheless use it as a preliminary description of a phenomenon that strikes every observer—the powerful absorptive effect on people coming from one hundred and two different countries, the tremendous physical and moral influence on them of a new environment in which nature, work, men and institutions make their daily impact and the combined effects of climate, society, culture, values and religion have forged a powerful instrument of human transformation.[1]

The crucible's power is manifest on all sides. The most striking demonstration is the young who tomorrow will occupy the responsible positions in the administration, the economy and the army. Among the students of the Hebrew University, though most are of Ashkenazi origin (young "orientals" still have little access to higher education[2]), it is impossible to recognize dominant morphological types by color of hair, skin or eyes or by size or features. Individuals with blue eyes and fair hair are by no means uncommon. The same is true in the factories, where the mixture is more complete, since there are many North

[1] There are those who resist the transformation. There are immigrants who for various reasons return to their country of origin or go to some third country, and there are also among the indigenous Jewish population a few hundred intransigents, the Natorei Karta, who refuse to acknowledge the new state.

[2] *Cf.* Chapter 6, "The Second Israel."

African workers (Tunisians, Algerians, and above all Moroccans), Egyptians, who are often skilled workers or foremen, and Iraqis, Persians and Yemenis.

In the *kibbutzim* marriages are rather more numerous than in Israeli society as a whole, and these young people take no notice, or very little, of economic or ethnic considerations, to which much more weight is still attached in urban areas, among the middle class, and even among intellectuals and in certain working-class groups. The most unexpected marriages are quite commonplace, and what handsome children result! I recall, for instance, those I saw at B.S., the offspring of Sarah, an American girl from Brooklyn, and the *sabra* Uri, whose grandparents escaped from a ghetto in Bukovina; and those at the G.H. *kibbutz*, whose parents were a young woman from the Yemen (many Yemeni girls are magnificent creatures) and the son of a German lawyer who arrived with the big *aliya* of 1935; and the two small boys I saw at R., children of a Polish agricultural expert and his Mexican-Jewish child-wife who, wearing a brightly colored dress for the feast of Purim, with her roguish little face and her black eyes shining under her sombrero, might have come straight from a dance in a Mexican village.

Wherever the traveler goes, by bus or by *sheirut*, on the beach at Eilat or Ashkelon, in the fields of Galilee or the streets of Tel Aviv, or on a factory floor at Dimona or Arad, he is plunged into the same biological caldron. This is also true of the *shikunim* of the Haifa area and those of Afuleh or Beit Shean, where the children of the last wave of immigrants mingle at their games and achieve the "fusion of communities" to which their parents often resist in their homes or at their places of work. One Friday afternoon on the Ashdod road I met a Moroccan with a long gray beard, wearing his best *kipah* and a big woolen cloak for the sabbath. He could speak nothing but Arabic. We gave him a lift in our car with his son, a boy of about ten, whom he was taking, or rather who was taking him (because the lad had already learned Hebrew at his *ulpan* and was very alert) to family prayers and ritual wine-drinking with relatives in the town.

The population of Israel resulting from such unprecedented mingling of populations has increased at a rate that is also unprecedented. Up to the foundation of the state on May 14, 1948, there had been six big *aliyot* which increased the Jewish population of Palestine from 24,000 in 1882 to 170,000 in 1930, 445,000 in 1939, after the fifth *aliya* which followed the Nazi persecutions, and 629,000 in December 1947. After the establishment of the state and the promulgation of the "Law of the Return," which abolished all restrictions on the immigration of Jews from anywhere in the world and invited them to come and establish themselves in Israel, the pace quickened. The population numbered 914,700 in January 1949, more than a million in December of the same year, 1,629,500 at the end of 1952, and 2,598,400 on January 1, 1966. It doubled in ten years (1949–59) and nearly quadrupled in seventeen (1947–64).

Before the establishment of the state, immigration was almost exclusively from central and western Europe; depending on the period, Russia, Poland and Germany provided the bulk of it. The armistice restricted the territory of Israel to an area of 12,500 square miles, and here 1,285,450 Jews immigrated between January 1949 and January 1966. But the majority of these were from Jewish communities in Africa or Asia. The 1949 Operation "Flying Carpet" removed 100 per cent of the Jews in the Yemen, and Libya (98 per cent), Iraq (97 per cent), Egypt (93 per cent), and Syria (89 per cent) were not far behind. The movement from Morocco (60 per cent) and Tunisia (70 per cent) was not on the same scale, and most Algerian Jews (80 per cent) chose to settle in France. At the beginning of 1966 the population of Israel included about 212,400 Muslims, 57,100 Christians (chiefly Arab converts) and 29,800 Druses (on the Lebanon border). In spite of the scale of recent *aliyot*, *sabras* born on Palestinian soil constituted 40.4 per cent of the 2,299,100 Jewish inhabitants. Of these 28.3 per cent were of Asian or African and 31.3 per cent of European or American origin. The displacement of the center

of gravity toward the so-called "oriental" countries has had immense consequences and caused grave problems for Israel in
every field.

REMOLDING ADULTS

It is easier to mold children physically and morally, to adapt
them to the progress made in fifteen years in the fields of
hygiene, education and health, than it is to remold adults. Many
of those who settled in Palestine in the course of the early
aliyot, particularly the Zionist pioneers, the idealist *halutzim*,
constituted an elite. Among the founders of the first *kibbutzim*
who laid the foundations for a socially and psychologically revolutionary experience there were a great many students, engineers, doctors and lawyers who came from petty bourgeois or
bourgeois environments. While draining marshes and irrigating
the desert they were themselves reborn. The first generation of
pioneers are dead, though there are still some survivors (the
comrades of Ben-Gurion) who occupy leading positions in the
state or are elder statesmen in the political parties, the Knesset, the Histadrut or the *kibbutz* federations. In Israel one still
comes across men and women in the fine flower of old age
whose radiant personalities are obviously the result of militant
and creative lives. Obviously there was first-rate material here
which flourished magnificently in an atmosphere of struggle and
hope. The official ideology of the Soviet Union for a long time
attributed the shortcomings of state-educated citizens to "survivals of capitalism" and claimed that a new kind of society
was producing a new kind of man. A new kind of man has
not been produced in Israel, but at all levels, in schools,
factories, "development towns," co-operatives in town and
country, in administration, the trade unions and the army, there
is an unusual proportion of human beings of high quality.

Such persons throng into my memory. There was Moshe
S., for instance, a strapping, handsome fellow who looked like
a suntanned Swede. He was the only member of his family to

escape from Galicia in 1940 (many of the builders of the new society in Israel are sole survivors of exterminated families). After escaping he became a worker at Saratov and then at Tashkent, immigrated in 1946, fought with the Palmah, entered the Hebrew University at the age of thirty-five, and became an archaeologist. He showed me the site he was excavating at R.R., at the gates of Jerusalem, with deep love and knowledge. He is perfectly relaxed and at ease, and is thoroughly at home in the fields of archaeology and history. He explained to me his theories about the dating and identification of the remains of Netofa, a town mentioned in the Old Testament, which he is excavating under the direction of Professor A. He is an agnostic, and is opposed to orthodox Judaism and its hold on public and private life and, of course, to the extremists of Mea Shearim. "The students of the Hassidic *yeshivot* and the young fanatics of Natorei Karta ought to be compelled to do military service," he said. "All those people, fathers and sons alike, belong not to the new age, but to the old."

Then there is Miriam H., a cheerful and vigorous woman in her fifties, who came of a solid bourgeois family in Basel. Her businessman husband professed Zionist principles, but was comfortable in Switzerland, where the small Jewish community had little reason to uproot itself. She accompanied him on a visit to Palestine and stayed on, allowing her husband to return alone to his business and his comforts in Switzerland, and she ended by settling in Palestine permanently. After doing various jobs at Tel Aviv, Haifa and Beersheba, she now has a responsible post in a government department. She still preserves the outward appearance of a plump and well-cared-for Swiss middle-class woman, but over and above that she is a cultivated and enthusiastic Israeli, taking part in a dangerous and enthralling adventure. If she had stayed in Switzerland, to which she returns every summer to visit her family, she would, as she says herself, have been irrevocably condemned to a comfortable life of receiving and paying calls, tea parties and cream cakes, interrupted at regular intervals by cozy but empty holidays. As it is, her work causes her to travel a great deal, spend herself, make decisions.

She represents an extreme case of personal transformation; a vast distance separates her point of departure from her point of arrival. In the old days in the Soviet Union, during the period of the first five-year plans, I often met men and women who were living as she is. I also know some in France, but mostly in a religious or stoical perspective, and they are rarer.

In Israel such types abound. Gideon F., for example, at the age of thirty-five was devoting all his thoughts and energies to the redevelopment of *moshavim* (the settlements on the frontiers which are required for both military and economic reasons and which are the responsibility of a special organization, the Karen Kayemeth Leisrael, or Jewish National Fund) that had been unwisely established among the rocks of the mountains of Judea, where agriculture was bound to fail (in the eyes of many of the founding fathers and their disciples agriculture was the panacea of the Jewish renascence). Gideon was retraining the inhabitants, most of whom were North Africans, teaching them goldsmith's and silversmith's work and working in bronze; and he had succeeded in imbuing these people, who had passed through so many trials, to which the disappointment of unsuccessful farming in Israel was added, with his own faith. I watched them and listened to them at work in their poorly equipped workshop. They were full of enthusiasm, confident that they were on the right road. They already had many orders for their simply and carefully designed chessmen, and their jewelry was going to be put on show at an exhibition at Tel Aviv. Gideon, a former skilled mechanic, is both a visionary and a practical man, as is Shmuel D., now in his fifties and a militant leader of the Histadrut, for which he fights on all fronts—against the mounting tide of the private sector, the *nouveaux riches* and the speculators who ridicule the very name of socialism, the young technocrats to whom the pioneers are a lot of old squares, the bureaucrats, and the lukewarm members of his own movement. Shmuel, rationalist and atheist though he is, has nevertheless preserved the messianic spirit. Thanks to a handful of men like him, the prophetic spirit still survives in the "White Kremlin" (the nickname by which the complex of buildings that house the Histadrut headquarters is sometimes referred to in Tel Aviv) and the principles for which the founders of the Histadrut stood are not yet dead.

Those principles also survive in the excellent athlete Jonathan P., secretary and leading spirit of a *kibbutz* in Galilee, where he practices them with unvarying simplicity every day. Naturalness and simplicity are the very stuff of the "new" men and women of Israel, the essence of their personality and all that they do. The best of the *kibbutznikim* are engaged in a daily struggle to ensure the success of the most remarkable experiment in communal living that has ever been attempted. Jonathan is one of those who irrigate it with their life-blood, defend it against hazards both within and without, face the special problems of their environment—those of education and the family, technical progress, the demand for privacy and private happiness, the needs of the aging and the aged, the constant readaptation of communal values necessary in a society in which selfishness and pleasure-seeking and the very human appetite for wealth and power are now raising their heads. At a distance of thousands of miles the memory of Jonathan and his wife Rivka is an inspiring one to anyone who has spent even a few days with them. No less tonic is the memory of Sarah, the young American student who came from Brooklyn to spend a holiday at the frontier *kibbutz* of B.S., near the Gaza strip, which was infested with *fidayim* ("Volunteers for death") and starving "infiltrators." She stayed, so she told me, "because there were a lot of good-looking boys there," or at any rate one particular boy, Uri, who was in charge of the fruit plantations. Their wedding party is still talked about at B.S. We spent hours discussing with them the economic difficulties of their young *kibbutz*, the aid provided in the form of technicians and advisers by a rich and famous *kibbutz* in the valley of Jezreel, and the new prospects opened up by the establishment of a small canning factory.

When I apologized for having taken too much of her time she replied: "No harm, we love the subject." There were many unforgettable meetings; many faces, both young and old, marked by exertion and serenity.

On all these people the Israeli crucible has had a happy effect. The process was certainly aided by the selection of individuals in a period of struggle and danger and an institutional framework in which Jewish idealism and pioneering energy remained alive and active. But a large part was also played by the physical and moral remolding of individuals in a new environment. Apart from the intellectual elite, many central European Jews belonged to closed communities traditionally restricted to commerce, in which small traders, artisans and shopkeepers were not entirely averse to sharp practice. Others lived on their wits. Is the level of honesty in Israel higher than it was in those communities from which many traders or their parents sprung? Reliable observers of the present and the past assured me that it is. It seems very probable that the moral quality of the *halutzim* has had a favorable influence over wide sectors of the society until very recent times. Nowadays the expansion of the private sector, the manifold temptations of affluence, the need for relaxation of tension, and an evident "post-war" psychology seem capable of reversing the order of values and the direction of the trend.

ARE THE YOUNG STILL JEWS?

The effect of new social conditions, evident in many adults, is even more striking among the young. The country's institutions have been devised for the purpose of molding the young, identifying them with the country's problems, struggles and dangers, bringing them up as patriotic citizens of Israel. One of the most important of these institutions is the Nahal. Theoretically it is a branch of the defense forces (i.e. the army), and is recruited by voluntary enlistment, like the air force and the navy.

In practice the youth movements[3] at secondary schools and at places of employment provide the nuclei around which future *garinim* (prospective members of the Nahal) gather. By the time they reach conscription age the young people of the Nahal have spent several weeks in agricultural co-operatives and have got used to *kibbutz* life. Their military training between the ages of fourteen and eighteen is also an apprenticeship in agriculture and the life of the pioneer, for which the Ministries of Education and National Defense are jointly responsible. They are soldier-farmers. Boys and girls live in separate quarters, but are trained in the same camps and mix at meals. The heads of the organization refuse to idealize it; one of them told me it was a "military unit like any other, neither better nor worse." But it is not immaterial that it is posted to the frontiers, the interminable frontiers of this small country, and that its young members spend more time clearing land and driving tractors than going on route marches. The frontier is continually before their eyes and in their minds, and they do not need to have speeches about their country's needs and problems rammed down their throats. For some time the government, stretching the voluntary principle, has used the Nahal as an instrument of re-education by drafting into it small numbers of recent young immigrants or other difficult or asocial urban elements. These are accepted and treated as equals by their comrades. Most of the experiments seem to have been successful. Some of the young soldier-farm-workers decide to remain and make their lives at the settlements they have helped to build.

The Nahal is a *corps d'élite*, and there is a proud ring to its name, which means "fighting pioneer youth." It is sent to

[3] The youth movements were for a time forbidden to compete for membership in the schools, but this right was restored in 1962. The change of policy seems to have been inspired by concern at the moral crisis among the young, which it proposed to meet by organizing them and thus combating an increasing "lawlessness," one of the symptoms of which was juvenile delinquency. This had been non-existent, but was becoming an increasing phenomenon in the towns. Each of the principal parties has its own youth movement; the biggest is Hanoar Ha'oved, affiliated to the Histadrut. There is also a scout federation, including a non-Jewish section for young Arabs.

the frontier wherever a new settlement, *kibbutz* or *moshav*, is being established. The detachment I saw at B.S., for example, on the borders of the Gaza strip, besides being subjected to military discipline and trained in squads in the methods of "modern" war, was also being given agricultural training by *kibbutz* specialists, under whose direction the members were working the fruit and tobacco plantations. Elsewhere, on the borders of Jordan, from the southern tip of the Dead Sea to Beer Menucha and Yotvata, it is often the Nahal that is sent to reinforce frontier villages or establish new ones.

The civic training role of the army as a whole is as important as its military role. It is a hard school, combining long marches in the desert, life under canvas, and heavy engineering work on the frontiers with courses in basic education and civic training. Young immigrants, after receiving a grounding at the *ulpanim*, improve their knowledge of Hebrew in the army. Men have to do two and a half years' military service between the ages of eighteen and twenty-six and unmarried women have to serve for two years,[4] and at the end of it their "Israelization" has made great progress. I talked in factories, *kibbutzim* and *moshavim*, and universities to young people fresh from military service, as well as others still in uniform, like Bathsheba, for example, a *sabra* of German antecedents, to whom we gave a lift from the outskirts of Tel Aviv to Jerusalem, where she was going to rejoin her family. (The visitor's instructive encounters are increased by the habit of hitchhiking, which is practiced throughout Israel on an enormous scale, and sometimes in the most insistent and audacious manner.) Bathsheba's straight nose and clear-cut profile stood out below the dark hair curled under her cap, and she looked neat and attractive in her well fitting gray-blue uniform jacket and trousers. Nothing about her recalled the physical features, gestures and in-

---

[4] The ultra-orthodox (i.e. members of Hassidic sects), and in particular the Natorei Karta, are exempted from military service on the grounds of conscientious objection. Many *yeshivot* (Talmudic college) students destined for the rabbinate are also exempted.

tonations that survive among many German Jews even after years in this country; nothing about the pale-complexioned, confident girl, sparing of speech and gesture, suggested she was the daughter of Augsburg shopkeepers who had immigrated here in 1935. On leaving Ramla we came upon a party of girls returning to their quarters, marching with springy step, their khaki shirts showing the shape of their figures. "Parachutists," Bathsheba said. Most of them were handsome creatures.

Some of these young people's parents miraculously escaped the death camps, or they had escaped them themselves. Others, brought from North Africa or Asia by the youth *aliya*, had eaten their fill and slept alone in a bed for the first time in their lives at Ramat Hadasseh, the youth *aliya* reception center in Lower Galilee, near Kiryat Tiv'on. Many of these offspring of Jews of the Diaspora have behind them generations, centuries of tribulation, in which the isolation of the ghetto, the stagnation of the *mellah* (the Jewish quarter in a North African town) alternated with persecution, anguish and sometimes horror. But each year sees an increase in the proportion of those born on Israeli soil, free of the complexes and anxieties of their parents, caught up in enthusiasm for an arduous task, plunged into a life in which everything is new—the country, the language, the institutions, the hopes. It is the birth of a new community. What will become of all those young people I met in lecture halls, buses, workshops and *kibbutz* dining rooms? What were they? Were they still "Jews"? Such were my thoughts, the naïve thoughts of a new arrival, while we drove down the narrow road along which an endless stream of cars and trucks flowed in both directions. On either side wrecked trucks bore witness to the fighting of the war of independence. I put the question on my mind to my neighbor, N.A., a Rumanian, the manager of a Histadrut factory and a typical pioneer of the early days. He leaned toward me and answered quietly in French, in order not to be overheard by Bathsheba. "They have lost the defects of their parents," he said, "and also their qualities." It took me weeks or months to explore the implications of those few words.

The schools, the youth movements, the Gadna (the organization inspired by the scout movement that gives boys and girls between the ages of fourteen and eighteen pre-military training and training in pioneering agriculture), the Nahal and the army plunge boys and girls into an intense social life. Girls of fifteen go on route marches or sleep under canvas in Gadna teams, and young women non-combatants of the three services mingle with the young men in camps and at military posts. Boys and girls get to know each other early, often, I was told, in the Biblical sense of the word. This state of affairs seems to be taken very much as a matter of course and to be regarded by both sexes as part of a free and necessary experience of life. Frequently it leads to early marriage.

ISRAELIZATION

The health and beauty of Israeli children are impressive. There are about 600,000 in the age group from three to fourteen, 425,000 of them Jews and the others Arabs (Christian or Muslim) or Druses. I shall never forget the way the children celebrated Purim at a *kibbutz* in the valley of Yezreel and in the North African *shikunim* at Beit Shean and Afuleh, and the carnival processions in the packed streets of Tel Aviv. From early morning processions of clowns, dandies in top hats and morning coats, cowboys, Renaissance courtiers, gypsies, Carmens, young ladies in crinolines escorted by musketeers, as well as Esthers with cardboard crowns and bearded Moseses bearing big bunches of grapes to symbolize the arrival of the Jews in the land of Canaan, crowded past my hotel at Hadar Acarmel on their way through the sunny pinewoods overlooking the Bay of Haifa. Their fancy dress was done with taste (Hadar Acarmel is a prosperous residential neighborhood), and they were on their way to the school, where their teachers were waiting for them to begin the great festival on that Friday morning before the sabbath.

Elsewhere, in districts inhabited by recent immigrants, in

the outskirts of Tel Aviv, the fancy dress was more makeshift, but the children's delight was no less.

At R., as in all the *kibbutzim*, the children were divided up into their "own" houses according to age. For some weeks past their parents had spent their spare time carefully rehearsing the turns that they put on. Two cleverly-got-up bearded dwarfs with enormous chests were seated facing the audience, violently agitating their short legs in a furious dispute. In the circle dances, in which parents and children, all in fancy dress, joined in, there were couples or husbands and wives from two different continents or twenty different nations. The "big" children, those between thirteen and sixteen, put on a performance of their own to which the parents went after leaving the small ones in charge of their "house mothers." Purim did not create the impression that the pleasures of family life are declining in the *kibbutz*. Instead of being a celebration limited to a small unit turned in on itself, restricted to a small group of parsimoniously and socially selected friends, as the traditions of bourgeois individualism often dictate, here it is a great carnival in which young and old mingle in communal relaxation and pleasure. It was the same thing again the next day; the children had invited their parents to see "their" garden and "their" zoo, to admire a chamois caught in the Moab Mountains, a pony, sheep, peacocks and geese. In comparison with their parents the children often have lighter hair and complexion. One of the numerous effects of the "crucible" is elimination of the physical differences between Ashkenazim and Sephardim, which many hold to be irritating to both, thus hastening the fusion of the communities.

There are, however, obstacles to this process. It is a difficult operation, and all the conditions for it are not yet present.

Its most powerful agents are the army and the linguistic monopoly of Hebrew. Knowledge of Hebrew is the *sine qua non* of integration and, when it has been acquired, its sign. Intensive courses in Hebrew, lasting from four to six months, are given at the *ulpanim* to be found in all towns, *kibbutzim* and *moshavim*. Newly arrived immigrants, who are frequently

illiterate, are visited in their homes by voluntary teachers, and
newspapers and magazines are published in "basic" Hebrew,
made easier by the addition of vowels. Special programs are
broadcast for the benefit of beginners in the language. I noticed
that ignorance of Hebrew earns a bad mark in the eyes of certain
Ashkenazim, and if Yiddish is not understood either, it makes
matters worse; it is a disturbing sign, capable of restricting the
hospitality so readily and generously practiced in the country.

In the crowded dining room of my hotel at Eilat two Israelis
—a Pole who emigrated in 1937 and his younger companion,
a *sabra* whose parents came from the Ukraine—sat at my table.
As they knew a little English, we were able to communicate,
but when they heard me talking French to the young waitresses,
one of whom came from Morocco and the other from Egypt
(both spoke Hebrew), they were obviously upset. "No one
worries about where people come from," the Pole said to me.
"Here one has to forget one's native tongue."

Such reactions are by no means exceptional in Israel. To be
a good Israeli you have to forget your native country, wipe it
and your native language out of your mind. Anyone who remains
excessively attached to the country of his birth in the *galut*,
whatever country it may be, runs the risk of being suspect
in the eyes of some patriots of the new state. No doubt this
jealous attitude is necessary. It is a vital ingredient in the
cement needed to combine such disparate elements, and it is
essential for establishing a means of communication between
them and making them assimilable. Another example of the
principle of breaking with one's origins is the Hebraization of
surnames, a trend that has now assumed large-scale proportions.
Some resist the trend and go on calling themselves Nussbaum
or Abramovich, but they are getting fewer and fewer, particularly
among technicians and members of the liberal professions.
Many Jews have changed their German-, Russian- or Polish-
sounding names for Hebrew names; Ben-Gurion set an example
for this long ago. Forenames are largely borrowed from famous
characters in the Old Testament, as well as obscure ones. Leafing

through the telephone directory, you come across the complete posterity of Abraham as given in the Book of Genesis, and all the heroes of Jewish history, from Yehuda to Bar Kochba. The obverse (or inevitable counterpart) of the rapid Hebraization manifested by all these signs is sometimes a kind of chauvinism, which conflicts with the Jewish spirit of universality, as understood in either its religious or merely lay and humanist sense. Hebraization is the potent yeast that daily leavens and fortifies the Israeli nation; it is also a bulldozer that serves to consolidate the foundations of the young state and a culture, both millenary and completely new, that has risen from the ruins of Jewish cosmopolitanism and internationalism.

But, even in its sometimes excessive forms, Israeli patriotism must also be interpreted as a defense reaction. This community of two million souls, split up into parties, divided on the problems of the relations between religion and the state, on the role of collectivism and trade unions, on policy toward the Arab world, would, I am convinced, in an emergency rise like a single man to defend its land and its liberties. The Arab world is disunited, but it will surely end by uniting. Nasser wishes to crush Israel as in a vise. On the eve of its sixteenth birthday[5] the young state seems to be facing severe tests. Are these happy boys and girls, these handsome young people saved from the death camps, now threatened by a cruel twist of history, which has concentrated and exposed them in this refuge?

Is Israelization everywhere and always equally effective? Of course not. But it is an immensely powerful force, fortified by feelings, fears and hopes shared by practically everyone. I met some Jews of German origin who had been settled in Israel for thirty years and seemed at first sight hardly distinguishable from others I had met during my stays in Germany before 1933. They dressed the same way, had the same gestures and intonations. This superficial impression is particularly striking

[5] This chapter was written in April 1964.

in the Had Hacarmel district of Haifa, where you hear German
spoken everywhere—in streets, cafés and shops. Is this an instance of resistance to the "crucible"? The reality is more
complicated. Many of those who live in this residential area on
the slopes of Mount Carmel are people in their fifties who
have benefited from the reparations paid by the Federal Republic of Germany to the victims of Nazism. They have preserved their style of life and family habits. They talk German
among themselves and even to their grandchildren, often to
the irritation of the intermediary generation, to whom Hebrew
has become the current and dominant tongue.[6]

Most of these veterans retired to end their lives peacefully
in this beautiful spot after working hard for more than a quarter
of a century, and their Germanic patterns of behavior do not
mean that they are less integrated to Israel in heart and mind
than other immigrants. Take W.T., for example, an outstanding
jurist. At first sight he looks a typical Herr Professor of the
old school, solemn and a trifle starched and stiff, but, despite
this appearance, he is a militant member and trusted adviser
of a *kibbutz* federation, a socialist and an Israeli patriot, whose
enthusiasm is not always tempered by a critical spirit. Both
his sons live in a *kibbutz* in Galilee, where they have taken

[6] S. N. Eisenstadt in a classic work (*The Absorption of Immigrants*, Rout-
ledge, London, 1954) made a comparative study of the absorption of immigrants
by the *yishuv* and the state of Israel during the first few years of its existence. He
explains the survival among certain groups of immigrants of islands of culture
characterized by a kind of inertia and a "relative apathy" toward the communal
principles of the *yishuv* and subsequently of the state of Israel. The fifth *aliya*
consisted almost exclusively of German Jews driven from Germany by Nazism
who came to Palestine simply to find a refuge and who had no trace of Zionist
or socialist ideology. Their motives, like those of the "oriental" Jews, differed
from those of their predecessors of the *yishuv*, and they also differed in their degree of readiness to change; in the sphere of communal values and in culture
their impulse to do so was smaller. They identified themselves less with the
yishuv, and consequently maintained islets of culture, regional associations, *Landsmannschaften*, and even German-language newspapers. On the other hand, their
adaptation to technical and professional jobs was swift and thorough (Eisenstadt,
pp. 103–104). These observations on the 1935–48 period explain certain already very attenuated cultural traits that we have mentioned.

root and founded families. Most of the *sabra* students of German
parentage whom I met are physically and mentally assimilated
Israelis, as was Bathsheba, the girl doing her military service.
There are still groups united by ties of origin in the towns and
even in some *kibbutzim*, where people from Riga, Lvov, Vilna,
Bucharest or Frankfurt meet and maintain declining "sub-cultures." These groups will die out with their present members.
Failing a catastrophe, a new exodus leading to a new Diaspora,
the process of Israelization is irreversible.

NEW TOWNS IN THE DESERT

This country, which is half the size of Switzerland and at present
has less than half the population, is a microcosm in which
men and values that seem to have been borrowed from the
most widely different periods of one and the same history co-
exist and confront each other. Traditional Judaism and the
Judaism of the central European ghettos rub shoulders with
Marxism, the most modern techniques, the most audaciously
forward-looking experiments in human co-operation, technological realism, and the most fervent pioneering spirit, the frontier
bastions of the *kibbutzim*, youthful enthusiasm and the building
of new towns.

I visited some of these towns. They are built both because
of the need to exploit the country's resources to the full and
to absorb immigrants. The new port of Ashdod, which was
expected to be finished in April 1966, after which Haifa would
be used chiefly as a fishing and pleasure harbor, was being built
completely on a deserted coastline between Palmahim and Ashkelon. It was to have the most modern equipment and handle
more trade than Haifa. Modern apartment buildings had already
been erected and were largely inhabited by Moroccans who had
previously never lived in anything but hovels. Kiryat Gat lies
in the center of the Lakhish district, which includes about
sixty villages, mainly *moshavim*, some big textile (cotton) factories and sugar refineries. This rural-urban complex on which

work was begun only in 1955 had more than 30,000 inhabitants in 1961. Of these, 16,000 were living in the villages. The population of the area included a minority of *vatikim*, who provided the original backbone (15 per cent), but the majority were Poles and Rumanians (40 per cent) and recent North African immigrants, mostly Moroccans, (40 per cent). Kiryat Gat was already an old "new town." It had established solid roots, and was a model for others, such as Arad, which were still at the stage of methodical survey and planning.

The road connecting Beersheba with Arad by way of Omer was opened on March 1, 1961. It is a long, smooth, asphalt streak across the desert, and is to be continued as far as Sodom (Sdom). So far Arad was nothing but a group of administrative buildings lying among the dunes; these formed both the "advanced camp" and nucleus of the future town. Architects, engineers and sociologists were working on the site, and building workers, most of them brought daily from Beersheba, were busy putting up housing units (the industrial zone had been leveled by bulldozers but was still an empty expanse), and an American town-planner surrounded by Israeli specialists was working out plans to cope with future waves of immigrants, the composition and extent of which had to be predicted—no light task. The pioneers of the advanced camp were proud of the palm trees, parkinsonias and bushes (clerodendrons) planted by Zvi Aharoni, the man who brightened Kiryat Gat with trees and greenery. For each young bush or sapling a hole two feet deep and two feet in diameter had to be made with a pneumatic drill; for each hole earth had to be sought among the outcrops of loess several miles away, and compost had to be brought from Tel Aviv. Efforts have been made to avoid the difficulties and setbacks that have occurred in other new towns, such as the formation of "ghettos" by new immigrants or friction between new immigrants and old. There is a nucleus of old settlers who are intended progressively to absorb the newcomers. A kind of symbiosis of *aliyot*, old and new, is aimed at in Arad, a new town in the desert, which will triumph over isolation, hunger and thirst.

Eilat is young too, but in comparison with Arad it is developed and flourishing. To appreciate it, one should go there, not by air, but by the road through the Negev, which is perpetually busy with two-way traffic between the Mediterranean and the Red Sea; the convoys of trucks and huge trailers are like trains. Eilat, Israel's gateway to Africa and, by way of the Indian Ocean, to Asia, should be approached after inspecting King Solomon's copper mines at Timna and then, after passing Beer Ora, seeing Israeli territory, wedged between the steep frontiers of Jordan and Egypt, contracting toward this point, this small casket of shining blue. The small and modestly equipped port is clean and well kept; soon, when the big modern docks a few miles away to the west have been finished, it will be a fishing port only. For some years yet Eilat will remain a pioneering town to which enterprising spirits such as my Algerian friend G. will come, to earn money and help their families climb the social scale. Every year an increasing number of tourists will be attracted by the dry climate, the perfect blue of sky and sea, the air-conditioned hotels and the bathing beaches that are being laid out. From my hotel window, just beyond the last-born *shikun*, I could see the beginning of the desert that stretches to the mountains of Egypt. While it remains unvulgarized and unspoiled, Eilat is still the Israeli deep south.

2

The *Kibbutz* Adventure and the
Challenges of the Century

The *kibbutzim* take us straight to the heart of what is not only
the most daring advance toward a social utopia that has ever
been made, but also a specifically Jewish contribution to the
realization of communal ideals. Understanding the *kibbutzim*
and the whole range of their current problems supplies a key to
the comprehension of the new Israeli society, the "other" society
in process of economic growth by which the collectivist sector is
now confronted.

This is not the place to summarize the history of the *kibbutz*
movement from its nineteenth-century origins, in which the various streams of Jewish idealism, both lay and religious, socialist
and Zionist, mingled and sometimes clashed, or to describe in
detail the organization of the federations of which it consists.[1]
I will merely draw attention to what seems to me to be their
essential characteristics and thus indicate their economic and
social importance, their difficulties, hopes and anxieties, and their
prospects sixteen years after the foundation of the state and
more than half a century after the first *kvutza* was established
at Degania.

[1] The three principal federations are the Artzi, Meuhad, and Ihud Hakvutzot
Vehakibbutzim (which we shall refer to as Ihud), affiliated respectively to the
Mapam (a labor group more leftist than Mapai), Achdut Haavoda (whose
position is between Mapam and Mapai) and Mapai (the Israel Labor Party)
parties. In 1966 they included seventy-three, fifty-eight and seventy-three
kibbutzim respectively. There are also two small federations, the Dati, affiliated to
the religious Hapoel Hamizrahi party (eleven *kibbutzim*) and the Hanoar Hazioni
(six *kibbutzim*) affiliated to the Liberal Party and connected with the Ihud.

The agricultural co-operatives known as *kibbutzim* were originally organized on a strictly communal basis, and their development has been closely linked with that of the doctrines of their founders. Each stage must be considered in its ideological and social context. From 1920 onward it must be considered in the light of the aims and ideals of the principal pioneering movements, such as the Halutz, Hashomer Hatzair and, up to 1929, the Communist-inspired G'dud Avodah.[2] The *kibbutzim* of the *halutz* period were founded by young socialists of various schools who came with the first *aliyot*, chiefly from central Europe, Russia and Poland, and included many students and even men who gave up medical or legal practices to return to the soil of Palestine. They believed that the Jewish state, the return of the exiles prophesied by Herzl, could be achieved only by sweat and toil, the reclamation of marshes and the irrigation of deserts, the rehabilitation of land abandoned for centuries or neglected by the Arabs; they wanted to show the opponents of Zionism that the soil of Palestine was not barren, and, with the aid of primitive tools, in exceptionally hard conditions, and at the price of prodigious efforts, they showed it. They also wanted to show that Jews, who for long ages had been excluded from possession and cultivation of land, could be successful settlers and farmers, could be *productive*. There is now a large institute of productivity in Israel with a whole network of branches, and the practical notion of productivity is very topical. But let us remember that at the very beginning of Jewish settlement in Palestine it was the same. Productive labor has been at the top of the scale of moral values ever since the establishment of the first *kibbutzim*. The good *haver*, respected by his comrades, is the productive worker. Whatever function in the community may devolve on him, he is judged by results.

The needs to which the *kibbutzim* responded have been dif-

[2] It should be noted that at this time the first *moshavim* had already been founded under the influence of Eliezer Joffé, but conditions were not yet ripe for these co-operative villages, which now occupy an important place in Israeli agriculture. *Cf.* pp. 297–299, where information about their organization and development is given.

ferent at different times, depending on the different waves of immigration, external events in the Diaspora and internal events in Palestine. Thus, at the beginning of 1933, when the youth *aliya* movement was founded to rescue the maximum possible number of Jewish children from Nazi Germany, the *kibbutzim* were given the extra task of providing reception and training centers for them. Then, when the Nazis had overrun nearly the whole of Europe, they did the same for orphans or young people cut off from their families who came from other countries. In the same way, in the armed struggle with the Arabs from 1936 onward, they were given a military role, particularly in Upper Galilee, the Jordan Valley and the Negev. They were turned into armed camps, which many of them have again become in the face of the renewed acuteness of the Arab threat.

But what is the function of the *kibbutzim* in the Israel of the present day? What is their essential role?

ROLE AND FUNCTIONS

Since the eve of the establishment of the state in 1947 their number and population have not ceased to increase. The *kibbutz* population rose from 47,408 in 1947 to 77,890 in 1959 and 80,600 in 1966; the number of *kibbutzim* increased from 115 in May 1948 to 228 at the end of 1959 and 230 on January 1, 1966. However, in relation to the growth of the population as a whole, there has been a decline in the population of the *kibbutzim*. From constituting 7.5 per cent of the whole in 1947, it fell to 5 per cent in 1955, 3.7 per cent in 1959, and 3.1 per cent in 1966.

Has there been a corresponding decline in the ideological and social weight of the *kibbutzim* in the state of Israel? We shall try to answer this basic question in the course of our survey. It should be noted in the first place that, if the *kibbutzim* are regarded as agricultural producers (many of them, as we shall see, have also become industrial producers), a relative decrease in the agricultural population in relation to the working population as a whole is normal in an economy at the stage of "take-off," to use W. W. Rostow's classic phrase. This trend is further accentuated by the increased productivity resulting from the very advanced mechanization of many *kibbutzim*. Their demographic development corresponds with that of the well-known relationship between the primary and secondary sectors in societies undergoing industrialization. In 1965 the proportion of the agricultural population to the population as a whole was 20.1 per cent. If the development of the Israeli economy continues peacefully, this figure is expected to decline to 13 per cent in a total population of about three million in 1970.

The relative decline in the population of the *kibbutzim* is also explained by the nature of the massive influx that took place between 1949 and 1952. This was chiefly from the Jewish communities of Asia and Africa, and these people, unlike the *halutzim*, were not prepared for agriculture and still less for collective agriculture. The *kibbutzim* cannot, except to a minimal extent, count on recruits from Zionist youth from western Europe or the Americas.[3] In the context of Israeli society as a whole, taking account of the attitude and values of the young, the *kibbutzim* are now having to look chiefly to the second or third generation of their own members for reinforcements.

I have already mentioned the rapid progress of mechanization in the *kibbutzim*. The modernity of their equipment is one of the features that most struck me. In their newspapers and the satirical revues they put on for their own entertainment on special occasions they themselves make fun of their mania for buying the latest—and most expensive—thing. There are certainly big differences on this point of view between the old *kibbutzim* and the new, such as Nahl-Oz, Eilata, Yotvata and Adamit (Idmit), which are in debt, and in difficult years receive technical aid from their seniors.

The "old" *kibbutzim* are those founded before 1936, the

[3] After 1960 the situation changed in Latin America, particularly in Argentina, where social and political instability and recrudescences of anti-Semitism led to emigration from which the *kibbutzim* benefited.

"middle-aged," those dating from before the war of independence, and the "new," those that have come into existence since 1947. I visited some "old" and "middle-aged" ones. Most of them were offshoots of the Artzi *kibbutz*, and they were neither the most famous nor the richest. Everywhere there was an observable concern to alleviate the toil of the *haverim* by modern techniques, with more or less successful or happy results. At the *kibbutz* Rechafim, founded in 1944 by pioneers from Rumania, Bulgaria and Israel itself, where I spent several days, the *haverim*, both men and women, who work by rotation in the kitchens, have at their disposal a fine battery of electric cookers, dishwashers and other labor-saving devices. The laundry is equipped with ironing machines and the dairy with milking machines. Most impressive of all, however, is the hen house, or rather the egg factory. Thousands of hens are stacked closely against one another on three floors in a room several hundred yards long. Within reach of each beak are two troughs, one containing food and the other water, and underneath is a channel along which the eggs travel to the place where they are collected, checked, packed and dispatched. The sequence of operations is completely rationalized and "wasted space" reduced to a minimum, as on a Detroit production line. The sight of these unhappy creatures can rouse various reactions, depending on the visitor's sensibilities. At all events, the output of eggs at Rechafim and elsewhere under these conditions is very high, and problems of marketing arise, as they do in the case of milk, poultry and other *kibbutz* products.

At Beit Alfa and Dalia the "cultural centers," including libraries, reading rooms, rest rooms and halls for theatrical performances or movies, can stand comparison with the most attractive and comfortable institutions of the same kind that I have seen in France or abroad, west or east. The one at Ginnosar, a "middle-aged" offshoot of the Meuhad organization superbly situated on the western bank of the Lake of Tiberias, actually defies comparison. The *kibbutzim* dining rooms are not always big enough, so that there is overcrowding at meals; and some of them are furnished in an old-fashioned style that seems to identify the community spirit with grimness and severity. However, at Hazorea, which was founded in 1934 by immigrants from Germany and produces an opera every year entirely from its own resources, the dining room is in simple good taste, furnished with Formica-topped tables for four. Others are as comfortable as the dining rooms of good clubs in England or the United States.

The living quarters of the *haverim* no longer recall the ascetic life of the first *kvutzot*. At the oldest *kibbutzim*, such as Beit Alfa, the first of the Hashomer Hatzair group (1920), a newly arrived young couple can straightaway be given a small flat including a good living room, kitchenette and pantry, making it possible for them to take their midday meal there alone or entertain a friend. At Rechafim the typical living quarters in a "middle-aged" *kibbutz* consists of a gaily furnished small house, with a living room in which bookshelves alternate with good reproductions, and a small kitchen and bathroom. They are situated among trees, flowers and lawns maintained with varying degrees of care according to the time available to the *haverim* responsible for them.

What needs do the *kibbutzim* fulfill today? What attraction can they have for the younger generation at the present stage of Israeli society? Originally tented encampments, they are now in many cases pleasant modern villages in which food, lodgings, working conditions, cultural facilities for adults and schools and playgrounds for children have continuously improved. Except for some new ones still faced with teething troubles, a *kibbutz* is no longer a "place where everyone is equal in poverty."

But are comfort and material prosperity to be the principal aim and primary justification of this way of life, and are efficiency and yield to be its principal criteria? To use the terminology of the debates at the *kibbutz* federations, does not the "economic" threaten to take precedence over the "social"? Darin-Drabkin, an authority on the *kibbutzim* who is always ready to grant them understanding sympathy, notes in this connection: "When the *kibbutz* first appeared in Palestine, it answered the needs of the workers who were looking for employment and for support in a desperate struggle for survival. It paved the way for the development of Jewish agriculture. These needs are still present to-day, but they have lost much of their primary importance. From these points of view, however, the *kibbutz* still has unique advantages in settling Israel's outlying districts. More than 70 per cent of the *kibbutzim* formed between 1948 and 1955 were settled either in the Negev or in Galilee, that is, in undeveloped regions. The lessening of tension after the inception of the state and increased capitalist development have worked to the detriment of the collective. However, the attraction of the *kibbutz* as a comfortable place to live has increased. It forms a solid base for people who are interested in social progress, in building the cells of the socialist society, and in developing the productive forces of the country."[4]

This paragraph puts in a nutshell all the great problems that face the *kibbutzim* in Israel today: the relations between the *kibbutz* economy and the capitalist sector; the extent and nature of the attraction the *kibbutz* has for young *sabras* and recent immigrants; the new aspects of its pioneering role; and the relations of the old ideal of socialist construction to the unprecedented satisfactions (and needs) of prosperity.

Anyone who has immersed himself in the life of one or two *kibbutzim* and watched their inhabitants at work and at leisure and taken part in their holidays and celebrations cannot help bring struck by the difference between them and the general run of people in the "other society," that of the urban areas, factories and offices. Not that the contrast generally is sharp, though it is sharp enough in some environments dominated by the Israel "N.E.P.," the business or pleasure quarters the "Dizengoff Squares,"[5] in the big towns, where the people you see do not seem to differ very much from those who make up the "lonely crowds" in the West or the United States, devoted to a gregarious search for the distractions and gratifications offered

---

[4] H. Darin-Drabkin, *The Other Society*, Gollancz, London, 1962, p. 83.
[5] In the eyes of many Israelis Dizengoff Square in Tel Aviv is the symbol of a new, easy, flashy life which attracts some and alarms others.

by a technological civilization. On the whole, as I have said, there is a remarkably high proportion of individuals of quality in Israel, and in the *kibbutzim* the proportion is especially high. Joseph Klatzmann, an authority on Israeli agriculture, insists on the vital role played by this elite. An important chapter of his *Les Enseignements de l'Expérience Israélienne* ("Lessons of the Israeli Experience"), in which he surveys the *kibbutzim*, is entitled "Men as the principal factor in success."[6]

The very conditions in which the *kibbutzim* were born—the daily struggle for life against nature and an external enemy (the Arabs), poverty and an unhealthy climate, their constitution, which insists on communal property, living arrangements, production and defense and denies the individual the stimulus of personal ambition, the acquisition of money or power or even of comfort for his family unit, and makes the mainspring of human activity the realization of a collective ideal—could only reinforce the selection of the original *halutzim*. "The country is of course not populated exclusively by heroes," Klatzmann observes. "Some give up and go back to their countries of origin. Others stay on and grumble."[7]

The *kibbutznikim* are neither angels nor supermen, and deserve something better than blind admiration or stupid moralizing. It does them a better service to discuss objectively the criticisms and anxieties aroused by their movement as well as their successes. The *kibbutz* experiment is of tremendous interest; its success, or even limited success, is worth careful study precisely because it is conducted by men exposed to all the difficulties of communal life, all the strains and tensions, on which social psychology has thrown light in recent years, to which interpersonal relationships are exposed in small communities.

The *kibbutznikim* are not angels. Nevertheless the *kibbutz* is both a selecting agent and a crucible. It is extremely rare for the general assembly to have to expel a member for "unfitting behavior." Things seldom get as far as that; the first

[6] P.U.F., Paris, 1963, Ch. IV, pp. 69–76.
[7] *Ibid.*, p. 76.

symptoms of "deviation" are soon noticed, for a *kibbutz* is a small group, averaging two or three hundred adult members. (In 1961 the average Meuhad *kibbutz* numbered 210 adults. In other federations the figure did not differ greatly. In "giant" *kibbutzim*, such as Guivat Brenner and Yagur, the average population, including children, is about two thousand.) Collective life is intense and close social control is exercised. Thus as soon as "deviations" appear they are dealt with by talking to the person concerned, and rarely lead to situations of conflict. If there is a deep disagreement with the principles of life in a *kibbutz*, or a new *haver* is incapable of adapting himself, the "deviation" may be the preliminary symptom of his departure.[8] Hence, too, the absence of crime in the *kibbutz* population. "Deviations" have not to my knowledge been studied by Israeli psychologists. But it would be interesting to know what they are and in what circumstances they arise. We also lack any systematic study of marriage and divorce in the *kibbutz*. During the period of the first *halutzim* socialism was in some cases associated with doctrines of free love, and the "bourgeois servitude" of the family was derided; but in the *kibbutzim* of the present day the family is the basic unit, and the stability of couples is greater. Crises sometimes arise when one partner to a marriage comes from the "outside world" and is chronically unable to adapt to communal life. In such cases the choice is often between both partners leaving the *kibbutz* and a divorce.

Is the attraction of the *kibbutz* for new immigrants and the young in urban areas declining? This is a very controversial question, depending on a whole complex of circumstances, in particular the economic situation, the stage of Israel's development, and the nature and composition of the waves of immigrants. The most sympathetic observers of the movement admit that, when opportunities for employment in the town are good, neither the young who live there nor recent immigrants choose to live in the country, particularly in a *kibbutz*, where their

---

[8] Rules governing departure from a *kibbutz* are laid down in the constitution of each federation.

liberties are restricted.[9] Intake by the *kibbutzim* depends on the state of the economy (now in a phase of growth) and also on the standard of living they can offer young people not motivated by collective principles. Most of the "oriental" immigrants who came with recent *aliyot* have been settled, not in *kibbutzim*, but in *moshavim*. Some better educated members of this group (Yemenis, North Africans and in particular Persians) have joined a *kibbutz* after being disappointed with their experience of town life, sometimes after a lapse of several years. On their first arrival in Israel there was too great a psychological distance between them and communal life,[10] though when they achieved greater integration into the Israeli environment but were repelled by urban life the *kibbutz* offered them a way out. Since 1961 the principal intake by the *kibbutzim* from the Diaspora has consisted of young Argentinians, who seem to adapt themselves well, both to the work and in human relations with their comrades.

The attitude of the younger generations is another matter of much discussion. To young people reared and educated in the shelter of a *kibbutz*, military service is often a critical experience. Another is marriage to a partner from "outside." These events normally occur between the ages of twenty and twenty-five. Many young people return to the *kibbutz* after being released by the army, even after tasting life in the "other society." Others leave the *kibbutz* because of economic difficulties, such as overproduction of agricultural products, or lack of jobs suitable to their education and ambitions. Other difficulties are of a social nature, e.g. the normalization of life in the *kibbutz*, which those among the young who have preserved a spark of the pioneering spirit of the *halutzim* object to as becoming more and more bourgeois. Young people mingling with representatives of the great mass of the population in the army are some-

---

[9] Darin-Drabkin, *op. cit.*, pp. 279, 280.

[10] *Cf.* the types of tension observed among oriental Jews by S. N. Eisenstadt during the early years of the state of Israel and analyzed by him in *The Absorption of Immigrants*, Ch. VI, *op. cit.*

times affected by the decline of the *kibbutz's* prestige in Israeli society as a whole and by the criticisms of it (with which we will deal later); and some of them end by losing their confidence, although this crisis may be countered by the new technical jobs provided by *kibbutz* industries and their regional centers.

In spite of these influences and the test of military service, only 5 per cent of young people leave the Artzi *kibbutzim* annually.[11] According to Shlomo Rosen, the joint secretary, the population of the seventy-two Hashomer Hatzair *kibbutzim* increased by 539 in 1962. Of the 14,500 *haverim* belonging to that federation, 2080 were born in the *kibbutz*, and 93 per cent of the children born there have remained. The same federation made an interesting inquiry into departures. Thirty-one per cent take place after less than two years of *kibbutz* life, and 23 per cent between two and five years. Then the proportion rises again to 27 per cent among those who reach their thirties after from five to ten years in a *kibbutz*, set up a family and decide on their future careers. After ten years in a *kibbutz* adaptation is more or less complete (departures decline to 9 per cent). Between 1948 and 1960 37 per cent of the growth of the *kibbutz* population was accounted for by intake, a figure unlikely to be repeated. But an intake of from 15 to 20 per cent will be sufficient to assure the future of the movement. The present figures, though they show that the growth of the *kibbutz* population is not proportional to that of the general population, do not show any psychological or moral alienation from the institution.

Moreover, it should be borne in mind that the *kibbutzim* constitute a selected society and have never been thought of as a way of life for everyone in Israel, still less as a way of life exportable to very different technical and cultural environments. The *kibbutz* as an institution is unthinkable apart from its Jewish origins. Apart from representing a special type of ideal-

---

[11] Darin-Drabkin, *op. cit.*, p. 205. In other federations the percentage is understood to be not substantially higher.

ism, it is a specifically Jewish contribution to the progress of co-operative institutions, the Jewish specificity itself being determined in the eyes of the historian and sociologist by a complex of conditions and circumstances, and therefore transient. (I am aware, and I greatly regret, that these views conflict with the faith of religious Jews in the messianic vocation and eternity of the Jewish people. I shall return to this subject in the closing chapters of this book.)

Will the *kibbutzim* react to the difficulties of outside recruiting and of their relations with the "other society" by accentuating their social and psychological turning-in upon themselves? I thought I saw some signs of this. The "sheltered" education of the young inveigles them into a kind of segregation in relation to the problems and realities of the "other society." One can feel a sense of pride among some *kibbutz sabras*, but awareness of being the "salt of Israel" does not provide immunity against resentment and ambivalent complexes (of both superiority and inferiority) in relation to those who live in the world of money and easy pleasures and struggles for power and prestige, the world of town dwellers, "who run after everything that offers," as a young *sabra* at the *kibbutz* of Nahal-Oz put it. If such feelings, sustained by their own image as reflected back at them by the outside world, are developing among the *haverim*, they will tend to make of the *kibbutzim*, not a sector, but an island in a society in which economic growth and models of the Western type are increasingly establishing themselves.

Fortunately, the tendency to fall back upon themselves is kept in check by other factors. *Haverim* have the right to annual holidays, and relatives, friends, visitors and temporary workers bring the breath of the outside world into the *kibbutz*. But, above all, an essential feature of the institution is detachment or, as it is often called in the federations, "mobilization," of the *haverim* to work outside the *kibbutz*. Every *kibbutz* is under an obligation to put about 6 per cent of its *haverim* strength at the disposal of the federation to which it belongs, and those so drafted have to work for it, either in Israel or abroad. This "mobilization" may last from one to five years, and it ensures the circulation, if not of all the *kibbutznikim*, at any rate of the important section of them that take a close interest in the movement and in federation affairs. Ever since the foundation of the state the number of *haverim* in the most varied (and highest) positions in the government, the army, the administration, the Knesset and the Histadrut has been very great, and their abilities and talents are still utilized in this way. Another factor that counters the isolation of the *kibbutzim*, as well as the accumulation of inherited benefits and the tendency toward "bourgeois respectability" of the most firmly established and richest of them, is the solidarity between the old institutions and the new ones.[12]

Groups of young people belonging to the former spend periods working at the latter, helping them, and sometimes settling in them. Thus, young people coming from the celebrated industrial *kibbutz* of Afikim were lending a helping hand to the Kfar-Azar *kibbutz*, near the Gaza strip on the Egyptian frontier; and others, "heirs" to the rich *kibbutz* of Guivat Brenner, in 1961 founded a new community called Eilata, on the Red Sea, and started again from scratch.

SOME ECONOMIC PROBLEMS

Having mentioned some aspects of these problems, let us take a closer look at how they appear to the militants and theorists of the movement who are actually faced with them. All those I met try courageously to pin them down and face them. The innumerable repercussions on the *kibbutzim* of the transformations of a society in a state of constant and rapid development lead to the liveliest discussions in the federations, partic-

---

[12] This form of solidarity recalls the *shevtsvo*, the system of mutual aid that linked schools, factories, banks, *kolkhozes*, etc., in the period of the first five-year plans, the working of which I described in "Quelques Traits de l'esprit nouveau en U.R.S.S.," in *Inventaires*, I, published by the Centre de Documentation Sociale de l'Ecole Normale Supérieure under the direction of C. Bouglé, Félix Alcan, Paris, 1936, pp. 113–121.

ularly the Meuhad and Artzi organizations. These enable one to discern the chief challenges to the *kibbutz* adventure thrown down by the world of affluence, automation and mass culture.

Since the foundation of the state the organization and methods of the *kibbutzim* have distinctly improved. Experts draw attention to the growth in average yields: for instance, in cotton (nearly three tons to two and a half acres) and in milk (more than 4000 quarts per cow per year). In 1960–61 the value of production per worker in Jewish agricultural production (that is, excluding Arab agriculture), was 12,000 francs, or 40 per cent better than the French average. If expenses are taken into account—and these, in view of the cost of mechanized equipment, are higher than in France—the "added value" per worker during the same year in Jewish agriculture in Israel amounted to 7000 francs, which is still 25 per cent higher than the corresponding French figure. These are not record figures. In the *kibbutz* of Maagan Mikhael to the south of Haifa the "added value" per worker was 13,000 francs, or more than double the French average.[13]

Nevertheless *kibbutz* agriculture is faced with great problems, which veteran theorists of the movement, such as Eliezer Hacohen, with whom I talked at his *kibbutz* at Beit Alfa, do not conceal. Modernization of equipment and increased output of certain products have outpaced the growth of markets; and the situation is aggravated by the fact that since 1949 many immigrants arrived without resources and thus only feebly reinforced the home market. In the spring of 1963 the co-operative purchasing and distributing organizations (i.e. the various branches of the Tnuva, which carry out these services for the whole of the collective sector, including the *kibbutzim*) had difficulties, particularly in disposing of eggs and poultry mass-produced by specialist *kibbutzim* at renumerative prices. The profitability of *kibbutz* agriculture cannot be properly evaluated without taking into account the capital invested in buildings, raw material and equipment. To ensure their *haverim* of an

[13] J. Klatzmann, *op. cit.*, p. 102.

adequate standard of living, many *kibbutzim* have borrowed and got into debt. Loans are normally granted by the Jewish Agency at from 3 to 4 per cent over a period of twenty-five years. In 1957 the cost of establishing a family unit in a *kibbutz* amounted to I£16,400 ($5460 at the present rate of exchange). Seventy-five per cent of that amount borrowed from the Jewish Agency at 3 per cent requires I£470 as repayment of capital and I£246 in interest, or I£716 annually in all. The remaining 25 per cent advanced by the government at 6 per cent over a period of twelve years calls for an annual payment of I£610. Thus the *kibbutz* has to pay out I£1326 yearly for each family unit; and these figures were greatly exceeded in some communities which, having failed to secure relatively favorable terms, pay out as much as I£2000 per family annually.

The grimness of this picture is somewhat relieved by some new facts which have come to light during the past decade. In the first place, an accumulation of capital has taken place in the oldest and richest *kibbutzim*. The amount is difficult to estimate because of the inflation of prices (particularly of equipment), and the process of accumulation has certainly been slow. Moreover, *kibbutzim* have had the benefit of loans granted by the government (the Agricultural Bank) and the Histadrut (the Labor Bank) at rates more favorable than those of the Jewish Agency. But Israeli agriculture still suffers from the lack of long-term, low-interest loans.

Thus the *kibbutzim* as a whole are heavily in debt. Information of varying degrees of accuracy about this situation leads to criticism in various circles of the "other society" to whom *kibbutz* ideals are alien and unsympathetic. It is said, for instance, that the *kibbutzim* are now subsidized by the more prosperous branches of the Israeli economy, that they are not adapted to the latter, and are therefore not viable. The impulses and needs in response to which they were founded are said to be obsolete, and the "heroes" of yesterday are said to have become the millstones of today—some go so far as to call them parasites. This sort of thing is said in Israel today by "realists" of all ages and types, even inside the government. The reader is asked to reserve judgment until we have gone a little more deeply into these difficult problems.

The efforts of the *kibbutzim* to put themselves on a sound economic footing and to keep their essential structure and ideals intact while adjusting themselves to the changes in Israeli society explain two other closely linked aspects of their development: the growth of *kibbutz* industries and the employment of paid labor.

To many observers of the *kibbutz* economy, the important part already played by the industrial sector is at first sight surprising. Most of the *kibbutzim* envisage supplementing agriculture with industry, which they look to as both a revenue raiser and a creator of jobs. Some, like Beit Alfa, have set up semi-handicraft industries intended to satisfy their own needs for furniture, clothes and minor mechanical or domestic equipment and at the same time to provide employment for older members or those who become unfit for land work. Others, such as Dalia, have set up factories producing for the home market and even for export. In 1960 the industrial income of the *kibbutzim* already exceeded one fifth of their total income,[14] and in "industrial" *kibbutzim* such as Guivat Brenner, Haogen, Ein Hahoresh, Kefar Mazaryk, Afikim and Dalia this proportion is much higher. In the case of the last two, industrial already exceeds agricultural income. In 1959 the export turnover of the celebrated plywood factory at Afikim, which employs about five hundred workers, exceeded I£3 million.[15] Dalia manu-

---

[14] According to Haim Barkai, of the economics department of the Hebrew University, it reached half in 1959; in other words, the net product of industries and workshops equaled that of agriculture. These claims were disputed by the traditional supporters of *kibbutz* agriculture at a symposium on "The role of the *kibbutz* movement in the society and economy of Israel" in August 1963, organized by the Inter-*Kibbutz* Committee and the Hebrew University of Jerusalem.

[15] This information is taken from an unpublished paper by Nicos Andreou on "pluralism in the *kibbutz*" (written at the École Pratique des Hautes Études under the direction of Henri Desroche). It contains valuable documentation about the principal federations.

factures water meters and detergents. In March 1963, only forty-five persons were employed in the former enterprise and about thirty in the latter, because manpower is reduced to a minimum by the use of automatic equipment and electronic control. The manager is of Swiss origin, and nothing in his manner suggests that he is the representative of a collective enterprise and not of commercial interests. He says he could not export at competitive prices if his overheads were burdened by one more operator. The fact of the matter is that one of the motives for introducing automation at Dalia is the desire to keep as many of its *haverim* as possible in the fields and plantations; the latter now employ only about forty full time. Nevertheless, in order to pay their way the two factories have been forced to employ paid labor, thus making a breach in *kibbutz* principles.

Some *kibbutzim*, like Dalia, have already come down on the side of industry, while others, like Rechafim, though mechanized and provided with modern equipment, have so far remained exclusively agricultural. The attitudes of the *kibbutzim* in relation to industry differ, depending on their special problems. Nevertheless, over and above their ideological variations, there are trends common to all the different federations, which are linked to the economic and technical changes in Israeli society, which in turn are linked to international trends.

Industry can be considered one of the principal challenges of the second half of the twentieth century to the *kibbutz* movement. The early *kibbutzim*, starting with Degania, were established in Palestine by *halutzim* in the first decades of the century partly to meet special and immediate needs (the rescue of Jews who had been discriminated against and persecuted and their regeneration by labor), but also as an answer to long-range, universal social problems—to put an end to the "exploitation of man by man" under the capitalist system and the passions, tensions and suffering that the system created. The *halutz* solution to this was the foundation of agricultural enterprises by small groups working on strictly communal principles.

Half a century later the *kibbutz* movement has to face the difficulties arising from the irreversible trend to industrialization of all human societies, including Israel's. The *kibbutzim* are affected by the problems of the distance between the decision makers and those who carry out the decisions, the fragmentation of labor, and the alienation of the workers. They take cognizance of these problems, and in their industries they hope to promote the spirit of their agricultural communities and the principles on which these are based. According to the theorists of industrial expansion, the organization of labor on the factory floor should be similar to that in industrialized agriculture. The principal branches of an agricultural *kibbutz* are not partitioned off from one another. Rotation of labor takes place between fruit, tobacco and cotton plantations, for instance, and those employed in, say, cotton have to know their job from beginning to end, from the selection of the seed to the dispatch of the bales. It is held that the growth and industrialization of *kibbutz* agriculture show the way to the solution of corresponding problems in industry. Study centers shared by the three principal federations work on these problems and undertake investigations in cooperation with specialists in rural scoiology from the universities.[16]

The *kibbutzim* took their first steps toward industry in the thirties, when they set up workshops to supply the needs of their own agriculture; this was followed by the establishment of small fruit-canning and milk products enterprises. The war stimulated industry in Palestine, in spite of the troubles of the time and the inaction of the British administration, and after the foundation of the state considerable progress in industrialization took place in the *kibbutz* economy. In 1959, apart from several hundred artisans' workshops, the *kibbutzim* had a total of about 150 large or medium-sized factories employing more than 10,-000 persons, or more than 7 per cent of the total population employed in industry in Israel. The advantages derived from this

[16] These inter-federation studies were encouraged by the establishment in 1963 of the Union of *Kibbutz* Movements (known as BRIT), which includes the principal federations. Its secretary, Haim Gvati, succeeded Moshe Dayan as Minister of Agriculture when the latter resigned from the Eshkol cabinet in November 1964.

have been considerable. Some *kibbutzim* that practice intensive cultivation with the most modern methods have reached the ceiling in this direction, having no more land and water at their disposal. The combination of industry and agriculture makes it possible to raise the standard of living in a *kibbutz;* the average return from industry in Israel has so far been higher than that from agriculture, and on a lower capital investment.[17] If the *kibbutzim* want to assure their future without relying too much on their members' asceticism, they must offer them a standard of living comparable with that of town dwellers and thus, in spite of the general drift away from the land, maintain their attractiveness to immigrants and young townspeople, who are in any case drawn more to industry than to agriculture.

Industrialization also helps the *kibbutz* to solve internal problems, such as providing jobs for new immigrants of working-class origin whose skills it is sensible to use and for its own members whom age or illness has made unfit for land work. In an environment in which such high moral prestige is attached to work, to aging *haverim* total retirement would be both economically and psychologically harmful, and even unthinkable. Industrialization can also provide employment for members still of working age whose jobs have been eliminated by mechanization. The *kibbutzim* as modern agricultural enterprises—some critics actually call them "modernist"—are necessarily affected by the technological pressures on employment that affect all developing agricultures at the present time, and the setting up of industries not subject to the hazards of climate (in particular, drought) and seasonal fluctuations offers them a graceful way out. It gives their members greater security and, in areas that are often isolated and have no alternative employment to offer, does away with the necessity of uprooting them from their familiar surroundings. Finally the *kibbutz*, faced with rapid expansion of the "other society" in the towns and the growth of the private

---

[17] In 1965, according to a report of the Bank of Israel, the average monthly earnings of an industrial worker were I£455, while in agriculture (in which non-Jews are numerous) these earnings were only I£265.

industrial and commercial sector, assures itself of a certain degree of independence by industrializing itself and its agricultural products and producing at least a certain proportion of the manufactured goods it needs; also, according to its leaders, it avoids as far as possible being "exploited" by the new capitalism developing in Israel.

It is interesting to note the ambivalent role of automation and electronic equipment in the readjustment of the *kibbutz* movement to the economic and social realities of the "second twentieth century." It reduces employment in the manufacture of certain agricultural products. But by enabling small factories to use only a minimal staff, it must ultimately, according to the theorists, make the employment of outside paid labor unnecessary and at the same time liberate *haverim* for work on the land, which, according to the spirit of the founding fathers of the movement, combines both economic and spiritual values and is the great redeeming form of labor. It is doubtful whether this article of faith is still tenable amid the technical and scientific revolutions of our time, and it was given rough handling at the meetings of the Artzi federation, and particularly at those of the Ihud, held at Degania-Bet in April 1964. It emerged that half the Ihud *kibbutzim* had one or more industrial enterprises, and that these provided one-third of the federation's total income.

Industrial expansion in the *kibbutz* is faced with other difficulties, to which its opponents in the movement willingly draw attention. *Kibbutz* industry, if it is to acquire the latest automatic equipment, must have substantial capital investment and highly qualified, specialized technicians. It has on the home and foreign markets, to compete with private industry, with the industry of the government sector, and with foreign firms, which have ample capital available to keep their equipment up-to-date. The *kibbutz* population can to only a limited extent supply the qualified staff and technical personnel required. New institutions are necessary to meet these difficulties in a systematic manner, increase profitability, recruit and train technicians and assure outlets for continually expanding production. Examples of such institutions are the Techen Company, established by the Artzi Federation, and, above all, the Union of *Kibbutz* Industries, which aims at their co-ordination. But it is necessary to go beyond the particularism of the federations, and an inter-federation economic commission is working on these problems. It has in mind appealing to the government and the Histadrut for methodical investment in *kibbutz* industry.[18]

PAID LABOR

Because it affects its very foundations, its basic moral principles, the gravest difficulty with which the movement is faced is the increasing employment of paid labor that is made necessary by the development of *kibbutz* industry. This has aroused and still arouses the most violent controversies in the *kibbutzim*, their assemblies and federations. The Artzi Federation, which is the most hostile to this development, admitted on the occasion of its anniversary congress in May 1963 that 27 per cent of the 1600 persons employed in its workshops and factories were not *haverim*, but paid workers. Other federations also have implacable opponents of the trend, as was shown at the meeting of the central committee (*merkaz*) of the Ihud in December 1961, which also commemorated the tenth anniversary of the federation. The veterans of the movement, several of whom—Haim Gvati, the general secretary, Meir Mendel, his predecessor, and Kadish Luz, the president of the Knesset—are well known, vigorously denounced industry as the Trojan horse of paid labor in the *kibbutz* movement. "The situation is grave," Mr. Luz declared. "This is the first time in my life that I have heard *haverim* defending paid labor by giving it an ideological plat-

---

[18] The setting up of "Regional Councils" and their modernization favors the expansion of *kibbutz* industries. These organizations, besides providing local municipal service, supply all the subsidiary services required by a group of *kibbutzim* and *moshavim;* each of these *kibbutzim* is free to join the "Regional Councils,"—co-operatives which provide them with equipment and machines and help them to convert or market their products.

form"; and he concluded by appealing to his audience to "remain faithful to our doctrine." Mr. Mendel recalled having heard cries of "Paid labor shall not pass," but, he added bitterly, it was passing. "The *kibbutzim*," he said, "on the one hand accept money from the banks, and on the other employ paid workers and profit from the surplus value that they create in the sweat of their brow."

It is understandable that the *kibbutz* pioneers should be extremely hostile to the employment of paid labor, which conflicts with their basic collectivist ideal. The *halutzim*, repudiating exploitation of man by man, joined together in scrupulous egalitarianism to clear and restore the fertility of the land of their ancestors. Having recourse to "outside" workers, even if they are Jews, conflicts with the principle that the *kibbutz* should be self-sufficient by reason of its own labor. This principle, a reaction to the conditions of Jewish life in the Diaspora, formed part of a whole system of *halutz* values based on the ideal of productive labor. Living by these ideals and practicing them would demonstrate to all the opponents of the Return, both Jewish and Gentile, the falsity of the anti-Semitic cliché that the Jews were condemned forever to remain middlemen, intermediaries in trade, commerce and finance, even moneylending, and prove that they were capable of succeeding in a direct struggle with the elements—earth, sand and rock in the case of the farmer, metal and wood in the case of the artisan, and raw materials in the case of the builder. The *halutzim* decided to carry out this demonstration on a communal, self-sufficient basis, without appealing to outside aid. The emphasis on productive (originally essentially agricultural) labor also explains why *haverim* often try to avoid domestic or maintenance jobs when the *kibbutz* secretariat organizes the periodic reshuffle. This is not because such work is considered dirty, disagreeable or monotonous, but because it is regarded as non-productive. A highly interesting study could be made at the present time of this ardent but sometimes naïve and intemperate search for "productivity" in the new Israel; it represents a swing of the pendulum, a reaction to the age-long exclusion of Jews from agriculture and industry. These are some of the complex motives that cause the *kibbutz* movement to shy at the employment of paid labor, which it admits only under the pressure of necessity and with a bad conscience. In agreeing to become even a partial employer of labor, it fears it is undermining its own moral foundations and is itself opening the gates to an exodus to the glittering lights and pleasures of the town.

The combination of opposition to paid labor on the one hand and the pursuit of productivity on the other have stimulated technical progress, mechanization and automation. This last is actually regarded by Meir Yaari, general secretary of the Mapam and "grand old man" of that party, as the panacea that will spare the *kibbutz* the dangerous temptations (and obligations) of employing paid labor.[19] The Ihud and Artzi federations are in agreement on a policy of progressively restricting their industries to those that, thanks to advanced automation, use a minimum of manpower, with a view to employing only personnel available on the spot, in the *kibbutz*.

But this policy is very difficult to apply, and it conflicts with realities, with decisions already made, with plans already on the way to execution. The *kibbutzim* of the Jordan Valley in their capacity as employers provide work for the inhabitants of Tiberias and other places, in their fields as well as in their factories. The extent to which paid labor has established itself in *kibbutz* agriculture is difficult to estimate, for in many cases it is used for seasonal jobs. The Ihud employs 20 per cent paid workers.

Among those who lack sympathy with *kibbutz* ideals—and lack of sympathy can range all the way from indifference to ridicule, from moderate criticism to outspoken hostility—the introduction of paid labor is a convenient target. It is a com-

[19] See his statements at the Mapam congress (April 1963). Benjamin Minz, when he was the head of the Poalei Agudat Israel, the orthodox trade union, also wanted to take advantage of automation, but for other purposes, (i.e. to enable the religious in an industrial society to respect the sabbath, when strictly speaking all work, particularly handling any tool, is forbidden). In other words, he wished to put electronics in the service of the Torah.

promise in which the "realists" who want everything to end in a return to individualism take pleasure. They also take pleasure in recalling the lofty and ambitious ideals of the founding fathers who toiled and struggled on what were then the unhealthy banks of Lake Kinneret (Tiberias), the peaceful reconquest of the land of their ancestors, the demolition by Jewish labor of the myths spread by their enemies, and their substitution for the exploitation of man by man of a social structure that had a significance going far beyond that of a few small settlements in Palestine.

But what the opponents of the *kibbutzim* fail to recall are the hard economic and political necessities of the state of Israel in the first few years after it came into being, when its very existence was at stake; they overlook the massive immigration that has taken place since 1948, the pathetic appeals of Ben-Gurion to all the enterprises of the country to absorb immigrants and find them jobs. The *kibbutz* federations responded to these appeals, even Hashomer Hatzair, which was in principle frankly hostile to them. The truth is that the employment of paid workers alleviated their manpower shortage while simultaneously serving the young nation's interests. Now it is difficult for them to go into reverse, at any rate in the immediate future. Will this breach with principles destroy the moral foundations of the movement? Does it contribute dangerously to keeping alive a crisis of values among the young and demoralizing them? Is it true that many *haverim* no longer know where they are or what their future role in the society and the nation is to be? The *kibbutzim* are certainly faced with a crucial decision, which they will have to discuss in broad daylight. If the employment of paid labor spreads, it will cause internal tensions and even splits such as have occurred in other co-operative ventures in other countries and at other times; and the *kibbutzim* would survive precariously as producer co-operatives whose members would be employers controlling agricultural enterprises and small, well-equipped industrial enterprises, a modernized form of decentralized domestic industry.

But things have not yet reached that stage. The flame lit by the founders of the *kibbutzim* still burns brightly in many men of the second generation and many young members of the third. The confrontation of the *kibbutzim* with the realities of our time presents a challenge to the practical idealism, the creative imagination, the courage of an elite that might have a tremendous regenerative effect far wider than this strip of territory in the Near East, on all the industrialized societies that, in spite of a century's efforts, have not succeeded in putting technical progress fully in the service of man, his physical and moral development, his happiness. This vast ambition could be a daily spur to the many young Israelis who, having thrown off their religious traditions, are in search of new motivations and new values. Here is a new frontier to be peacefully conquered, defended and maintained. By setting themselves the goal of superseding the employment of paid labor by spreading education and prosperity among their paid workers, whom they would progressively raise to the status of full partners, the *kibbutzim* would assure themselves of their complete loyalty. In an economically developing Israel the *kibbutz* can save itself from isolation and decline only by boldly tackling the whole complex of the human problems of industrial society and making a frontal attack on the difficulties unresolved by the most powerful nations. This experiment, though on a small scale, will be the more difficult in that it will have to be devised and conducted in a period in which a huge military effort is necessary to ensure survival in the face of external threats. But that is the only way that seems to me to assure the *kibbutzim* both economic and spiritual salvation.

KIBBUTZ DEMOCRACY

At a symposium at the Hebrew University in August 1963, on the role of the *kibbutz* movement in the Israeli society and economy, a number of speakers, including Professor Ernest Simon and Moshe Unna, a member of the Knesset, warned the federations against adopting a written constitution having the force of law and permanently laying down both their internal organization and their relations with the state. This, it was pointed out, would be equivalent to acknowledging that their aims had been accomplished, would mean the abandonment of all dynamism, and would involve them in the risk of losing their independence. It would also mean congealing themselves into the co-operative society pattern, while their real aim should be constantly to represent, both within Israel and without, the ideal of a democratic micro-society.

That, indeed, from the political aspect, is one of the movement's principal aims. Democracy is enshrined in the constitution of the *kibbutz*. It requires frequent meetings of the *haverim* (generally held on Saturday night after the end of the sabbath), the election of responsible officers, participation of a large number of members in the day-to-day management of the community, the greatest possible respect for individual tastes and wishes, the substitution of discussion for coercion and the absence of a privileged class of managers and bureaucrats. Such are the basic aims. But clear-sighted *kibbutznikim* admit that they were more easily attainable when the *kibbutz* was a small community of pioneers, a restricted group with an intense collective life and a high degree of participation. Nowadays, in a *kibbutz* divided up into different branches of production, often including one or more industries, the situation is more complicated. In the old days the general meeting was able to discuss and itself decide on its investment program; nowadays this is in practice impossible. Professional knowledge, economic and technical expertise, specialization, are becoming more and more indispensable, and the federations are having to create special institutions accordingly. In the early days the *kibbutz* could itself give its members the instructions necessary for the carrying out of their work. Nowadays, like all the enterprises of our time, it is confronted with the problems of information. This has to be made interesting and attractive, and has to be communicated rationally and at the right time. The most up-to-date *kibbutzim* are equipped with intercoms, and some that cover a large area have an internal radiotelephone system.

Is the participation of the members of a *kibbutz* in its management less extensive and more superficial than it was thirty years ago? That is a controversial question, on which research has been done, in particular by Erich Cohen of the University of Jerusalem. In the case of some *haverim* the spirit of participation seems to have been weakened by the new forms of organization, the growth of centralization and the increasing importance of technicians. They have the feeling that the important decisions affecting the life of the community are no longer really made at the general meeting, but elsewhere, by special committees, by those responsible for the various branches of the *kibbutz's* activities, by the secretariat, etc. When such feelings creep in among the members of a community, the result is skepticism, apathy and less regular attendance at meetings.

Internal democracy in a *kibbutz* is also linked with the principles and practice of egalitarianism in consumption, that is, the successful application of collectivism. With the transition from the limited field of the first *kvutzot* to the extensive and many-sided enterprises of the contemporary *kibbutz*, the problems grow more complex. The basic principle of *halutz* communism was and remains "from everyone according to his capacities, to everyone according to his needs." Because of the "informal" social control exercised continually by all the members of a restricted group, this kind of egalitarianism could be effectively achieved without any apparatus of laws, police or magistrates. The *kibbutz* ideology attaches a great deal of importance to egalitarianism of this kind, which, in the apparent absence of all coercion, is not "mechanical" but "qualitative," as one of the leading spirits of Hashomer Hatzair puts it. But when a *kibbutz* grows, diversifies, modernizes itself, one of its chief difficulties is to avoid declining from "qualitative" egalitarianism into "mechanical" constraint.

To do this it has to devise an egalitarianism in pluralism that takes into account to the maximum possible extent (or at all events to a far greater extent than in the old days) the individual tastes and needs of its members (in clothing, furniture, home comforts and personal quirks and fads). This is a continuing process, and the degree to which it is successful certainly depends on the policies devised by the masterminds of each federation, and even more on the chief officers of each *kibbutz*. These include the treasurer, the economic secretary, the internal secretary, the work organizer and the responsible members of the committees (or "branches"). The period of office varies from one to three years, after which there should theoretically be a reshuffle. But the growth of the *kibbutz*, increasing specialization, and the increasing technical knowledge required do not always enable rotation to take place. The role of the internal secretary, who is often called the social secretary because he devotes himself principally to the problems of community inter-relations, is vital. He has to deal with all matters not dealt with by those responsible for the different sectors, and to compose differences between them. Most of the groundwork for important decisions on economic or technical matters is done in advance by discussions at "the top," that is, federation level. It is not the same in the social sphere.

When a *haver* accepts an absorbing and responsible position in his *kibbutz* from which he derives no material advantages, he does not seem to be motivated by considerations of prestige. The source of his authority, unlike that of many officeholders in the social field both in East and West, is not the prestige of his position, but the manner in which he carries out his duties from day to day under his comrades' eyes. Nevertheless, *haverim* who are clear-sighted observers of their communities admit that the position of secretary does in fact involve prestige; to fill it satisfactorily the incumbent has to possess a certain informal authority, have organizing experience, understand people and be able to handle them. On an average, about 50 per cent of the *haverim* are members of the various committees and groups responsible for daily decisions; they are the nursery from which the "top management" and in particular the secretaries are drawn. This method of recruitment has important consequences. The smallness of the group from which the choice is made has to be borne in mind. The ablest and most experienced *haverim* sometimes occupy the post of social secretary several times, and the "rotation" of those who carry out these difficult duties takes place within a restricted group. But they all eventually return to the rank and file, and there does not seem to be any danger of the growth of a "managerial" class.

There is more risk of the latter's developing among those who are "mobilized," as the phrase is, or sent on detachment to the federations, or on *kibbutz* missions to the outside world. *Haverim* have occupied so many important positions since the establishment of the state that the whole state apparatus can be said to have been riddled with them. In the early days, the *hevra*, that is, the inner circle from which the leaders of the government, the Histadrut, the Knesset, the army, and even Israel's ambassadors to foreign countries were drawn, consisted to a great extent of *haverim*. "At the time when the state of Israel was founded the *kibbutznik* was king."[20] In a society in a state of economic growth there is an ever-increasing diversification of jobs. Nowadays, apart from deputies to the Knesset and leaders of political parties and trade unions and youth movements in Israel and in the Diaspora, the federations have to be supplied with technical advisers, specialists in economic problems have to be found at inter-federal level, and young *kibbutzim* have to be provided with advisers and instructors. The *haverim* supplied to the federation originally constituted a kind of "human tax" levied on each *kibbutz*. The rule was that this must not exceed 7 per cent of the *haverim* in each community, and the percentage has remained practically unchanged. No material advantage accrues to those sent on these "detached" duties; I was assured that a *haver* who becomes a minister remits his salary to his *kibbutz*, at which, incidentally, he frequently spends his weekends. One of them, Z., received me very hospitably in his *kibbutz* one sabbath. Actually only the outside of his small house resembled that of the other *haverim*; inside there was much more luxury and comfort. I see no cause for alarm at this inequality. Z., in spite of his youth, has been on the political scene for a long time. In his *kibbutz* he entertains, not only academics like myself, but also ministers from foreign countries and ambassadors. No doubt his drawing room was furnished out of his expense allowance.

Technically, the minister's official expense account is reimbursed. Unless the mobilized *haver's* work forces him to spend several years abroad, his family goes on living in the *kibbutz*, preserving moral and material ties with his community of origin; this is a "centripetal" factor, which counteracts the "centrifugal" influences to which he is inevitably subjected.

I pose this problem without being in a position to suggest an answer. It is among neither the most urgent nor the most worrisome with which the *kibbutzim* are faced. On the contrary, I regard the number and quality of these "detached" individuals, who assure contact between *kibbutz* society and Israeli society as a whole, the labor movement and the political and cultural life of the country in all their complexity, as a guarantee against isolation and self-centeredness. And those who are "detached" are not removed from the ideological and moral world of the *kibbutzim*; the leaders and advisers of the federations and those deputed to act as advisers or instructors to other *kibbutzim* remain within it. If the *kibbutzim* are to survive and develop, they must know the "other society" as it really is, come into close contact with it, and even clash with it.

FAMILY, EDUCATION, CONSUMPTION

Not the least of the problems that face the *kibbutzim* by reason of their own development and that of the "other society" in Israel are those involving inter-personal relations—the family, collective education, and relations between the generations (the young, the adult, and the aged).

Only those who have spent years, or at any rate long periods, in *kibbutzim* of different types, ages and ethnic composition are qualified to make generalizations on the subject. Let us rely on the evidence of qualified observers, such as H. Darin-Drabkin and Yonina Talmon. In their view the restriction of the functions of the family in the *kibbutz* community has a favorable effect, on relations both between married couples and between parents and children. The marriage rate is high and divorces are few.[21] In choosing a marriage partner young people are not swayed by financial considerations or expectations or opportunities for "getting on" or making a career such as often arise in western and even (insofar as making a career is concerned) eastern countries, where position in the party is a powerful lever of mobility in the economic and social scale. The links that bind both husband and wife to a shared communal life no doubt help to preserve stability, and love, free of "economic impurities," is enriched by moral intimacy in an atmosphere of friendship, advice and mutual support. (In the "outside world" I was often told that *kibbutz* women fade early, worn out by the life they lead.)

The parental role in bringing up children is far from being abolished. During the time that the child spends with them they are freer than other parents to think of him and for him, and the child is free to relax and play, either with them or with his friends, as he may feel inclined. In these circumstances he may be more drawn toward his parents than he would be in the "outside world," because they do not have the ungrateful task of "disciplining" him, which is the responsibility of the "socializing" institutions of the *kibbutz*—its trained nurses for the younger children and teachers and their own age group for the older. Some observers[22] actually claim that the consequence of this educational system is that affective relations between parents and children are stronger and deeper in the *kibbutz* than outside it. They claim that parents, relaxed and free after their day's work, are in a position often to say yes to the child (who is free of the cares of school) and have a "permissive" attitude to him during the hours of leisure and play that he spends with them. It is only at this time that the children enjoy care and attention

[21] Darin-Drabkin, *op. cit.*, p. 183.
[22] Z. Shefer, A *Developing Society: the Kibbutz*, Am Oved, Tel Aviv, 1960 (in Hebrew).

they do not have to share with other members of their age group, and the result is that the gratitude and affective credit for this daily privilege goes to the parents.

This system of upbringing, removing the responsibility from the parents and entrusting it collectively to the *kvutza*, was based on the scientific rationalism of the first *halutzim*, who relied completely on modern methods of applied education, not by parents often ill-qualified for the task, but by qualified teachers. Also, being hostile to the tradition of paternal authority, they wanted to assure women strict equality, both at work and in social status, and give them full opportunity for personal development.

The success of this part of the program is vigorously, and sometimes passionately, denied by some *haverot*, particularly among the "under forties." Women's work in the *kibbutz* seemed to me to be an acute current problem, even though it had not yet been officially discussed in the councils of the federations. Some of the reasons for their latent tensions and frustrations most frequently given by women are: (1) many employed in domestic tasks without the benefit of modern equipment do not in the eyes of *kibbutz* "public opinion" enjoy the prestige enjoyed by every *haver* who does his work well; (2) the very nature of their work, which is more exposed to scrutiny and criticism, puts them under constant collective pressure; and (3) (and this is no doubt the most serious of the complaints) girls, after receiving the same education as boys, if they wish to qualify for a career of their choice, have little opportunity to pursue it in the *kibbutz*; the labor market and the opportunities are too restricted.

Boys are not exempt from this difficulty either. This problem, like others previously mentioned, may be alleviated or superseded by modernization and mechanization, which will do away with many domestic tasks or turn the women responsible for them into responsible "technicians."

Collective education (*hinuch meshutav*) in the *kibbutzim* has been studied by the Israeli sociologists mentioned above. In the course of my visits I was particularly interested in the application of the "project" method—the connection between the work done by the children in the workshop or the various branches of agriculture on the one hand, and the general teaching given in the school on the other—and the basic educational role that is given to the class magazine, which the children themselves write and criticize. At the secondary school of the Beit Zera *kibbutz* we found Haim, the fourteen-year-old son of our friend B.N., engaged in a "multidisciplinary" study of feudalism, involving geography, general European history, Jewish and Islamic history, and medieval, and in particular Sephardic, literature. He was also the editor of his class magazine; one of the subjects chosen for this by his "collective" was the place of the voluntary principle in everyday life. Teachers play no part in either the choice of subjects or the writing and editing of the articles, but Haim and his comrades criticized their own lack of spontaneity and the dangers of organization. Of the words written on the blackboard that my companion translated for me I singled out the happy phrase: "We are activized, but not really active."

Among the many questions that occurred to me in relation to collective education in the *kibbutzim*, I recall two. In spite of the optimistic assurances of internal observers, I wonder whether in the new generation of adolescents—in the oldest communities it is the third—there is the same intellectual tension, the same creative restlessness that was so amply demonstrated by their elders. In reply to this it may be said that, *mutatis mutandis*, we are confronted here with the change in mentality that is to be noted among many young people outside the *kibbutzim* and outside Israel—that, in fact, what we have here is an instance of a universal phenomenon. We will return to this question in a wider context in connection with the crisis of values and problems of the young.

Here and now it leads us to another question. May not the apparent "normalization" of *kibbutz* youth be connected with their sheltered situation, particularly in communities where there are few or no children of immigrant parents, or children who came to Israel in a youth *aliya*? As long as they remain in the solid framework of educational institutions in which they progressively pass from one age group to the next, from the cradle to secondary school, there is no problem—outside critics say that in this closed, now artificial world there are perhaps not enough problems. The values and standards that they imbibe as a heritage seem natural to them—until the day when they discover the "other society." When this happens the shock is capable of causing some of them mental crises and heartbreaks of the kind that a young man brought up in a priests' seminary may experience if he is flung too suddenly into the world. Watching a swarm of these boys and girls coming back from school in a truck and dispersing in their *kibbutz*, and seeing them next day when the sabbath was over, healthy and cheerful, full of simple happiness and health, I could not help wondering whether there might not be harsh awakenings and ordeals ahead of some of them.

The efforts made by the *kibbutz* communities to cope with the problems of their aging members have been the subject of careful study by Yonina Talmon.[23] In the *kibbutz* the family is "extended" to several generations. But young couples who look after their aged parents only supplement what is done for the latter by the communal institutions, and their duties, as laid down for them by the society in which they live, do not interfere with their daily lives. The relationship between the generations is not spoiled (as it often is in our western societies) by a sense of guilt or resentment on the part of the young resulting from excessive responsibilities toward their aged parents. Because their responsibilities are limited, the young couples of the second generation are able to exercise them spontaneously

23 Among her publications in English and French are "The Family in Collective Settlements," *Transactions of the Third World Congress of Sociology*, International Sociological Association, Amsterdam, 1956, IV, pp. 116–126; "Social Structure and Family Size," *Human Relations*, XII, 1958, pp. 121–146; and, above all, "Aging in Israel. A Planning Society," *American Journal of Sociology*, November 1961, pp. 284–295. *Cf.* also *Esprit*, special number on aging, May 1963, "Jeunes et vieux dans les communautés israéliennes."

and generously. Here again the institutions of the *kibbutz*, far from weakening family relationships, reinforce them. These conclusions of Y. Talmon have not been invalidated by the work of others in this field.

In devising a new policy toward the problems of the aging, the *kibbutzim* have partially revised the ideology of the *halutzim*. The latter, as we have seen, laid stress on labor and productivity, that is, on youthful values. Many Zionist pioneers were revolutionary intellectuals and exalted the virtues of non-conformity and rebellion against patriarchal authority; in other words, they stood for discontinuity between the generations. The pioneer who reclaimed marshes and brought the desert into cultivation was necessarily a young man or a man in the prime of life, a symbol of national renascence and of the personal redemption of the Jew by manual labor, and Zionist youth movements were (and to an extent still are) impregnated with these ideals. From this aspect, aging looks like a moral as well as a physical decline, "a gradual privation of grace."[24] From the point of view of the strict *halutz* ethic, as from that of the Protestant ethic according to Max Weber, grace is recognized by "works," that is to say, by their quality and success. Apart from these ideological resistances, there is another obstacle, this one arising from concrete circumstances, to the retraining of aging *haverim*, namely the pace of technical progress and the "modernist" spirit of the *kibbutzim* which makes them continually strive to be up-to-date. The frequent replacement of equipment and the introduction of complex machinery devalue the experience of the old on the one hand and on the other increase the prestige of specialization among the young, who are still pliable and find readaptation easier.

Thus, in devising a series of new measures for the benefit of their aged members the *kibbutz* federations have rigged their sails toward a vision of life wider than that of the *halutzim*, less rigidly centered on the cult of youth, manual labor and productivity. After systematic analysis of all the work done in

---

[24] Y. Talmon, *American Journal of Sociology, op. cit.*, p. 285.

the *kibbutz*, they have reserved certain jobs for older members, particularly jobs combining responsibility with relatively little physical exertion (fish-breeding, bee-keeping, dairy work). Jobs are also reserved for them in light industry and in workshops, which are sometimes especially established for the purpose. Older members are also retrained for employment as social or agricultural instructors in a young *kibbutz* "adopted" by an older one, or as accountants or librarians; suitable older persons are sent "on detachment" as representatives of the *kibbutz* in the federations or other organizations, such as the co-operative organizations or the Histadrut.

In reassessing the institutions on which family life, the role of women, collective education, relations between parents and children and the treatment and retraining of the aged depend, the aim is to secure a maximum of advantages for the members of the *kibbutz* and at the same time reduce to a minimum the tensions or frustrations of communal life. But are the latter not bound to increase in an age when the basically ascetic principles of the *kibbutz* (or at any rate the strict communal regimentation of *kibbutz* life) are, in spite of its relative isolation, constantly confronted with a stream of "models" of "affluent" societies and of the race to prosperity imported from the West (particularly the United States) by the mass media of communication? These "models" are very widespread in Israel. The *kibbutz* is no longer a place where "all are equal in poverty," but it cannot become a place where "all are equal in affluence" without denying its principles. The policy of "liberalization" carried out in varying degrees in different federations during the past ten years or so shows that the movement as a whole is aware of these problems and is determined to find an answer to them. If the *kibbutz* ignored the findings of contemporary psychology—the nature and strength of the impulses that it has revealed and the dangers to both the individual and the group involved in their blind repression—it would be condemning itself to failure. Since the first *kibbutzim* were established man has acquired greater knowledge of himself, and big breaches in the intellectual and pseudo-scientific rationalism with which the idealism of the *halutzim* was combined have been made by the work of Freud, Janet, Adler, Jung, Lewin and their successors. Man cannot be fashioned in a collective mold as easily as the "founding fathers" of the movement believed, though in the early stages, in the economic and psychological conditions of the *yishuv* (need for survival, pioneering enthusiasm, the general poverty), there was greater plasticity than there is today.[25]

The resistance, the revolt, of certain impulses and human needs are now more evident. The individual cannot really repress them, even if he makes up his mind in principle to do so. If he succeeds in repressing them, he suffers for it, and his personal difficulties are daily reflected in his relations with his family and his fellow workers. In spite of all his efforts, it becomes impossible for him to find his equilibrium in the life of the community.

What are the principal causes of the tensions with which liberalization is intended to cope? Liberalization is still the subject of lively discussion in the federations. Meuhad and particularly Artzi are on the whole more attached to original principles and more resistant to change than Ihud. Thus "personal grants" of money with which to buy clothes, which were authorized by the Ihud council meeting at Einat, are not available in the two other big federations. But the general trend in the *kibbutzim* is the direction of meeting the *kibbutznik's* need for intimacy and relaxation in a small circle of relatives and personal friends after working hours and on the sabbath. The addition of a kitchenette in old living quarters and the inclusion of one in the accommodations at new *kibbutzim* enable those *haverim* who desire it to have light meals at home at midday and also in the evening; the *kibbutz* supplies the utensils and the food. A still more important reform is the easing of the rules for collective child-raising, diminishing the separation of

[25] *Cf.* J. Ben David, "Professions and Social Structure in Israel," *Scripta Hierosolymitana*, Vol. III, Studies in Social Science. The Hebrew University, Jerusalem, 1955, p. 126.

mother and child (which is the subject of lively criticism), and strengthening the family unit. About fifteen *kibbutzim*—most of them belonging to the Ihud and including Degania—have agreed to the provision of a room for the children in their parents' quarters. They spend the night there, and return to their "house" next morning, where they work all day and take their meals.

The trend evident in these domestic arrangements is even more noticeable in the attitude of the federations to personal possessions.[26] Originally, during the period of total collectivism, the *haver* had no personal possessions except a pair of slippers and a toothbrush. Clothes were redistributed after being cleaned. This system, known as "Commune A," was progressively modified from 1935 onward. Today the *kibbutzim* allow their members to choose the "style" of their clothing, and the more liberal ones allow them to choose that of their furniture as well, but personal cash allowances to permit a *haver* to go to town and buy the clothes and underwear of his choice instead of drawing them from the *kibbutz* store has been the subject of lively controversy. The principle used to be that cash allowances to meet holiday expenses or minor purchases (e.g. presents for the children) must not exceed 4 per cent of the annual cost of living of a *kibbutz* family. Some *kibbutzim* have increased this and allow money to be spent on personal purchases of a kind considered to be relevant to individual tastes. Strict regulations apply to the utilization of inherited property or funds received as reparations from the German Federal Republic. In principle such funds go entirely to the community, which assumes ownership of them and then decides on the share that the *haver* may use for his personal needs or pleasure. The mere admission of some personal entitlement on his part (the proportion varies in different cases) is a modification of the strict collectivism laid

---

[26] Eva Rosenfeld has made a study of the early stages of the trend in the years that followed the establishment of the state. See her *Institutional Change in Israeli Collectives*, thesis, Columbia University, and "Institutional Change in the Kibbutz," *Social Problems*, Vol. 2, 1957. *Cf.* Albert Meister, *Principes et tendances de la planification rurale en Israël*, Mouton, Paris and The Hague, 1962, p. 106.

down by the formula "to each according to his needs." Many *kibbutzim*, particularly in the Artzi federation, resist the trend and stand by collective principles as the moral foundation without which the whole edifice would collapse.

Here, too, the *kvutza* has to walk the razor's edge between intolerable rigidity and dangerous compromise. Can it ignore the increasing pressure of individual consumption? The daughters and wives of *kibbutznikim* cannot be entirely deprived of the pleasures of looking smart and attractive. The federation leaders (even those of Hashomer Hatzair) certainly no longer regard Soviet society as a model in the establishment of new kinds of socialist-inspired human relationships. Nevertheless they observe the whole path followed by the Soviet Union since the October Revolution toward the differentiated satisfaction of needs that have revived and increased with industrialization and the rise in average income. The policy makers seem to have realized that too much must not be demanded of the individual, that the *haver* is not an artificially constructed superman, and that there are deep tendencies in him that cannot be suppressed. If the *kibbutzim* insisted on remaining in the strait-jacket of a permanent and omnipresent collectivism and tried to impose on their members by the force of "public opinion" a niggling and increasingly impatiently tolerated social control, they would inevitably end by foundering in the midst of a society in full economic growth, whose models of varied consumption, prosperity and abundance would inevitably gradually penetrate their defenses. But let us not conceal from ourselves the fact that the concessions made to individual consumption, limited though they may be, constitute a "serious breach in the collectivist ideology"[27] of the communities.

Such, in broad outline, is the psychological and social background behind the slogan "more individual liberty" which I often heard being attacked or defended in discussions of the *kibbutz*. The *kibbutz* federations, anxious to study the effects

[27] A. Meister, *op. cit.*, p. 107.

of major economic and social changes on their institutions and the readjustments made necessary by them, have promoted research into the problems involved under the scientific direction of specialists from Israeli universities. The research for which the Artzi federation is responsible, in which Erich Cohen of the University of Jerusalem is taking part, is devoted, among other things, to job analysis in modernized *kibbutzim*, and a study of work satisfaction and internal democracy in *kibbutz* institutions. Other work, inspired by the question of group dynamism, is to be devoted to the relations between *haverim* during the period of the *kibbutz's* adaptation to Israeli society in a stage of economic growth.

THE *KIBBUTZIM* AND THE "OTHER SOCIETY"

The difficulties for the *kibbutzim* arising from the economic growth of Israel are plain, and the signs of their confrontation with the "other society" are many and obvious. The observer notes daily the diversity and contrast of the impact made by the *kibbutzim* on the minds of his interlocutors. Except perhaps to the less developed new immigrants from North Africa, the *kibbutzim* are not just institutions like any others to the people of Israel. An investigation of the reactions to them in different environments and levels of the population would be as interesting as it would be difficult to carry out, and to my knowledge no one has yet attempted it. I met critics whose attitude was ironical, even sarcastic, who took a malicious pleasure in pinpointing the compromises and retreats that have taken place in comparison to the idealism of the pioneers. These critics regard the *kibbutzim* as privileged groups indirectly subsidized by the Israeli economy as a whole, and they claim that a great deal of tension and neuroticism exists in them, particularly among the children. (These latter claims have not been substantiated by any study of mental health in the *kibbutzim*.) A kind of Voltairian skepticism toward all Jewish enthusiasms, whether lay or religious, is discernible here and there in the new Israeli so-

ciety, and attitudes of this kind are not surprising in an economically developing society in which the private sector is developing and western "models" directed toward the "normal"
satisfactions of individual and family life are more and more
widespread. I also believe there are other reasons for it. Some
Israelis, who in the Diaspora had the traditional religious upbringing and strictly obeyed the dietary laws, have been caught
up in the realities of the age and seem to be reacting violently to
the traditions they have shaken off and to all forms of what in
their eyes is outdated and even dangerous asceticism.

Apart from hostility of this sort, whose origins are often social
or emotional, there is the critical, would-be aloof and "objective"
attitude that prevails in certain academic circles. These critics
already regard the *kibbutzim* as part of history, and attribute
their present difficulties to their inadaptability to the present
age.[28] They say that it is no longer possible to put the chief
emphasis on the *halutz* virtues of asceticism and selflessness and
even of personal achievement, for Israeli society is being directed
toward other aims—prosperity, the amenities of urban life, technical efficiency, and productivity in the service of abundance.
The communal spirit was not only an ideal but also a means
toward Zionist ends. But now that the Jewish state has been
established, ideals have changed, and the new society as a whole
recognizes the legitimacy of the profit motive. With the aid of
statistics these critics claim that both the economic and moral
importance (the defenders of the *kibbutzim* make the question of "importance" the central issue) of the *kibbutzim*, whose
80,000 members (families included) do not represent even 4 per
cent of the Jewish population of the country, has declined. They
met the needs of a heroic age, but cannot survive in radically
different conditions without undergoing radical change themselves, involving the sacrifice of their principles, which would

---

[28] Among the best work on rural sociology in Israel that attempts to do justice
to the *kibbutzim* and at the same time places them in the context of economic
and social development is that of D. Weintraub and his colleagues (Hebrew
University of Jerusalem).

mean their rapid disintegration into the "other society." The *halutz* spirit of perseverance, heroic toil by small groups in a struggle with the elements, is obsolete in an age when the clearing of land, the irrigation of deserts, the reclamation of marshes, can be done more quickly and more cheaply by a whole battery of machines than by taking "pioneers" to the spot and maintaining them there. Nowadays a different form of pioneering spirit is required, my friend D., a sociologist, says. The education of the young in the *kibbutz* is one of the best pieces of evidence of this inadaptation. Children are still indoctrinated with *halutz* values, which in most cases are no longer embodied in and demonstrated by their parents who belong to the second generation, are more modern and more "liberal," and have revised the ideologies of the founding fathers on their own account. These views coincide with those of the "realist" group of statesmen, whom we shall discuss later.

In these conditions it is legitimate to ask whether the *kibbutzim*, now largely populated by the second generation of *haverim* and their children, plus a few thousand recent immigrants, have preserved their spiritual ardor. Are they still as firmly cemented by communal values? Any general reply would be hazardous. There are distinct differences between different movements and *kibbutzim* of different ages in this respect. Artzi seems to have a livelier ideological life than Ihud; there are differences between old and young *kibbutzim*, particularly when the latter are engaged in a real pioneering struggle on the threatened frontiers; there are also differences between rich and poor *kibbutzim*, and those that have been penetrated by industry and others that have remained exclusively agricultural.

Let us pass quickly over the comments made in Israel both by the skeptics on the lookout for every sign of "normalization" in the *kibbutzim* and by young idealists in search of a new mystique. The sort of thing the latter say is, "Nowadays in the *kibbutzim* you find nothing but well-fed animals," or "The *kibbutzim* are dead, they send you to sleep," or "All they've got to offer you nowadays is comfort." The material comforts that make these faithful apostles purse their lips were obtained at the cost of the most fantastic privations and efforts. On the other hand the hesitations shown by Darin-Drabkin, an *a priori* sympathetic observer, are worthy of note.[29] He admits that with the new generation the intellectual climate in the *kibbutzim* has changed: "Ideological discussions are infrequent and do not arouse much interest." He also states that the "*kibbutzim* devote much attention to political and ideological problems," and that in these fields they exercise an influence out of proportion to their demographic weight.

These two observations are in fact less contradictory than might appear at first sight. The second is based on the proportion of *haverim* who are deputies to the Knesset (sixteen, or more than 25 per cent of the sixty-three representatives of the three labor parties). The federations send their ablest political minds "on detachment" to the outside world, while inside the *kibbutz* intellectual life concentrates increasingly on the arts and literature or the sciences and technology. Undoubtedly there is justification for considering it less rich and ardent than in the period of the *halutzim*. As for the unifying values that sustain the "morale" of the group, though shared economic hardships have diminished or even vanished and participation in democratic management has declined, there remains pride in belonging to a *kibbutz*. This is accompanied by a feeling of "superiority" to an environment in which social justice is not considered the highest aim and people are less concerned with pioneering activities and the nation's needs.[30] But in a *kibbutz* besieged by an affluent society and penetrated by its values this sense of superiority runs the risk of transformation into a sense of inferiority, isolation and bitter and impotent contempt.

There are four main trends hostile to the *kibbutzim* in Israel, and these sometimes mingle and reinforce one another. The first is indifference or hostility to socialism, and this is now reinforced by the second, the disappointment caused by the

[29] *Cf.* Darin-Drabkin, *op. cit.*, pp. 315 and 319.
[30] Darin-Drabkin, *op. cit.*, p. 179.

course of development in the Soviet Union and the whiffs of anti-Semitism from there, to which the Hashomer Hatzair movement, which was very much oriented toward Soviet communism, has been particularly sensitive. This has both diminished the confidence of the socialists and reinforced their opponents' case. Moshe Dayan expresses the opinion, not only of a group of politicians but of a large section of public opinion when he declares (in his caustic tone) that the old socialist ideals—still defended in the Mapai congress by such accredited leaders as Levi Eshkol, Golda Meir and Zalmann Aranne—"simply have nothing whatever to do with the kind of people who nowadays live in Israel."[31] He describes ideology as a luxury that developing countries simply cannot afford. This is the section of public opinion that riddles with its irony the ideals and outdated illusions of the leaders of the Mapam, and thus by implication also those of Hashomer Hatzair and its *kibbutzim*. The Mapam, it is said, "will play a very feeble constructive role in the labor movement and the nation if it persists in behaving like a group of students belonging to an atheist *yeshiva*, barracading itself behind the barbed wire of its *kibbutzim*. The credit acquired by past merits is rapidly evaporating in the face of the challenges of the present."[32]

The picture of the *kibbutzim* barricaded behind their barbed-wire brings to mind a third danger, a trend toward segregation and isolation, with consequences both economic and moral. Isolation would involve inability to replenish their population from the outside world. Shortage of manpower would then lead to a fourth danger—increasing recourse to paid labor.

These various trends affect public opinion, primarily that of the young in urban areas, who are undergoing a crisis of values, to which we shall return. Many young *sabras* mistrust intellectual systems, ignore or would like to forget the struggles of the recent past, and take the liberties they enjoy as a matter of

---

[31] Speech to the Mapai congress, October 15, 1963.
[32] J.P.W., April 19, 1963.

course. Their pragmatism tends to make them lukewarm or even indifferent to the ideals of their Zionist and socialist parents, and consequently to the *kibbutz*, which for long was their symbol. The *kibbutz* no longer stands in the forefront of the scene. Immigration is now legal, and the defense of the country is the responsibility of the army. Not only the young, but also a considerable cross-section of the adult population, particularly in the big towns, react to the changes in the social climate. The prestige of the *kibbutznik* is not what it used to be. By taking over the tasks formerly done by a voluntary army of pioneers and youth movements the government has accentuated this development.[33]

I have drawn attention to the grave problems noted by the observer on the spot and confirmed by reflection. On the other hand I have not concealed my feeling that, notwithstanding these difficulties, the *kibbutzim* represent the most successful attempt yet made to substitute communal principles for private interests as the foundation of social life. The *kibbutz* experiment, though on a far bigger scale than the communal experiments of which history offers us examples, from the Essenes to co-operative ventures by small producers in the twentieth century, is nevertheless relatively minute; it is a "micro-sociological" phenomenon in relation to the ambitions of the communist societies of the Soviet Union, the European popular democracies, or China, whose population is more than three hundred times that of Israel. The success of the *kibbutz* way of life may be contrasted with the tensions, the "survivals of capitalism" in Soviet society exemplified by such things as social differences, the emergence of new forms of inequality, the role of personal ambition, hedonist trends, the race for prosperity, and "economic crime." The reality of human relations, whether in Moscow or in a *kolkhoz*, is more remote from the ethical ideal laid down in Marx's philosophy (e.g. in relation to the role

[33] *Cf.* Darin-Drabkin's admirable summing up of the situation, *op. cit.*, pp. 324–325.

of money, the conflict between manual and intellectual labor, and family life) than it is in an average Israeli *kibbutz*. The latter is more than a "contribution to the micro-sociology of socialist societies"[34]; it is, on a limited scale, an original and successful application of communist principles.

But the contemporary social sciences have demonstrated that small groups cannot be considered in isolation from society as a whole, as if they were autonomous, impermeable cells. On the contrary, they are part of a living tissue. Constant interaction takes place between small groups of all sorts (family, educational, occupational, trade union, religious and also leisure groupings) and the society out of which they were born. If large-scale attempts to create a "new kind of man," new human relations inspired by the communist doctrine, have partly failed, it is because the authoritarian, centralized institution of state socialism subject to the dictatorship of a single party—in practice that of a restricted circle of leaders—has been incapable of giving birth to this "new kind of man" and enabling him to live and prosper. Similarly it would be a great mistake to believe that the micro-communism of the *kibbutz* could survive in the long run in an economically developing society penetrated by models of abundance.

The *kibbutz* will not survive in Israel unless it adapts itself to the economic and technical imperatives of profitability and productivity and at the same time preserves its driving force and essential standards and values, remaining all the time a myth, a living, formative utopia. It will not be able to survive against a background of daily conflict between these essential values and those of Israeli society as a whole. Nor will it be able to survive if the long-term development of the encompassing society takes place in a direction opposite to that of the *kibbutz* experiment, that is, if the socialist sector is progressively reduced in relation to the private sector, and if the new generation of technically equipped and realist *sabras* turns Israel in the years to come into a society "just like the others," a model of modern capitalism in the Near East.

---

[34] Darin-Drabkin, *op. cit.*, p. 341.

Many representatives of middle-of-the-road opinion take the view that the *kibbutzim* no longer stand for the central problems of Israel, which have now moved elsewhere. They argue that the main task of the present day is that of integrating into the nation that large section of the population represented by the immigrants who have entered the country since 1948, the great majority of whom, unlike most of their predecessors, were not motivated by pioneering ideology. It is generally admitted that the *kibbutzim* do not represent a form of social organization that is attractive to these immigrants or is capable of absorbing and molding them. But, while the pioneering activity efficiently undertaken by the state is highly praised, there is no desire to jettison that other kind of pioneering which, thanks to the energy of their members, was and remains the mainspring of the *kibbutz* communities. State pioneering and individual pioneering are indivisible. Devaluing the ideals represented by the *kibbutzim* would mean rejecting their invaluable contribution to Israeli society as a whole. "Realist" technicians and bulldozer drivers inspired solely by personal interests would have to be paid very highly indeed to irrigate the Negev, if they were not to be tempted to throw up the job at the first opportunity and hurry to the city lights of Tel Aviv to find more agreeable and remunerative work.

Devaluing the pioneering spirit, the spirit of disinterested service to a collective ideal, would also mean depriving youth movements in the Diaspora of their strongest appeal and sacrificing all chance of attracting an elite of young people to Israel. As Dan Leon, a *haver* at Yasur, a *kibbutz* in western Galilee, pointed out in a closely argued plea, the *kibbutz* is not a "place of retreat."[35]

In discussing the critics' arguments one by one, he drew particular attention to the progress made by *kibbutz* agriculture. In 1963 the Artzi *kibbutzim* derived 70 per cent of their income from agriculture, 23 per cent from industry and 7 per cent from "outside work." During the same year the number of paid

[35] "The *kibbutz* remains faithful to its ideals." J.P.W., June 28, 1963.

workers was reduced by 30 per cent in agriculture and 16 per cent in industry.[36] The lack of markets for certain agricultural products was certainly a cause for concern, he pointed out, but it was less serious, after all, than the poverty and semi-starvation from which so many other young states were suffering. "The hardest nut to crack" for the movement as a whole during the next few years remained the problem of paid labor.

In the last resort, he continued, it was a fact that the *kibbutznik* was nearer than any other category of Israeli to the new type of Jew of whom the movement of national renascence had always dreamed—productive, rooted in the soil, and the creator of a culture. If the essential values of the *kibbutz* were rejected, as the realists and skeptics rejected them, and if the slogans of affluence and "Why should we do without?" were adopted, they must accept the consequences. It was not only the *kibbutz* that was condemned; all Israelis, all Zionists, all socialists and ultimately all Jews were condemned with it. There is more than an emotional reaction in this moving *cri du coeur* by a *haver*. The future of the state of Israel as a "different" society and of Jewish idealism in Israel are closely linked with the fate of the *kibbutzim*.

However, the dangers the federations make no effort to conceal may yet be surmounted. The game between the *kibbutzim* and Israeli society as a whole is far from over. The latter forms a closely knit structure reinforced by the rapid growth of industrial production and linked with the economic success of the *moshavim*[37] introduced into the collective sector controlled by the Histadrut. The *kibbutz* adventure has increased importance

[36] Report presented by Shlomo Rosen, general secretary of the Artzi *kibbutzim*, —to the executive committee of that federation (January 1964). Taking the *kibbutz* movement as a whole, the growth of its annual income during the ten years 1953–63 was proportionately greater than that of the Israeli gross national product during the same period. According to a communication of Haim Barkai to the inter-federation symposium held at Jerusalem University in August 1963, the net product of *kibbutz* industry, including factories and artisans' workshops, equaled that of agriculture as early as 1959.

[37] For the economics of the *moshavim* and a comparison with those of the *kibbutzim* see J. Klatzmann, *op. cit.*, pp. 150–156.

in a world in which the supersession of the "old type of man" molded by capitalist society has been postponed and the two great communist states have quarreled bitterly and accuse each other of heresy. Faced with the psychological and moral results at the individual level achieved so far by experiments in a planned economy, some observers of the eastern countries wonder whether the models of the humanization of inter-personal relations—particularly labor relations—contained in the philosophical works of Marx and Engels should not be considered utopian. They should be kept on the horizon, they say, but can be approached only by bearing realities constantly in mind, using a carefully devised system of trial and error, a policy of experimental reforms—such being the policy in fact practiced by the "socialist" states.[38] The *kibbutz* movement, in spite of its limitations and difficulties, is the biggest and most successful "utopian" revolutionary experiment that has been attempted and the closest approach to the way of living at which communism aims. In the *kibbutzim* I met men of wide culture, and also creators, artists, writers, technicians, in whose daily lives the contradiction between manual labor and the work of the mind, which Marx denounced, has been overcome.

Let us not idealize the *haverim*. The best of them are men struggling with their weaknesses and with a society that is often alien and sometimes actually hostile to their enthusiasms. They are at grips with the century of automation, nuclear strategy, mass culture, the dramas of the Third World which surround and sometimes involve them. Nevertheless they represent a human advance, not based on any contemplative wisdom or mystique "separated" from the social body like that of the Hassidim, and still less on unconditional retreat such as that of the Natorei Karta, who are entirely absorbed in waiting for the Messiah and defying the world about them. Neither do they

---

[38] This seemed to me to be the attitude of Professor J. Hochfeld, of the University of Warsaw, in a talk delivered at the École Pratique des Hautes Études on May 15, 1963, and inspired by his book *Studia o Marksowskiej Teorii Spoleczenstwa* ("Essay on the Marxist Theory of Society") and in particular the chapter "Two models of the humanization of labor."

seek to pluck these rewards like a fruit inevitably ripened by new productive relations which automatically deliver the old type of man from his egoisms and passions. Instead they seek to advance through difficulties, setbacks, the ever-changing problems of their original institutions, ennobling collective life and continually rising again. I have indicated enough of the shadows not to have to veil the light, and I have drawn attention to enough dangers not to overlook their successes and indicate their hopes. The *kibbutzim* are nowadays Israel's most effective contribution to the millenary messianic promise of justice and peace; and this contribution is in large measure due to unbelievers inflamed by the same ardor that consumed Isaiah.

3

The Histadrut and the "Labor Economy"

Looked at in the context of the Israeli economy as a whole, the *kibbutzim*, in their role as producers' co-operatives, form part of the "labor economy," which itself constitutes one of the three sectors into which the productive activity of the country is divided: the public sector, the private sector, and the collectivist sector controlled by the Histadrut, the General Federation of Labor.

A STRANGE LABOR FEDERATION

It is impossible to stay or travel about in Israel without constantly coming up against the direct or indirect presence of the Histadrut, its institutions, influence and power, and the differing and sometimes violently contrasting images of it reflected in people's minds, depending upon their age, income level, occupation or ethnic origin. Though it is nearly half a century old, it has not yet been the subject of the exhaustive study that Israeli historians and sociologists might have devoted to it. The truth of the matter is that it is a highly complex and emotionally charged subject and such a study even if it were carried out by highly qualified teams would inevitably lead to passionate controversy; the Histadrut today represents the whole structure of state socialism in Israel.

It was founded in December 1920 by a convention at Haifa, and was intended to meet the urgent need of organizing the workers of the Jewish national home, the outcome of the Balfour declaration of November 2, 1917, then still in its early stages. A High Commissioner of Palestine, Sir Herbert Samuel, himself of Jewish origin, had been appointed under the British mandate a few months earlier. The founders of the Histadrut, several of whom were later among the founders of the state of Israel, were inspired by the ideals of Zionism and national liberation. At first the organization had barely 4500 members. In 1966, including the families of members, it had nearly one and a half million, or nearly three-quarters of the Jewish population, plus fifty thousand Arabs. The three other federations of labor, supported by the religious parties or the revisionist organization, could together claim only about one-tenth of that figure; moreover two of them have been practically absorbed by the Histadrut.[1]

In its own chart of operations the Histadrut presents itself as a departmentalized organization, and indeed it is better understood if its four principal functions are distinguished: (1) its trade-union function proper; (2) its economic function (control, ownership and management of the most varied productive enterprises); (3) its social-security function, which it exercises through a complex of social insurance and other institutions; and (4) its cultural function, including adult education.

In the first of these roles it has under its wing trade unions representing about 90 per cent of the working population in all three sectors of the economy, not only in industry and agriculture, but also in administration, trade, transport and the liberal and technical professions. All members have a vote in the election of delegates to the conventions (the ninth of which was held in February 1960). Members of the general council (Moatza) and the executive council (Va'ad Hapoel) are elected from among these delegates, and the Central Committee is elected from the council.

The near-monopoly of social-security benefits exercised by the Histadrut certainly contributes to the stability of its massive

---

[1] Cf. pp. 299–300 for additional information and statistics about the Histadrut and its organization, as well as details about the other trade-union organizations.

membership. All its members are *ipso facto* members of the sickness-insurance organization, the celebrated Kupat Holim, and to benefit from the numerous advantages that membership in the Kupat Holim provides it is necessary to be in practice a member of the Histadrut—a state of affairs that its opponents regard as unacceptable. In certain cases the Kupat Holim grants benefits to non-members of the Histadrut—members of the religious trade-union organizations, new immigrants during the first few months after arrival, orphans, and others recommended by the appropriate authorities, as well as families of members of the police force.

I met clerical workers and holders of academic posts who admitted that their principal motive for belonging to the Histadrut was the Kupat Holim, whose admirable service includes more than a thousand clinics, sixteen hospitals, eighteen convalescent homes, two hundred nurseries and maternity homes, etc., and which has an annual budget more than double that of the Ministry of Health—which is not surprising considering that it receives 46.5 per cent of the subscriptions to the Histadrut (which amount to nearly 4.5 per cent of each member's pay). Thus the Kupat Holim receives about 2 per cent of the national payroll, increased by a supplement amounting to 80 per cent of the ordinary subscription paid by members of the Histadrut who wish to assure their families the full range of available benefits. It should be noted that, thanks to the Kupat Holim, every new immigrant gets a medical examination on his arrival and free medical care for three months, whether or not he finds work and joins the Histadrut during that time. For the nine months that follow he pays a very low trade-union subscription rate. The Kupat Holim covers the great majority of Israeli citizens, but its benefits do not extend to those who are not members or dependents of members of the working population. This disturbing situation provides the advocates of a national health service one of their principal arguments.

To understand the problems that the Histadrut raises, which are psychological as well as economic and social, it is necessary to bear in mind at least in broad outline the original link between its various institutions.

Apart from being a trade-union federation entrusted with the defense of the workers' interests and its monopoly or near-monopoly in the field of medical care and social security, it is also the master of one of the three great sectors of the national economy, owning and controlling productive enterprises whose value amounts to thousands of millions of Israeli pounds, and is the employer of a large proportion of the workers whose interests it is its duty to protect in the public and private sectors, and theoretically in its own as well.

If I may hazard a philosophical comparison, the Histadrut resembles the substance of Cartesian philosophers, which is completely but differently expressed by its several attributes. Similarly, the attributes of the Histadrut correspond to the different functions of this remarkable trade-union federation. One of them is the Kupat Holim; another is the Hevrat Ovdim, which represents its economic function. The Hevrat Ovdim is the "general association of co-operative labor in Israel." All members of the Histadrut are automatically members of the Hevrat Ovdim. In other words, the Hevrat Ovdim is the whole Histadrut in its role as an association of co-operatives. The trade-union movement is coextensive with the co-operative movement. The convention, general council and executive council of the Histadrut can meet as the bodies responsible for laying down and carrying out Hevrat Ovdim policy.

The Histadrut's purpose in organizing itself in this fashion was to accelerate the economic growth of Israel, create employment for the successive waves of immigration and, above all perhaps in the minds of its leaders, reinforce and extend the collective sector, whose means of production and management are in the hands of the workers' organization that owns them.

THE TRIPARTITE ECONOMY

Let us pause for a moment to note some features of the economic growth to which the Histadrut wishes to contribute by demonstrating the superiority of its methods, which dictate the path of "Israeli socialism," over other forms of production and distribution.

Between 1950 and 1958 the annual increase in gross national product per inhabitant exceeded 5 per cent, which represents an average rate of increase in the national income of 12.5 per cent.[2] The massive absorption of immigrants is a no less remarkable achievement, although it has created still unresolved difficulties to which we shall return.[3] The rate of absorption was 26.6 per cent in 1949 and 13.2 per cent in 1951—figures that have never been reached in any other host country; and this was done without incurring an unemployment rate much greater than that of such highly industrialized countries as the United States, Canada or Japan. The unemployment rate reached a maximum (11 per cent of the working population) in 1953, but the average rate for the period considered by Sitton (1950–1958) was 7 per cent. At least 85 per cent of workers who came to Israel found jobs, and unemployment fell to 3.3 per cent in 1964. It is true that, according to Don Patinkin in his masterly survey of the first decade of the Israeli economy, workers on part time and the disguised unemployed who unduly swell administrative offices and the tertiary sector ought to be included in the unemployment statistics.[4] Unemployment particularly affects the so-called "orientals" from North Africa or Asia, whose original skills or qualifications were unusable in a society undergoing industrialization, the structure of whose working populations tends to resemble that of western models. The problem of readaptation has been difficult ever since the beginning of Jewish immigration, for a considerable proportion of the immigrants were small tradesmen or artisans or came from a few light industries (e.g. the clothing trade) or the liberal professions. Commerce has absorbed only about 12 per cent of

[2] Shlomo Sitton, Israël: immigration et croissance, Editions Cujas, Paris, 1963, pp. 307 and 309.

[3] Cf. Chapter 6, "The Second Israel."

[4] Don Patinkin (dean of the faculty of economic sciences in the Hebrew University), The Israel Economy, The First Decade. Falk Project, Jerusalem, 1960.

the immigrants, agriculture nearly 20 per cent, and industry 11.6 per cent. The hypertrophy of the tertiary sector, which still employs more than half the Jewish population, as it did before the establishment of the state, remains disturbing.[5]

Other shadows on the bright picture of economic growth are the country's adverse trade balance, which diminished in 1963,[6] and, above all, the symptoms of inflation. Money in circulation increased six and a half times between 1948 and 1958 (i.e. at an average rate of 17 per cent a year). The cost of living index trebled and the Israeli pound had been devalued by 16 per cent in relation to the 1948 rate calculated in dollars. Capital imports largely from the United States (funds raised by the Jewish Agency and the Jewish National Fund, i.e. unilateral transfers) and also from Federal Germany (reparation payments to the victims of Nazism) accentuated the inflationary trend. Israel, while simultaneously providing herself with the military resources necessary for her defense, has thus been living beyond her income. The beginning of 1962 marked a turning point in the policy of the young state, and in becoming more independent it is trying, in the words of S. Sitton, to "live on the fruits of its own labor." The success of this policy, however, will partly depend on its relations with the Common Market. Taking full account of the external aid it received, it is still remarkable that in recent years Israel's gross national product increased at an annual rate of 10 per cent in a tripartite "mixed economy," in which the share of the national wealth attributable to each of the three sectors in 1960 was: public sector, 21.1 per cent; private sector, 58.5 per cent; and the "labor economy," 20.4 per cent.[7] The public sector includes companies controlled by

[5] Cf. Klatzmann, op. cit., p. 247.

[6] Exports covered only 22 per cent of imports in 1962. The figure rose to 40.9 per cent in 1961 and 50.1 per cent in 1965.

[7] H. Barkai, The Falk Project for Economic Research in Israel, Sixth Report, 1961–63, Central Press, Jerusalem, 1964. The Falk Project included in the collective sector only enterprises in which the Histadrut was the majority shareholder. The precise determination of percentages in the above is complicated by the frequent investment in the same enterprise of capital from two different sectors.

central or local government, companies in which the state is the majority shareholder (e.g. the railways), companies producing and distributing electricity (i.e. public services) and heavy industry—all fields in which large-scale capital investment is required. The private sector engages in light industries in which profitability is relatively assured and is responsible for a large part of the commerce; it seems at present to be expanding. The favorite field of the collective sector was originally construction and primarily agriculture; 70 per cent of the arable land is still worked by various types of co-operatives—*kibbutz, moshav* or *moshav-shitufi*. In recent years it has made a pioneering excursion into the industrial field, and even into heavy industry.[8] There are no rigid demarcation lines between the three sectors. There are many mixed companies in which state and private capital co-operate, and also co-operate with Histadrut capital; the last frequently goes into partnership with government institutions, and also on a fifty-fifty basis with Israeli capital, and in particular private capital from abroad. In principle this is peaceful co-operation, but future developments are unforeseeable and will be of prime importance to the future of Israeli socialism.

TWO ASPECTS OF COLLECTIVISM

The collective sector represented by the Hevrat Ovdim itself consists of two forms of organization and control.

In the first place independent co-operatives of the three kinds

---

[8] The distribution of employment in the labor sector of the economy in 1961, according to Noah Malkosh, *Histadrut in Israel*, Tel Aviv, 1961, p. 64, was as follows:

Agriculture	93,000
Industry	29,000
Building and public works	17,000
Transport	12,000
Trade, finance and various	25,000

already mentioned are engaged in all branches of the economy, but chiefly in agriculture as well as in transport and trade. They are run by their own members, but the general trend of their economic policy and their working conditions are supervised by the Hevrat Ovdim, which is represented on the managing committees of their central associations and supervises their accounts and their long-term projects. All the co-operatives recognize the Hevrat Ovdim's authority; in return they enjoy the benefits of the social services associated with it.

There are producers' co-operatives and service co-operatives. Among the latter are the remarkable enterprises responsible for road transport throughout the country. Most of the bus or coach drivers own shares in them. The ordinary man's dream in Israel, according to current folklore, is not to work harder than a clerk, to have a teacher's holidays and to be paid as well as a bus driver. These drivers, who also collect fares and are the sole masters of their vehicles, rather like the captain of a ship, often seemed to me to be persons of a certain social status and to be very well aware of it in their dealings with the extraordinarily variegated public characteristic of the Israeli Tower of Babel with its teeming new immigrants in need of help and advice. They carry out their duties in difficult conditions, often with coolness and courtesy. Long before I discovered their special status as members of co-operatives, I noticed attitudes and a kind of professionalism about them that marked them off from their wage-earning comrades who drive buses in other countries.

There are 370 consumer co-operatives with 1100 branches serving 150,000 families. Co-operative loan and savings banks provide credit to 250,000 users. All these societies are responsible to central organizations that control and co-ordinate them in the name of the Hevrat Ovdim, avoiding duplication and friction (at any rate in theory, for it is a difficult task). Thus the producer, service and transport co-operatives are affiliated to the Co-operative Center, the consumer societies to the Hamashbir Hamerkazi wholesale society, the building co-operatives to the powerful Shikun Ovdim, which is an offshoot of the Histadrut, and all the banking and finance societies to the over-all control of the Labor Bank, the second largest in turnover in the country, whose impressive headquarters in Tel Aviv I admired from the top of Beit Hadar.

The second form of organization and management in the Histadrut sector of the economy consists of enterprises directly and collectively owned by the members of that organization. The Hevrat Ovdim is incorporated into each enterprise in the form of finance company and shareholder, with full powers to ensure a management policy whose characteristic feature is the reinvestment of all profits. The constitution of the Hevrat Ovdim lays down that profits shall in no circumstances be distributed to its members.

The co-operative sector of the Histadrut, because of its co-ordination, its simultaneously democratic and centralized structure and its industrial and agricultural ramifications under the wing of a trade-union federation, is an original achievement of the labor economy. The sector that directly owns means of production is no less original.

The most famous of the Histadrut companies, and the subject of sharp controversy, is the Solel Boneh, which specializes in construction and public works and since 1949 has built more than 100,000 dwellings, three-quarters of which were reserved for new immigrants and 19,000 for aged workers. The Solel Boneh is also responsible for the construction of harbor work in Israel and abroad; it has carried out big contracts in various countries in Asia, Africa and Europe. It developed into the biggest enterprise in the country, with financial resources and modern equipment at its disposal that were superior to those of the Ministry of Labor. Its breakup into three separate companies in 1958, an event for which Pinhas Lavon, then general secretary of the Histadrut, was held to be responsible, was an event of national importance, and a 1963 book about it by Hillel Dan,[9] who was

---

[9] *Along the Unpaved Road*, Tel Aviv, 1963.

director of the organization at its apogee, revived controversy on the subject.

This huge organization, the most important in the country because of its activities at home—to say nothing of its ramifications from Cyprus to Nepal, from Nigeria to Burma—was disturbing to certain members of the government and, according to them, also to foreign capitalists, whom it discouraged because of its privileged and near-monopolist position. The advocates of division, who ended by winning the day, argued that divided into three it would develop even more rapidly than in the form of a huge, hypertrophied "combine." In the cautious terms of an official comment, "the rapid rate of expansion of the Solel Boneh necessitated a revision of the company's structure and organization."[10]

Accordingly it was split up into three companies, each under its own management, but co-ordinated by a central administrative committee: (1) The core of the original Solel Boneh company, responsible for harbor works in Israel and overseas. Not content with the activities implied in its name it also builds airports, apartment and office buildings, tunnels and pipelines, and undertakes all kinds of public works and civil engineering. It has metal works in the Bay of Haifa and at Givat Rambam and Holon, and operates the port of Haifa, for which it provides all services, through a company (United Harbor Services), in which it has a 60 per cent interest. It also operates the port of Kishon and Eilat, owns and runs shipbuilding yards at Hayama and Ogen, and acts as management company for enterprises belonging to all three sectors of the Israeli economy. (2) The Solel Boneh Construction and Public Works Company in Israel. (3) The Koor Company, consisting of a complex of enterprises of impressive size and variety. It occupies a leading position in heavy industry, in which it specializes, and produces steel, metalwork used in building, pipes, concrete, rubber, electrical equipment, etc. In 1961 it earned 7 per cent of the total income of Israeli industry, contributed 12 per cent by volume

[10] Solel Boneh Overseas and Harbor Works, Tel Aviv, 1961, p. 3.

of industrial exports, and absorbed 10 per cent of the total industrial capital investment.[11]

When one sees these shipbuilding yards and factories, or the port of Haifa, where all the workers are employed by the Israeli trade-union federation, and when one is told that the Solel Boneh has branch offices at Rangoon, Addis Ababa, Teheran and in Nigeria; that the total turnover of its three branches is nearly $200 million; and that the whole is owned and managed by a trade-union organization, one can hardly believe one is not dreaming.

JANUS

Faced with this strange and monumental Janus the first question that occurs to one is how it plays its employer's role and how it is regarded by its employees. Noah Malkosh, stating the official Histadrut view, admits that its double role is often a "formidable stumbling-block to the understanding of our movement by trade-union leaders and sympathizers from other countries." When he comes to the key question, how workers' trade-union rights are protected in Histadrut enterprises, he concludes with a great deal of assurance that "in practice there is no real problem of inadequate protection of employees."[12]

Wages in Histadrut enterprises are theoretically kept in line with those in the other sectors, which are set by collective bargaining, and regulated within certain limits by the Ministry of Labor in order to combat cost inflation. Managers of the labor economy sometimes complain that wage freezes are not respected by many firms in the private sector, who "entice" skilled workers and technicians from the collective sector. On the other hand, I heard managers in the private sector complain of numerous

[11] Cf. annual report of the president, I. E. Eilam, for 1961–62. In addition to Solel Boneh, the Histadrut through the Hamashbir Hamerkazi and the Tnuva controls rolling mills, glassworks, foundries, canning and soap factories, the manufacture of oils, etc.

[12] N. Malkosh, op. cit., p. 78.

privileges said to be enjoyed by the other two sectors (e.g. preferential access to capital and less rigid application of the social laws). The workers' interests are supposed to be protected by the character of their managers, who are chosen from among the trusted leaders of the Histadrut. I was in no position to judge whether working conditions and social services there were better than in other sectors. In any case, when a dispute cannot be settled at the local labor-council level, it may go straight up to the national executive.

Critical observers object that even men who have risen from the ranks of the Histadrut and have been appointed by it begin playing a very different psychological and social role as soon as they assume managerial responsibilities, which impose a new viewpoint on them and confront them with necessities and difficulties and the compromises that these imply. Numerous examples of conflict between management and workers on joint management committees in Poland and Yugoslavia,[13] and the tensions that exist and sometimes come to light in Soviet factories,[14] show that in a collectivist economy things are not as simple as that. So the claim that conflicts between labor and management in a Histadrut factory are essentially different from those in the private sector, because in the former there can be no opposition of interests, but only a "temporary failure in the federal machinery of the Histadrut"[15] cannot be taken seriously. Such claims are an irritating reminder of Soviet propaganda in the Stalin era, which held that there could never be economic conflicts for workers in Soviet factories, or human problems resulting from technical changes, because "they were the masters now."

In fact, conflicts of interests in the full sense of the word are

[13] Cf. the discussions devoted to Régimes et institutions de la Pologne et de la Yougoslavie, Centre d'Étude des Pays de L'Est, Institut Solvay, Brussels University, two vols., 1959; and Albert Meister, Socialisme et autogestion. L'expérience yougoslave, Éditions du Seuil, Paris, 1964.

[14] Cf. my article "Les salaires et le travail dans l'U.R.S.S. de Khrouchtchev," La Nef, July–August 1958.

[15] N. Malkosh, op. cit., p. 79.

possible in Histadrut factories. This is demonstrated by the occurrence of strikes, which are, of course, all "wildcat" strikes by definition, since they take place without trade-union support and even in spite of its disapproval. Here again I am not convinced by the Histadrut's spokesman's claim that strikes are rare (a relative statement that is difficult to check) and "can hardly be regarded as official" (a claim that, coming from the source it does, is not without a certain savor), although "it has happened . . . that this technique has been used to hasten a resolution of the issue by the national executive."[16]

Let us grant the Histadrut that in some of its enterprises, in which disputes tend to be settled in the workers' favor, workers are more likely to abuse their privileged position than be deprived of trade-union protection. On the other hand (and incidents of this sort took place during my first stay in the country), when conflict between workers and management arises in a Histadrut factory, as in the private sector, if trade-union headquarters refuse to back the strike and throw the weight of this refusal into the balance, the strikers' morale is affected and their movement is morally and materially broken. "Employees of Histadrut enterprises may unduly exploit their position of privilege, thereby undermining the progress of the labor sector of the economy."[17] But at what point can labor claims be considered "undue" from the point of view of the Histadrut, a socialist entity in a mixed economy in which it has to succeed if it wishes to establish itself or even simply survive? The borderline is hard to define, and that is the root of the problem. It is here that conflicts arise, and here that the sharpest criticisms in Israel itself of this great trade-union federation's role as employer of a substantial proportion of the working population have their source.

These criticisms are the more substantial in that strikes or strike threats in defiance of the authority of the Histadrut have been numerous in recent years. In 1963 the local labor council

16 N. Malkosh, *op. cit.*, p. 79.
17 Malkosh, *op. cit.*, p. 80.

at the Histadrut factory at Yuval Gad, which manufactures pipes, brought the workers out against the leaders of the "White Kremlin." There was chronic unemployment in the area, and the strike was in support of fifty dismissed workers who claimed compensation from the Koor Company. Similar strikes were started by local councils during the same year at Ramat Gan, Kyriat Gat and Ashkelon. During my visits to Israel there were strikes among teachers, as well as in the transport co-operatives, whose importance and prosperity have already been described. Even in the time of Lavon, who was considered the "strong man" of the Histadrut, the transport co-operatives never admitted that the Histadrut controlled their rules, particularly the conditions under which paid workers could become full-fledged members. The paid workers of the Dan transport co-operative complained that they did not enjoy working conditions similar to those of the members, who are also the shareholders, and the price of the shares is high. Faced with workers who have often been small tradesmen or artisans, with imperfectly integrated immigrants and with individualists who regard arbitration as tyranny and prefer complete liberty of action, often to the detriment of their own long-term interests, the Histadrut leaders have a hard task. The local labor councils, who follow rather than lead them, complain that they are not consulted or listened to by the general staff at Tel Aviv. Their frequent conflicts with the "White Kremlin" are evidence of a structural fault: the "democratic machinery" of the Histadrut is too centralized and bureaucratic, unadapted to the new conditions of the Israeli economy and population structure. We shall see other examples of this. In any case, in view of this situation it is difficult for the Histadrut to claim that it is the representative organization of the workers in Israel and recognized as such by them. That image is increasingly denied by facts. It is further damaged when strikes in the public services (such as that of post-office workers in May–June 1964) are obviously directed against the Histadrut and not against the government, which was finally called in to arbitrate.

JOINT MANAGEMENT EXPERIMENT

The difficulties the Histadrut encounters in reconciling its conflicting interests as employer and workers' representative are illustrated by its experiments in joint management. It is absolutely essential for it to attempt to give workers a share in control of its enterprises, and those of its leaders with whom I discussed the matter make no bones about it. They have to be able to answer the questions put by many workers as soon as they appreciate that their trade union is also their employer. What difference is there between their conditions and those of workers in the private sector? Should they not be different and superior in every way? As G. put it to me himself, in the long run the only justification for a Histadrut industry is full participation by the workers in management.

The first stage in the experiment began in 1958 in a sample of about thirty enterprises chosen for the purpose. The worker members of the joint councils[18] were fully informed of the management's chief problems: production programs, investment and re-equipment policies, rationalization, quality control, raw materials, prices, markets and accounts. The experiment was guided and followed by a division of the secretariat of the Hevrat Ovdim set up especially for the purpose. This was intended to be merely a preliminary phase, aimed at developing in the workers a sense of their joint responsibility with management. The committees were to be a means of communication and consultation; responsibility for decisions remained the management's. At a later phase, that of joint management in the full sense of the term, the workers' representatives were to share in the daily responsibilities of management.

While the workers responded favorably to the offer of co-

---

[18] These should not be confused with the normal union representatives; workers' representation on the management council is not a substitute for normal trade unionism.

operation, the Histadrut admitted that the managers tended to be reluctant to accept the innovation.[19] Actually it goes much further than that. Many managers took the experiment amiss; they resented it as an encroachment on their responsibilities and an obstacle to the smooth running of the enterprise. The workers for their part, were ill prepared for the experiment too. Some seem not to have desired the additional responsibility, particularly as it was unpaid. Some experts outside the Histadrut think that the 1958–60 experiment was launched too hastily, that both workers and managers should have been better informed in advance about joint management. It was, however, preceded by lively discussions between senior representatives of the Histadrut and a majority of the managers. Are the latter already an incipient "managerial class," a potential threat to the "labor economy"? Whether they are or not, their pessimistic expectations were confounded on two points. No serious incidents or conflicts took place at the enterprises where the experiment was conducted, and the reaction of the workers was better than they had expected. About 8000 out of 35,000 voted in the secret ballot to appoint their representatives.[20]

The experiments were shelved after two years, but it would be wrong to describe them as a complete and discouraging failure. The most ardent advocates of workers' participation in the Histadrut take the view that the experiment's principal fault was that it was conducted in a test-tube, while what was really wanted was large-scale reform affecting Israeli society as a whole.[21] For it to succeed, they add, the extension of the private sector, the reinforcement of a "labor-made capitalism," made, that is to say, by a "government with a socialist label," must be checked. They argue that the Histadrut should persist with the project, prepare a campaign of information covering the

19 Malkosh, *op. cit.*, p. 82.

20 These figures were supplied by the Histadrut offices at Tel Aviv.

21 This is precisely where the major difficulty lies, because the Israeli economy is mixed, and public opinion as a whole is far from favoring collectivization of the means of production. The Mapai, which holds most of the key positions in the Histadrut, is itself divided on the question.

whole country and plan the introduction of joint management with very great care. This program indicates the efforts being made by the most militant members of the Histadrut, those close to the Mapam and the Lavon group, to extend to industry the principles of democratic participation adopted by the agricultural communities and make the *kibbutz* ideology prevail in the Hevrat Ovdim. This is certainly necessary if a "different" industrial society is to arise in Israel.[22]

But the immediate difficulties with which the Histadrut is faced are those common to societies "like the others" all over the world. One of the best examples of this is the attitude of the professional classes in Israel, the engineers, technicians and specialists in all sectors, including the public, the members of the "liberal professions," doctors, architects and teachers—all those who have a university degree. These people know they are the backbone of the new state and how much they are needed. Many are *sabras*. Far from accepting any trend toward a leveling-out in pay, they claim special recognition for their qualifications. The recommendations of a committee of fourteen (including Louis Guttman, a famous psychologist who agreed to sign the committee's report only with some important reservations and emphasizing the necessity of settling salary scales after scientific job analysis) formed at the instigation of the Prime Minister and presided over by David Horowitz, the Governor of the Bank of Israel, to examine the grading and remuneration of work in the public services, caused them to revolt. The committee's report, published at the beginning of 1963, was based on the principle of equal pay for equal work. The aim, Horowitz said, was not to impose egalitarianism, but to do away with anomalies and injustices by establishing a

[22] At the time of writing the tenth convention of the Histadrut had not yet been held. Soundings on the subject of joint management made by its research department among workers and staff were not very encouraging, but also, in the absence of an information campaign, not very significant. The breakaway of the Lavon group (the Min Hayesod), which left the Mapai in November 1964, may aid the council of the Histadrut in a left-wing regrouping, influencing the reorientation of its policy and a reform of its structure.

unified system of twenty grades, which would be extended to all the public services. He said that it was absurd, for instance, that a public official should receive an extra allowance simply because he was able to display a framed diploma in his office. The essential criterion in the classification of jobs was not a diploma, but the work done and its value to the state.

Nevertheless the members of the professions reacted to the report as if it were a threat to their status and their careers, and they did so violently and unanimously in all three sectors of the economy. In their view, the committee's recommendations would lead in practice to "putting everybody in the same boat," to the abolition of stimuli, and to discouraging the efforts necessary to acquire by a long period of hard work the qualifications Israel had urgent need of. The economic importance of specialized training and knowledge and technical expertise is universally admitted, and failure to recognize it is going against the facts. The principle of equal pay for equal work is a utopia that fails to take psychological and social realities into account. In all industrial societies, including the planned economies in the East, technical education is encouraged and rewarded.[23] At the same time the Israeli "professional men" vigorously refused to merge their defense associations into one. Their opposition to the Horowitz report was shown in the strong pressure put on the government and in strikes, and was even marked by open conflict between the Histadrut trade union and the headquarters general staff (the trade-union department) at Tel Aviv. In the course of this battle an alliance, strange only in appearance, was formed between the leaders of the Histadrut and the government that instigated and defended the much abused report. At the end of 1963 the professional men ended

---

[23] The controversies that raged around the Horowitz report reminded me of those that took place in a quite different context in the Soviet Union at the beginning of the period of the five-year plans (1930–35) and led to the abandonment of egalitarianism in pay (*uralinovka*) and the institution of a very wide range of remuneration to the advantage of those with scientific and technical qualifications and all engaged in "creative work." (*Cf.* my *De la sainte Russie à l'U.R.S.S.*, Paris, 1938, pp. 112–123.)

by gaining a double victory. Aharon Becker, the general secretary of the Histadrut, and Pinhas Sapir, the Finance Minister, agreed that they should each keep a salary scale of their own and their own unions. On the other hand the recommendations of the Horowitz report on simplifying the salary scales of state and municipal officials seemed to be making progress, with the support of the Histadrut. It had been realized in high quarters that certain recommendations of the Horowitz committee in the form in which they were put forward were schematic and inapplicable.

PUBLIC IMAGE

The public image of the Histadrut is as diverse and conflicting as its functions. It would be extremely interesting to make a systematic study of this image, based on representative samples of different ages and ethnic, educational and occupational groups, etc., although, in spite of the freedom of opinion and expression that the citizens of Israel enjoy, I am not sure that such a study could actually be financed or published at the present time. In the absence of the information that such an investigation would provide, here are some random, rapid impressions based on chance encounters and experiences.

In circles outside the labor economy, among administrators, young technicians in the service of the state and also, of course, leading figures in private enterprise, the image one comes across is "realistic" and unflattering, occasionally touched up with sharp criticisms. If one is to believe certain young *sabras* who are already in control of the levers of power—men whom one would gladly describe as technocrats—the Histadrut, through its patrons or representatives in the government,[24] is putting a brake on nationalization in order to prevent the expansion of

---

[24] In 1963 there was talk of a Histadrut "pressure group" supported by Y. Ben-Aharon, Minister of Communications, and several of his government colleagues.

the public sector that is in competition with the labor economy. They say that the *kibbutz* movement, that flower of the socialist economy, has become a reactionary force, protecting small-scale enterprise and retarding the industrial concentration that is necessary to progress. One of them added that it was a strange kind of socialism that favored protectionist tariffs and opposed nationalization. Among the prosperous merchants and industrialists of the private sector and in "labor-made capitalist" circles the enormous and ambiguous power of the Histadrut, as might be expected, causes irony, anxiety or mistrust as the case may be. What is less predictable is that the same reactions are to be found in labor and university circles, where the Histadrut is considered to be conservative and suffering from hardening of the arteries.

Some internal observers of Israeli society, priding themselves on their realism, are fond of saying that it is a very useful institution, after all, which, like Voltaire's God, if it did not exist would have to be invented. It looks after the workers' interests, but does still more to discipline them. In view of the problems created by the recent waves of unskilled, "undeveloped," "oriental" immigrants, it does invaluable work in organizing and training them and encouraging them to engage in useful and regular work. It sets in motion and accelerates the process of integrating them into the national framework. It also discourages or even breaks unjustified strikes. "But in that case," I pointed out to S., who was painting this picture, "you ought not to abuse these trade-union leaders, but crown them with laurels." "With pleasure," he replied, "particularly when they act as whipping boys for the government." If other aspects of the Histadrut were not superimposed on this picture, S. and his friends would be perfectly willing to compare its role to that of the trade unions in the Soviet Union. In any case, according to them, one of its essential functions, in the absence of a single party, is to aid the state (in a period of greater peril than the inter-war period was to the Soviet Union) to develop its economy as rapidly as possible and feed a population whose rate of growth, immigration included, is unparalleled in the world, and all this under constant threat from enemies who encircle it and proclaim their desire to wipe it out.

As trade-union headquarters serving the workers' interests and simultaneously a state agency devoted to promoting their education, discipline and productivity, the Histadrut obviously has no chance of producing a distinct and unanimous image in the workers' minds. The vagueness is reinforced by the difficulties encountered in the joint management experiments, which were due not only to the resistances of the "managerial class," but also to the workers' mistrust. Many workers in Histadrut enterprises seem to feel that the organization is not primarily theirs, devoted above all to the protection of their interests, but is in the first place an instrument of the government—whose restraining influence on the economy as a whole they recognize—and an employer. Moreover, in view of their control of the labor economy through the Hevrat Ovdim, the leaders of the "White Kremlin" are committed to ensuring its success, and its more or less long-term over-all requirements do not necessarily coincide with the immediate interests of this or that group of workers. From this point of view, to quote my friend B., is not the Histadrut a product of the subtlety of the traditional Jewish mind? Is it not over-subtle in view of the harsh realities of the growing society of Israel, and the conflicts of interest of a dichotomized industrial world in which the alienation of labor is no empty phrase?

On the credit side, the defenders of the Histadrut do not fail to refer to the adverse opinions of it held in employers' circles. I listened to the complaints about it made by the heads of firms and their colleagues. According to them, it uses different standards, depending on whether a concern is run by itself or by a "capitalist." The employers complain that they are not protected by the state, which is to say, that they are obliged by trade-union pressure to keep unsatisfactory workers on the payroll if they have been on it for three months, while the corresponding period in the collective and public sectors is a year.[25] Like the workers, although from a different angle, some employers criticize the Histadrut for not being a real trade union, a positive force, a genuine opposite number speaking in the name of the workers, but an emanation of the government.

Others complain of its demagogy. Many workers are recent immigrants from North Africa or Iran, Iraq or other Asian countries; they are unskilled, with no experience in industry, and manual labor has no prestige and is not even an honorable occupation in their eyes. Whether employed by private enterprise or by the Histadrut, they do not "give a good day's work for a good day's pay." The Histadrut, it is said, instead of instilling them with pride in their work, encourages the spirit of complaint said to be "innate in so many Jews who always consider themselves paid below their real worth, frustrated."[26] Nearly all employers regard the Histadrut as a force capable of exercising pressure on the government, while they themselves, they say, are politically underrepresented and have little protection for their interests. "Our association [that is, The Manufacturers' Association]," one of them said, "is a poor association of a few rich men, while the Histadrut is a very rich association of a great many poor men." If industrial relations in Histadrut concerns are bad, it is because the workers expect to find in them "something different from the private sector." Fortunately, however, the managers of Histadrut enterprises are themselves increasingly becoming "masters"; they have been forced to realize the need for profitability, the necessities that flow from the necessity to maintain regular working, productivity of personnel, etc.

In the course of a visit to a "private" factory producing refrigerators and other domestic appliances in Jerusalem, I was told a story by an engineer, which I heard repeated in another concern in the same sector. No doubt it forms part of Histadrut folklore, which is rich but constantly changing—probably no ethnologist of Israeli life will have time to catch it on the wing.

25 This assertion is disputed by the Histadrut leaders.
26 *Mekupah* in Hebrew.

This is the story: A sufferer from insomnia went to see his doctor and took the pills he prescribed. He was soon not merely sleeping normally again but having marvelous dreams about pretty girls. When a friend complained that he, too, suffered from insomnia, he warmly recommended him to the same doctor. The doctor prescribed the same pills, and his sleep duly returned. But instead of dreaming about pretty girls he had the most horrible nightmares; every night he was pursued by wild beasts. He complained to his friend, who went back to the doctor and demanded an explanation. "It's simple," the doctor replied. "*You* were sent me by the Kupat Holim." Other stories of the same kind betray the disquiet of part of the population at the Histadrut's power, especially its monopoly of medical aid.

A complete study of the public images of the Histadrut among the Israeli population would include those in the minds of its own leaders, which vary according to their age and political views. Certain survivors of the "old guard" regard it euphorically as a tutelary organization in a state of constant and harmonious development that, overriding any temporary compromises, will in due course extend the benefits of a socialist welfare state to the whole country. Many important personalities of the present day, with Ben-Gurion at their head, were among its founders, and one can sometimes detect nostalgia for the old days among them. The general secretary is still a power in the land. Left-wing militants regard the Histadrut as excessively subject to the "conservative" influences of the Mapai, but, in spite of its supineness and political compromises, they still consider that it carries the hopes of Israeli socialism. Their image of the Histadrut is critical, they find fault with its lack of dynamism; the labor economy, although it was established before 1948, has made little progress in the state of Israel. Circumstances (the Arab threat, the need to absorb massive immigration) have been unfavorable, but the policy of the leaders of the Histadrut has been responsible too. In developing its industrial sector it concentrated on huge organisms conceived more from the point of view of power and prestige than from a desire to promote cooperation, do away with paid labor and establish new forms of human relations in Israel. The image that these militants project for the future of the Histadrut is a transition from the economic to the social, the achievement of joint management in the collective sector and the introduction into Israeli industry of the pioneering spirit of the *kibbutzim*.

THE CHANCES FOR AN ISRAELI SOCIALISM

To what extent does this image of the Histadrut as a missionary of Israeli socialism take account of present social and national realities? Those who struggle courageously to have it accepted by others appeal in the first place to the difficulties the Histadrut has encountered during the past fifteen years as a consequence of the influx of a new kind of immigrant, which has brought about a tremendous change in the occupational distribution of its members. In 1947 the proportion of those belonging to co-operatives of various kinds (i.e. the labor economy) constituted about 25 per cent of its strength. Forty-five per cent of the remainder was made up of paid blue-collar workers and 28 per cent of white-collar workers and government employees. Today the labor economy accounts for barely 14 per cent of its strength, while the proportion of clerical workers (half of whom are technicians or qualified personnel) has risen to nearly 40 per cent. How could such changes, reflecting a transformation in the structure of the working population, fail to react on the policy of the Histadrut? Many immigrants who arrived between 1948 and 1954 had ten years later become citizens who were fully integrated into the Israeli nation, but not into collective ideals, which had not been inculcated in them and had never been theirs. They are individualists, interested in that part of the national income that accrues to them and their families, and not in the abstract principle of equality of distribution.

Moreover, the leaders of the Histadrut are disturbed, not without reason, at the expansion of the public sector. The state tends to take over many services originally provided by them.

Employment has become the responsibility of the Ministry of Labor; pensions and family allowances are becoming the responsibility of a national social-security service; there is even talk of turning the Kupat Holim into a national health service. How could the Histadrut, established in 1920 under the mandate (i.e. a colonial regime) survive in the free state of Israel without undergoing an agonizing change? Has this change taken place? Are not the rigid structure, the centralism, the imperious and meddlesome control that the "White Kremlin" tries to maintain over local labor councils, nowadays an anachronism? In short, are not most of the difficulties of the Histadrut, as of the trade-union organizations of the West, attributable to a delay in adaptation to a new world?

Has socialism any chance of being extended to the whole Israeli economy by legal means, by rallying a majority of the electors to its side? There has been much discussion of this question in recent years, at Mapam and Mapai congresses, at a conference organized in June 1963 by the Lavon group at Ma'ale Hahamisha, and in a miscellany of views on socialism published by the Meuhad *kibbutz* federation. When the Mapam leaders refuse to support the government, they criticize it for dragging its feet in introducing socialism, and show that this is not merely an intellectual controversy.

Except among the Mapam *kibbutznikim* and the left-wing "opposition" in the Histadrut, I did not come across many partisans of a complete socialization of the economy. To judge from the general election results from 1949 to 1961, there is little prospect of a majority vote for socialism in the course of the next ten years, chiefly because of the prevalence of many small businesses and the family-centered individualist tradition that exist among many Jews, the persistence of mistrust between ethnic communities and, above all, the tensions between Ashkenazim and Sephardim and the dependence on capital from abroad. Until Israel has achieved a complete fusion of its communities and has made itself independent of aid from abroad, it is hard to see any government engaging in large-scale socialist experimentation. Two-fifths of the population are already employed in the public or collective sectors.

The state could have carried out far-reaching nationalization, but has not done so, knowing that the majority of the nation remains attached to private enterprise and competition and criticizes the public sector for its poor productivity and profitability and slowness in establishing new industries and in undertaking regional development projects. It also knows that a great many people, including voters for the Mapai, the labor party, are more interested in the size of the national income (the "cake" to be divided up) than in the methods, whether capitalist or socialist, by which it is generated.

There was a highly significant clash at the Mapai congress in October 1963 between the "veteran" leaders, such as Levi Eshkol and Reuven Barkatt, and the "young" ones, among whom the chief figures are Moshe Dayan and Shimon Peres.[27] The former cling firmly to the ideals of egalitarian socialism and regard the Histadrut and the *kibbutzim* as the instruments by which it is to be spread throughout the country, and the general secretary of the party said that Mapai-type socialism implied joint management by workers. Moshe Dayan criticized the views of his seniors, sometimes with sharp irony. Ideological considerations, he said, were a "luxury" to a developing country confronted by dramatic problems. He was prepared to agree to the enrichment of those who invested productive capital in it; speculative gains could always be taxed. "Technology is not a matter of ideology; it determines our way of life. Stone-crushing is done better and more cheaply by machines than by pioneers." Dayan, while taking his hat off to the *halutzim*, gently ridiculed their out-of-date ideals, which men of the old school had tried to keep alive by sending young volunteers to make a road from Gadna to Ein Gedi, although the job could have been done more cheaply with bulldozers. But the sharpest barb he aimed

27 There is no correlation between political opinions and age groups. Thus, at the elections on August 15, 1961, many young *sabras* in uniform voted for the Mapam, the party most attached to the "old" principles of socialism.

at Eshkol was his statement that the latter's view of the future of Israeli society, his belief in the "strengthening of ideological potential" through the Histadrut and the *kibbutzim*, "simply does not correspond to the sort of people who live in Israel today." Returning to the charge, he said he did not understand how the picture painted by Eshkol[28] could be imposed on Israeli society as it existed.

Apart from Dayan's strong personality, his criticisms of ideals, methods and institutions handed down from the past but inadequate to the present often hit their mark. They express the view of those who hold that Israel should become a society "just like the others," a model of prosperity in the Middle East, equipped with everything that technical progress can provide and inhabited by an efficient population of "Hebrew-speaking Gentiles."

Yet behind all the devastating criticisms one can sense the spirit of the technologist, that is, a dangerous propensity to believe that all the problems, including psychological and sociological problems, that the reform of institutions and individual happiness and equilibrium involve are soluble by the application of techniques derived from the physico-mathematical sciences.

These criticisms of the *kibbutz* movement and the Histadrut and of the hopes that they keep alive are made in the name of realism.

But are such criticisms as realistic as they are claimed to be? Are not moral forces and their psychological foundations, closely linked as these are, a reality in Israel, even in the age of automation, electronics and jet aircraft? That was the question that I asked myself, and that was present in my mind until my last day on the soil of Israel.

[28] See *J.P.W.*, October 18, 1963, for reports of the Mapai congress.

4

The *Sabras:* the Crisis of Values

Underlying many current problems in Israel are the questions raised, in the minds of both foreign observers and their own parents, by the new generation of native-born *sabras.*

RUB IT AND YOU GET PRICKED

Sabra is the Arab nickname for the prickly pear (the Hebrew equivalent is *tzabar*). It is said to date from the period immediately after the First World War and to have originated at the Herzlia secondary school at Tel Aviv, the most important in Palestine under the mandate. Young people born in Israel and brought up in hard conditions were often outpaced in the classroom by the children of European immigrants who came from a more cultured environment, and to make up for the inferiority feelings that resulted they would challenge the star pupils to peel a prickly pear; they themselves were well able to do this and get at the sweet flesh under the prickles. Thus in the early twenties there were already *sabras* in Israel who are now reaching retirement age. Others occupy important positions in the administration, the army, the economy and all the activities of the state.

Since those early days the prickly pear image of the *sabra* (a decent fellow under his rough exterior) has evolved. Let me make a rapid survey of this image as it appeared to me; later work by Israeli investigators will correct and complete the picture.

The reader has already come across *sabras* in the course of

the preceding chapters. About one-third of the present population of Israel was born on Palestine soil. Most of the
sabras are young. Like Bathsheba, the young girl of German
parentage doing her military service to whom we gave a lift from
Tel Aviv to Jerusalem, they differ from their parents in physical
appearance, manners and behavior. They are the original products of the Israeli crucible, which has brought about striking
changes in the course of a single generation, changes that sometimes seem to border on the miraculous. My fellow passengers
in the bus in which I returned from Ramat Rahel could hardly
have been more incongruous. There was a family of American
Jews, tourists, very busy with their cameras, and a bearded, expansive Canadian rabbi. Seeing the Biblical sights of Jordan so
close at hand on the hills, he announced his intention of going
to visit them and protested when told that it would be an
excursion from which he would certainly not return. He exhib-
ited his passport as if it were a trophy and asked me and all
his neighbors our names, occupations and where we came from.
I satisfied his curiosity. A girl student from the Hebrew University, who was with me, came from Philadelphia. M.S., an
Israeli archaeologist and former combatant in the Palmah, came
originally from Kiev. His assistant, a young man who looked
almost smart in his open-necked shirt and blue jeans and was
rather aloof (or shy) and as reserved as the rabbi was expansive,
said to him simply: "I am an Israeli."

Several times I heard replies of this kind, delivered ostenta-
tiously, almost provocatively. Talking to *sabra* students in Jerusalem, Tel Aviv and at the Technion at Haifa, I gathered that
they have mixed feelings toward Jews of the Diaspora. After
the victories won by their elders, in which they themselves often
participated, during the war of independence or the Sinai operation, they have confidence (and sometimes a trace of pride)
in their soldierly qualities, their skill and fighting spirit. In talking of the victims of the Holocaust some of them said to me,
and I quote literally: "They let themselves be slaughtered like
sheep." I have since learned that this is a hackneyed phrase
which was heard more frequently than ever at the time of the

Eichmann trial.[1] I had difficulty in getting these young people to talk about major political or intellectual questions, which they seemed not to want to discuss, particularly in a language other than Hebrew, although all of them have some knowledge of English. They are much less extroverted than their parents and grandparents and are as simple in their speech as in their clothing; they are reacting against the subtleties of the traditional Jewish mind and (as one of them told me) are opposed to "socialist pathos and Talmudic quibbles." Their ambition seems to be to do their jobs properly and without fuss.

But in spite of the way *halutz* ideals of manual labor, whether agricultural or industrial, are instilled in them at school and in the army and vigorously propagated by part of the press, young *sabras* seem little inclined to accept and live them. A minority in the *kibbutzim* continue to follow in their parents' footsteps, but even the *kibbutz* will not be able to hold them for long unless, in addition to manual tasks, it is able to offer them technical education and modern working conditions. These *sabra* attitudes should help Israel to overcome the present shortage of qualified personnel and achieve a more rational structure of the working population, half of which is still engaged in the tertiary sector, particularly in trade.

These *sabras*, whose apparent guiding principle is "action without ideology," as one of their elders put it, seem to me to be an Israeli version of a youthful "model" familiar in the West. Are they, besides being "realists," also "materialists," indifferent to all spiritual values, which is what members of their parents' generation are apt to accuse them of being? To what extent is there a return to religion among the *sabras*, and what form does it take? These are questions awaiting investigation by Israeli sociologists and psychologists, for they alone can answer them authoritatively.

The *sabras* are very conscious of their Israeli nationality, their

[1] *Cf.* Simon N. Herman, Yochanan Peres and Ephraim Yuchtman, "Reactions to the Eichmann Trial In Israel: a study in high involvement," *Scripta Hierosolymitana*, Jerusalem, 1965.

attitude to the Jews of the Diaspora is often not very understanding, and they are ill-informed about the historical causes
and circumstances of anti-Semitism. Are these *sabras* still
"Jews"? To immigrants who came from Europe before 1947
the answer seems pretty clear. "They are Israelis," they say, "but
we do not really know what 'being Jewish' means to most of
them."

To many people in Israel this is a matter of great concern,
which can be felt running like a thread through the work of the
social psychologists. An extremely interesting study of the
reactions to the Eichmann trial in different sectors of the population was undertaken under the direction of Professor Simon
N. Herman of the Hebrew University. Those questioned were
classified according to the nature and extent of their personal
or family suffering at the time of the Holocaust.[2] It helps to
clarify what Professor Herman calls the "internal debate of
young Israelis on their identity as Jews and their ties with the
Jews of the Diaspora." Work such as this is of great interest to
educationists and politicians in those lay or religious circles
that are anxious to re-create or fortify among the *sabras* the
feeling of belonging to a universal Jewish community, a "Jewish
people," and at the same time ensure their understanding of the
Jewish communities still scattered about the world and
strengthen their ties with these. With this end in view courses
have been arranged for Foreign Ministry officials and instructors
of young recruits in the army by the Institute of Studies of
Contemporary Judaism at the Hebrew University of Jerusalem,
the head of which is Professor Moshe Davis.

Those *sabras* who were willing to talk freely to me seemed
to me to be free of complexes, anxieties and self-interrogation
from which their parents suffered in a discriminating and hostile
environment, but they also seemed to me to be lacking in their
tormented and fertile curiosity. I put questions to them that go
to the heart of the present difficulties of Israel—the rapid
growth of capitalism in the private sector, orthodox religious

[2] *Ibid.*

intolerance and its encroachments on public and private life (marriage, sabbath observance, etc.), the tensions between "old" and "new" immigrants, between the Ashkenazim and "oriental" immigrants of recent date. Generally speaking, they did not seem to worry very much about these problems. In the face of the Arab threat they were calm and confident in the strength of their army. Bearing in mind these conversations and other experiences and encounters I had, I believe that a "*sabra* sub-culture" is establishing itself in Israel, where several such sub-cultures can already be discerned: that of the solidly established, thoroughly integrated immigrants of long standing (the *vatikim*), most of them Ashkenazim in responsible positions in all sectors of Israeli life; that of the *kibbutzim;* that of the "old" *moshavim* established before the massive immigration of the fifties; and finally that of the new generation of *sabras,* aged under thirty, the children of the *vatikim,* who must be distinguished from the young "orientals" who have arrived in the country since 1950.[3] The *sabras* have given birth to a sub-culture of their own in a new country that has not yet had time to create a culture on a national scale. That is the explanation of a number of attitudes and problems that are peculiar to them.

I found a schematic, sometimes brutal expression of these attitudes and problems sometimes pushed to the point of caricature, among young *sabras* more or less directly associated with the "Canaanite" group, so called because they take their stand on the land of Canaan, in other words, on a Palestine antedating Abraham's coming from Chaldea and also by several centuries, perhaps by a thousand years, Joshua's establishing the Jews there. They are strongly influenced by archaeological discoveries that demonstrate the existence of a civilization more ancient than the exile in Egypt and even older than the time of Abraham, and they leap over four thousand years of Jewish history to rediscover at their source the principles of a coexistence of the

[3] I must thank Uriel Foa, Louis Guttman's colleague at the Israeli Institute of Applied Social Research, for drawing my attention to the existence of these "sub-cultures" in a society undergoing ethnic integration and economic growth.

Semitic peoples that would enable Jews and Arabs to live in peaceful symbiosis in the Middle East. If, as one of them said "with a grain of salt," "the state of Israel goes far beyond the Jewish accident" why should it not come to an understanding with the Arabs? That is the primary problem, which takes precedence over all others. The Canaanites are not numerous, but they are indicative of an attitude that they follow to its logical conclusion. They like saying that they are not interested in the Jews as such. When the decline of "Jewish culture" and the end of its universal values are talked of in their presence, it leaves them cold; some actually show pleasure at the prospect. What they want is that the new state should be capable of giving birth to a new culture, attracting Jews from all over the world and turning them into relaxed and happy Israeli citizens after finally exorcising all their internal dramas and anxieties. They want this culture to be original and different from that of other Near Eastern nations: of limited scope, making no claims to universalism and with no mystical aura about it. They see nothing shocking in the Israeli trend to normalization, to becoming "a society just like the others"; far from regretting it, they welcome it. A young *sabra* engineer at Haifa, who sympathizes with the Canaanites and is a positivist and something of a technocrat, told me that this was exactly what those who had escaped from the ghetto needed. In spite of their willingness to come to an understanding with the Arabs, the *sabras* are prepared to fight to re-establish the integrity of Palestine under the star of David and to recover the ancient city of Jerusalem. But if there is a holy place to which they are indifferent, it is the Wailing Wall, the symbol of a past all trace of which, in their view, should be obliterated.

THE *SABRAS* IN THE EYES OF THEIR ELDERS

I am well aware of the fragmentary and superficial nature of these personal impressions, which have been clarified and modified in the light of the work done on the new generation of *sabras* (though the truth of the matter is that there is not yet very much of it) by Israeli sociologists. I am especially indebted to Simon Herman and Joseph Ben David.[4] The latter, Professor of Sociology at the Hebrew University, is the author of a penetrating study in which he follows the evolution of the image of the *sabra* among Israelis as a whole since the time of the mandate. Some of his principal points deserve to be mentioned here.

The Israeli observer has to make a special effort to keep a cool head on a subject that is so topical and so charged, and one can sense the efforts made by Ben David to rid himself of all Jewish feelings and wishful thinking. To enable us to understand the origins of the current image of the *sabra*, he reminds us, as if it were a law of nature, of the inevitability of the decline of revolutionary ideals in a society where the object of the revolution has been achieved; in this case the inevitability of the decline of the collectivist, ascetic and nationalist ideals of the *halutzim* after the establishment of the state of Israel. Once an "exploited" social group or "subject" nation has attained its aim, social changes take place that are different from those the revolutionaries prepared and hoped for. Instead of the equality and fraternity of which they dreamed, the new liberty is accompanied by new social inequalities and new inter-group tensions. Specialization of functions and administrative and economic necessities create differences of status among the militants of yesterday, and are the more irritating in that henceforth they are permanent. The collectivist ideals in the name of which the new society was created lose their attractiveness, which cannot be restored by condemning the prevailing apathy since it arises from and is nourished by the daily observation of new inequalities.

These reflections enable us to place in historical perspective

---

[4] S. N. Herman, Y. Peres and E. Yuchtman, *op. cit.*; J. Ben David, "Conforming and Deviant Images of Youth in a New Society," *Actes du Ve Congrès Mondial de Sociologie* (Washington, 1962), Louvain, Association Internationale de Sociologie, 1964, Vol. IV, pp. 405–414.

some important aspects of what are currently referred to in Israel as the crisis of values among the young. The discontinuity between the ideals of the pioneering period and those of Israeli society after the proclamation of the state comes to light with striking clarity in the second generation. If the young feel there is a gap between themselves and their parents, it is created by the sacred myth of the "heroic age." This rouses ambivalent feelings in them. On the one hand they admire their parents who fought and pioneered, but on the other they begrudge them their ties with a world from which they are excluded.

I shall not here enumerate the successive images of the second generation that arose and spread after the First World War. What did the educators hope for? "It was assumed . . . that Israeli youth would possess all the virtues that Jews traditionally attributed to themselves, such as willingness to help their neighbors, love of learning and sobriety; but also qualities that Jews felt relatively deficient in because of their deprivations: spontaneity, physical prowess and love of nature."[5] They expected them to surpass intellectually and morally both their parents and the Jews of the Diaspora.

However, the real image of the *sabra* that presented itself to the observer of the *yishuv* in the twenties and thirties was very different. Even then the young *sabra* had little interest in creating an ideal society or solving the problems of Jews. There was plenty of work to be had, and he was surrounded by his family and friends and lived a relatively "normal" life. Nevertheless he had his difficulties. The *yishuv*, while continuing to exalt the ideology of the *halutzim* (asceticism, collectivism, redemption by tilling the soil), made him feel inferior to young immigrants from Europe who, brought up to cultivate these virtues by their parents—who were often intellectuals—set about living them. Thus there arose the first stereotype of the *sabra* as most immigrants found him or thought they found him in the Promised Land: a rather tough prod-

<hr>

[5] J. Ben David, *op. cit.*, p. 409.

uct of hard living conditions; like the prickly pear, good inside although the inside was difficult to get at.

With the forties, the first children born in the *kibbutzim* and *moshavim* began growing up and a new generation appeared on the scene. It worked in the co-operative villages and agricultural communities, and the "other society" considered it "idealistic." In fact, our sociologist observes, not without a trace of irony, "there was nothing idealistic for them in living and working in the settlements where they were born; it was just part of their inherited way of life."[6] However, under the influence of exceptional circumstances during a period in which there was a practically uninterrupted state of war,[7] the stereotype changed. *Sabras* played a leading role, and many officers and senior commanders of the Palmah and the Army of Liberation were recruited from their ranks. During this period a new image of the *sabra* established itself, which had lost most of its negative connotations. If the *sabra* was abrupt in manner, it was because he liked prompt decision and effective action. He detested verbiage, including moral verbiage, which did not prevent him from being a patriot willing to make greater sacrifices than most for his country.

The *sabra* now became an ideal image, closely linked with the older ideal image of the *halutz*, the altruistic pioneer. In other words, being a "typical" *sabra* was a good thing and the highest possible recommendation in the *yishuv*. Thanks to their real qualities, but also aided by the image that floated around them, *sabras* had meteoric careers in Israeli society. Simultaneously they created an image of themselves for their own use. The succession of unusual experiences they had shared constituted a bond between them, and they regarded themselves as constituting what was called the *hevra* ("group" or "clan"), of which each one of them was a member. In the jargon of that

[6] J. Ben David, *op. cit.*, p. 411.

[7] 1936–39: Arab terrorism directed mainly against the Jews; 1939–44: Second World War in Middle East and Europe; 1944–47: military action (by the Haganah) and terrorism against the British; 1947–48: war of independence.

sabra generation, the *hevra* had a highly favorable connotation. Society appreciated the services it had rendered, it was a proud privilege to belong to it, and it represented the best of the younger generation.

After the war of independence this splendid image deteriorated and rapidly gave place to another. J. Ben David gives an ingenious explanation of the process. The ideal image of the *sabra*, a rejuvenated version of the *halutz* image with the same aura, was based on a mistake. Altruism and devotion to duty are always displayed in wars of national or social liberation. During the period of the heroic fraternity of wartime the *sabras* had shared the collectivist ideals of the first generation only in appearance. The return to settled conditions brought to the surface the moral discontinuity between the generations that had been temporarily papered over, first by the clandestine struggle in the Palmah and then by war.

Individualism revived among the young, who were eager to make up for lost time by studying, seeking careers, enjoying themselves and establishing families, all things that, as J. Ben David remarks, are elsewhere considered perfectly reasonable and normal. But in urban areas they also showed signs of disarray and "moral void," illustrated, as in western societies, by a desire for pleasure "beyond good and evil" and by acts of delinquency.

Parallel with this, the collective principles of Israeli society propagated in the schools and by the youth movements, the press, the radio and the army implied a critical image of the *sabra* that is a revised version of that of the thirties. According to this image, the *sabra* thinks only of himself; *halutz* ideals are alien to him, indeed, in his "egoism" all ideals are alien to him. In short, he is a "materialist." His manners are not just offhand, they are positively discourteous and rude.

In literature there are new notes of criticism in novels in which *sabras* appear. Before 1950 essayists and humorists treated the ideal type of *sabra* rather as Cervantes treated chivalry, but now writers go beyond treating them with humor or even ridicule. In novels, such as those of Pinhas Sade, David Shahar, and Yael Dayan,[8] the *sabra* is depicted as fundamentally "alienated" from the society in which he lives, deliberately opposing everything for which it stands; he is a frenzied individualist, in some cases not even recoiling from crime.

Are these merely literary images that do not correspond to any real "lawlessness" or behavior in real life? That they are not unreal is suggested by the appearance in recent years of juvenile delinquency in Israel, where it was previously practically unknown, and by new forms of delinquency among the middle classes. Incidentally, it would be interesting to inquire why literature, which in Israel is influenced by both western (particularly American) and Soviet models, tends at any particular time to choose from one side rather than the other. Official values in Israel as transmitted through schools and the army tend on the whole to favor collectivist ideals, and hence are nearer to the East than the West. Between 1940 and 1955 this influence made itself felt in the fashion in which the ideal image of the *sabra* was presented and spread. Since 1955 the retouching applied to the asocial "deviant" image of the young Israeli has been inspired by the *nouvelle vague* or "beatnik" models of western youth.

The discontinuity between the generations and the resulting problems are a source of serious concern to politicians and educators in Israel at a time when a new *sabra* generation— that is, the third in relation to the immigrants of the second *aliya*—is beginning to undertake the responsibilities of public life and to occupy key positions.

IDEALS OF A PAST AGE

Full understanding of the image of themselves that the *sabras* have projected in Israeli society would require a comparison of the principles that the society attributes to them in the abstract with those it actually permits them to practice. For lack of a

[8] *New Face in the Mirror*, London, 1954.

complete study of the subject, which would go beyond the framework of this book, here are some rapid notes.

The instruction given in *kibbutz* schools and in urban secondary schools, besides including a more or less religiously oriented knowledge of the Old Testament, is still impregnated with the traditions of the *halutz* period, that is to say, it exalts the virtues of manual labor, the greatness of the pioneers and their collectivist and egalitarian ideals. But the life lived by the students' parents does not in practice always come up to these. Far from it, in fact. The older generation, even if they are *kibbutznikim*, have become less ascetic, more liberal, more adapted, in urban areas often totally assimilated, to the hedonistic aspirations of Israeli society. When a *sabra* aged twenty reads in an officially inspired handbook published in 1964 that "belonging to a *kibbutz* brings with it a prestige that is recognized by all workers in Israel, a prestige based on a great tradition—that of pioneers who mark out the way and build the roads," he may react with surprise, embarrassment, skepticism or irony. Even if such statements are made by a teacher in the *kibbutz* school, he knows, or will soon discover from his own experience, that they do not correspond to reality. They are obsolete, illusory, a kind of propaganda. The pioneering spirit cannot be permanent, a stable investment handed on from father to son, and it is useless to claim that it can. Pioneering implies transformation and joint struggle. The young *sabras* refuse to be guided by the enthusiasms of a past in which, though it was certainly heroic, they did not share.

Apart from being exposed to obsolete enthusiasms, they are also subjected to depressing and sometimes destructive influences. In Israel there is as great a diversity of minds as there is of ethnic origin. The multiplicity of outlook, which sometimes hampers government action, imposing procrastination or compromise, is also a source of strength, a permanent source of reinvigoration. Israel, a variegated spiritual family, has a sizable number of skeptics, whose aggressive rationalism recalls that of some Christians who have lost their faith. I met some former *yeshiva* students, for instance, whose childhood and youth were spent in the rigid framework of a Jewish orthodox home in some small Hungarian or Polish town. Now they are free-thinkers, agnostics, and, except when their aged and still practicing parents come to see them, they have abandoned the dietary laws and considerably relaxed observance of the sabbath. They are especially irritated by the manifestations of rabbinical clericalism and its intrusions into public and private life, but they also indulge their irony at the expense of the survivals of *halutz* idealism and the theorists of "Israeli socialism." Nothing is sacred to Jewish humor in intellectual circles of this sort, not even what they call Israeli "chauvinism." These reactions are part of the present situation in Israel where, among those who experience them, they are socially and historically necessary.

They are, however, disturbing to the young, plunged as they are into a society on the road to normalization that is riddled with the western models propagated by tourists, the cinema and a large part of the press. Many adults seem satisfied with their freedom of thought, and some even take pleasure in the ruins of the traditions that they carefully sweep away. They make no effort at reconstruction and, apart from pride in success, the race to abundance and prosperity, and technical progress, offer their children nothing to take the place of the values, beliefs and ideals that were theirs and their parents'.[9] True, a large number of young people in the West are in a similar position, faced with the same disintegration of traditional values and the same "void." But in their case the discontinuity is less abrupt; they do not fall from the same height as their contemporaries, the young *sabras* of Israel.

Thus it is not incorrect to speak of a crisis of values in Israeli society, particularly among the young. "The old dream has come true," a fifty-year-old engineer who emigrated from

[9] We shall return later, when we discuss the religious problem, to the place of the traditional values of orthodox Judaism in Israeli life, particularly among the young, but let us note here and now that the influence of orthodoxy, though far from negligible, is restricted to a minority.

Rumania in 1940 said to me, "and nothing has taken its place." By "the old dream" he meant the Zionist and national ideals. The moral "void" can be said to exist in the wide gap left open between the religious groupings (which are themselves very varied and conflicting, ranging from the Hassidic enclaves to the orthodox old guard), technocratic positivism, and the pioneering idealism that is trying to survive and acquire a new lease on life in the *kibbutzim* and the left wing of the Histadrut. The young have to live in these conditions and, so to speak, act and establish themselves in the interstices, and they manage as best they can. Some of the ablest are equally dissatisfied with skeptical rationalism on the one hand and formal, intolerant orthodoxy on the other. They remain attached to religious traditions, which, they feel, form a whole, but want them to be reformed and brought into harmony with the needs of a modern society. But is that possible? "If you remove a single stone you risk bringing down the whole edifice," a girl student said to me in Jerusalem. "But we need both a new culture and something to live by. Those who think that Israel can solve its problems without an ideal are mistaken." So obvious are the difficulties of the young that in 1962 the government gave permission to the youth movements attached to the political parties, both lay and religious, to enter the schools and engage in peaceful competition for the hearts and minds of their pupils.[10]

Nevertheless the gravity of the situation should not be exaggerated. Daily awareness of the many obstacles that still lie on Israel's path to prosperity and of the external dangers that might at any moment jeopardize its very existence are re-

[10] The Institute of Contemporary Judaism, which is part of the Hebrew University of Jerusalem, takes an interest in and studies the ideology of the young *sabra* generations. The specialists with whom I talked (in particular Israel Kolatt) believe that on the whole the young have retained little of the collectivist ideology characteristic of the *halutz* spirit. They note that few show keenness to work in the development towns. "Young people in revolt against the affluent society and its values are individual cases, not a movement," was how one of them summed up his views on the matter.

straining factors. It is impossible for the psychological and moral void to be widely felt in Israel, a tiny country that in a few years has received hundreds and thousands of poor and uneducated immigrants, many of them ravaged by privations, illness and old age, and is determined to make Hebraized, productive citizens of them, or at least to provide them with a decent shelter for their last years; a country that is bringing fertility to the desert, carrying out herculean labors throughout its territory with the aid of the most modern techniques, and, thanks to an active minority, is developing new forms of human relations in its agricultural and industrial communities. At the end of a symposium held at a delightful spot near Tel Aviv in February 1963, in which engineers, heads of enterprises belonging to all three sectors of the economy, senior civil servants and army officers (for the army, too, is concerned with education) took part, a number of speakers, varying in age, origin and education, agreed in believing that, after a period of faith in *halutzic* ideals, a new phase had set in, characterized by the spirit of technocratic realism, which was likely to remain dominant for some time yet. But a third phase was already on the horizon. The country's leaders and educators must give the young the sense of working effectively for a purpose, but must also make them aware of the psychological and moral needs on which individual happiness in an industrial society depends, and of the special difficulties that have to be faced in Israel to achieve this. Perhaps that is the direction in which the energy of youth should be oriented and mobilized.

We shall come across this trend toward a new humanism again in considering other aspects of Israeli life. Thus defined, it remains too abstract and too vague. To be widely accepted by the young *sabras*, it will have to be filled in and clothed with flesh and blood by them. Some of them, it is true, are not satisfied with scoffing at the "luxury" of ideologies, which are anything but a luxury to those who feel the need of them. What keeps them Jewish in spite of their elders' doubts also offers them their best chance of finding what they are more or less confusedly seeking. They live in a country that still offers those who want it (and, who knows? may one day offer all, even those who now are the most apathetic, the most bemused by material prosperity) a difficult, dangerous and dramatic life.

5

Normalization, "N.E.P.," New Environment

Israel is a remarkable experiment in every respect, including the economic.

In May 1948, the new state inherited from the Palestine of the mandate an impoverished country ravaged by endemic terrorism. Its finances were in constant deficit (more than I£48 million sterling in 1946), and it had to meet the costs and cope with the widespread damage caused by the war of independence while burdened with a first flood of immigrants consisting largely of survivors from the Nazi camps—destitute, sick, women, children and old men. Then huge floods of oriental Jews, suddenly precipitated out of the Middle Ages, poured in. Housing had hastily to be provided; hospitals, villages, new towns and new ports, roads and railways, factories and collective farms had to be built to shelter and feed and put to work these wretched and disparate multitudes, who simultaneously had to be trained and Hebraized. All these tasks had to be tackled at once. It is possible, of course, to point to failings, imperfections and mistakes, but the over-all energy and efficiency that were displayed were wholly admirable. Eighteen years after its establishment as a state Israel is still at grips with some of the classic difficulties of an underdeveloped country while at the same time part of the population is faced with problems characteristic of a society on the way to affluence; in other words, economic progress has been made in record time.

GROWTH AND COMPROMISE

A great many new factors have to be taken into account in explaining how this extraordinary leap forward was possible. In the first place, the *yishuv* was not an underdeveloped society as were its Arab neighbors. Many of the "veterans" who came from Europe before 1945 were educated and often highly cultivated men, intellectuals or members of the liberal professions, who chose to work as agricultural laborers for ideological and quasi-mystical motives, which combined the aim of redeeming the Jewish people with the quest for personal salvation. They were able, first potentially and then actually, thanks to their children—the first generation of *halutzic sabras*—rapidly to assimilate the techniques and institutions of a modern society. The "first" Israel (i.e. the whole Jewish community in Israel immediately after the proclamation of the state) was not an "undereducated" society condemned to underdevelopment for that reason. It has rightly been emphasized that "Israel, unlike the underdeveloped nations, is characterized by a transplanted economy. The men, the ideas and the techniques on which it is based come from elsewhere, chiefly from the West."[1]

Even capital investment in Israel has assumed unusual forms. It has come in the form of gifts from funds collected by Zionist organizations, particularly in the United States; there has been a considerable inflow of foreign capital into the private and public sectors, and loans have been raised abroad (state of Israel bonds). There have also been substantial reparation payments by Federal Germany, though this source is beginning to dry up. Total public and private investment of foreign capital has exceeded the amount received in gifts since 1962. Up to 1960 inflation was serious (the cost of living increased by 53 per cent between 1951 and 1952 and by 173 per cent between

---

[1] André Chouraqui, "Israël, carrefour de l'Orient et de l'Occident," *Tiers-Monde*, October–December 1962, p. 668.

1952 and 1960), and the danger has not been eliminated; in March 1963, the government issued an urgent appeal for a voluntary freezing of bank deposits, which were swollen by German reparations, big profits and speculation in certain branches of the private sector. Between 1962 and 1965, the cost of living increased by 30 per cent. In 1965 exports rose by 13 per cent, but because of an increase in essential imports, the deficit in the balance of payments in 1961–62 grew from $344.8 million to $354.8 million. In 1963 the deficit was reduced as a consequence of increased exports and stable imports, but in 1964 and 1965 it increased again.

Israel has no unemployment in the ordinary sense. The daily average number of workless was 5143 in 1961 and 4380 in 1965. Its unemployment problem is of a special type. For one thing, the unemployed, as everywhere where industrialization is under way, are often "potential workers" whom the economy has not yet been able to absorb, and for another the state undertakes public works to create employment. The difference between one country and another in the Third World (in which Israel is in some respects included) is the pace at which this absorption takes place. Increased foreign exchange receipts are assured by the development of exports and tourism, but other sources (German reparations) are declining, while there is the increasing pressure of old demands and new ones constantly appearing. There is the defense bill that has to be met, the "development towns," the reception of immigrants, a vast program of public works (capturing the waters of the Jordan, irrigation of the Negev, construction of the ports at Ashdod and Eilat, etc.), the requirements of the Ministry of Education, whose present expenditure needs to be doubled to ensure the rapid integration of new immigrants and their children. In short, the state of Israel has to find about $350 million worth of "external receipts" to balance its budget at the existing level, that is, without providing the funds necessary to tackle at their roots the problems posed by the "second" Israel.

Thus in the course of fifteen years there has been a transition from the egalitarian and mainly agrarian economy of the time of the mandate to a diversified economy, including an expanding private sector in which a class of industrialists and traders make substantial profits and a hierarchy of technicians and administrators demand a high range of salaries and privileges to consecrate their high status in Israeli society. The state contributed 30 per cent of capital investment in the private sector in 1961 and only 16 per cent in 1962. The pro-government press admits that this sector has benefited from sometimes excessive concessions, that cartels and monopolies, undercover deals and cost-plus contracts, have been tolerated, infringing competition and efficiency, that there have been real estate transactions "that have verged on scandal," and that the "current boom" has led to loose business morality and faulty management, fiscal and accounting practices.[2]

The socialist opposition, particularly the Mapam, the left wing of the Histadrut and the Lavon group, vigorously criticizes the government's compromises.[3] Israel, one of its theorists said to me, is "the only country in the world in which a government with a socialist label is creating an increasingly vigorous capitalism with its own hands." It regards the expansion of the private sector, which has been tolerated and even encouraged by the Ben-Gurion and Levi Eshkol cabinets, as a challenge to the establishment of socialism in Israel. Conversations on the possibility of unification of the three "labor" parties and a return of the Mapam to the government, which took place in the course of 1963 and 1964, broke down on this stumbling block, among others.

The "realists" reply that the government has to compromise. The multiplicity of problems that have to be faced simultaneously, above all the ever-present external threat to the very existence of the Jewish state, force them to press on with economic development, to turn everything to account, to utilize all the capital that is offered without frightening off private enterprise by ideology or discouraging it by bureaucracy, and,

---

[2] "Socialism in Israel," *J.P.W.*, June 28, 1963.
[3] Since the constitution of the new Levi Eshkol cabinet (January 12, 1966), the Mapam participates in the government.

above all, to do nothing to dry up the precious generosity of American Jews. When the realists are men of the left, they often deplore the attitude of the Mapam, which, by taking refuge in the purity of its principles and the comfort of sterile opposition and depriving itself of the opportunity of constructive action, has been itself partly responsible for the evils that it denounces. "We too found the compromises with the capitalists, like those with the synagogue, hard to swallow," some of them say. "But just wait till Israel's security has been assured, and then we will see." During a lively discussion of these matters in a Jerusalem restaurant, my neighbor, an agricultural expert from Vienna and a veteran *halutz* attached to his principles, rounded on his critics with the adage *propter vitam vivendi perdere causas*. I do not know whether in the heat of the argument others besides myself noticed this unusual outburst of erudition.

CITY LIGHTS

In urban areas—very definitely at Tel Aviv, but also at Haifa, which is more hard-working, and in certain districts of Jerusalem—one notes a combination of signs to which it is impossible to give a name without at the same time more or less arbitrarily putting forward an explanation. It is a phenomenon in which many trends mingle and many causes interact— the "normalization" of a formerly doctrinaire, ascetic society which has apparently attained its major aims and ended a period of major stress; relaxation and desire for material comfort, withdrawal into the pleasures and satisfactions of private life, a whole complex of attitudes characteristic of a post-war period; relative prosperity in certain sections of the population thanks to German reparations and also to industrial and commercial profits—concessions to free enterprise made by a socialist government, which in the Israeli context amount to a kind of N.E.P.; the rapid enrichment of a category of businessmen by financial operations and speculation in real estate; the social and psychological aspects of economic growth colored by the special features of a community traversed by the Third World. All these tendencies, dominated by industrialization and the rapid development of an advanced technical environment in a highly variegated society, must be taken into account if the Israeli nation eighteen years after its foundation is to be understood.

Tel Aviv, including Jaffa, has barely 400,000 inhabitants and, of course, is not Israel; and the district between Dizengoff Square and Ben Yehuda Street is, of course, not Tel Aviv. The brilliant, noisy, conventionally cosmopolitan town center, abounding in shops and luxurious cafés, which sometimes give one the impression of being in a Levantine town touched up with a trace of *dolce vita* in spite of some survivals of local exoticism—bearded Jews in black hats and picturesque *schnorrers*—seems to justify the saying of the inhabitants of Haifa, its great rival, that Tel Aviv enjoys itself while Haifa works and Jerusalem prays. Tel Aviv works too, of course, and some astonishing specimens of the Israeli "new wave" are to be seen in certain bars at Haifa and Jerusalem.

After immersion in the life of a *kibbutz*, with one's head still full of talks with men and women who are absorbed in a communal life in which each *haver* receives about I£100 pocket money a year, when one returns to Tel Aviv one is struck by the violence of the contrast between the two worlds. After getting out of the *sheirut* that brought me back from Rechafim, I went into an expensive café on Allenby Street. The boss, who was one of those unpleasant, bullying, self-made men that one can come across anywhere in the West, was noisily rebuking in French a young "oriental" waiter who had made a trivial mistake in writing out a check. On the terrace— it was eleven a.m.—middle-aged and young women, all strikingly well dressed, were basking in the sun. Some were knitting to kill time, others were sipping an *espresso* or browsing through a magazine. They exchanged greetings and were obviously regular customers—women of leisure who had no domestic duties to bother about at that time of day, because they had servants to see to these. Some were accompanied by their male counter-parts. This is a commonplace sight in the center of Tel Aviv. Farther down, other cafés seemed to cater chiefly to boys and girls, all looking modern and "emancipated"; they were hand-some young *sabras*, looking healthier and cleaner than most of their western "models." In the evening they cluster outside the cinemas, whose mainstay they are, absorbing tirelessly and (to the best of my belief) unprotestingly American films, which are rarely the best of their kind.

There is a great deal of discussion in Israel about the "gilded youth" of the towns. Some admit their existence and regard them as a danger, which others deny. The question is difficult to decide. Also, as Albert Meister notes,[4] the phenomenon itself is less important than the debate about it and what this symptomizes. In this connection we must recall some facts whose importance we have already noted. Since the establishment of the state, agriculture, 80 per cent of which is still in the hands of the *kibbutzim* and *moshavim*, has lost its attraction and influence. Urbanization is making rapid strides. The centers of the big towns and even of the new ones, with their cafés, cinemas and shops, which are increasingly supplied with goods and gadgets corresponding to the "needs" that have arisen in the most advanced industrial societies, proclaim an economic bond of which many Israelis are proud. But they also mark the appearance of the technical environment common to all these societies.

The acculturation to a new environment of the various levels of Israeli youth is taking place in remarkable conditions. A new technical environment, rich in the most violent contrasts, is arising in the land of the Bible. The desert landscapes seem forever reserved for the wanderings of a few Bedouin and their flocks, but in the Negev, at the turn of a red chain of mountains, huge pipes stretching over many miles are waiting to be joined up to bring the waters of the Jordan, drill holes are searching for oil, and bulldozers and mechanical excavators are preparing

[4] *Op. cit.*, p. 105.

the foundations for a new town, complete with bathrooms and lavatories, to which immigrants will go straight from the *mellah*.

In Israel, urban youth, whether "gilded" or not, is as everywhere on this planet, affected by the stimuli of the technical environment. But here the stimuli are applied in a post-war climate, in an atmosphere of "normalization" in which collectivist principles and pioneering idealism have been pushed back and concentrated in the bastions of the old *kibbutzim*. Although living and working conditions are from the start far better than they were in the old days of the *halutzim*, few young people's *kibbutzim* have been established. In spite of the time boys and girls spend in *kibbutzim* during their stint in the Nahal, few return to them after the end of their military service. Pioneering life in the new towns, the noble but uncomfortable and difficult task of training "oriental" immigrants, does not appeal to young people, who prefer city lights.

This is not surprising. Their parents, who came from Germany or eastern Europe, largely from families that had been urbanized for generations, are for the most part employed in public service or in trade, that is, in the tertiary sector, which is highly, indeed excessively, developed in Israel. (In 1961 it absorbed 60 per cent of the national revenue.[5]) These people welcome "normalization." Alien, sometimes fiercely hostile, to all pioneer ideology, they have no thought of moving to the Negev or sending their children there. If one of them takes a job in a development town—Ashdod, Dimona or even Eilat—it is only because he is heavily compensated for the heat, the distance and the discomfort. Ben-Gurion is said to have remarked (though the exact words are probably apocryphal) that, if he could only move 200,000 of the inhabitants of Tel Aviv to the Negev, many of the problems of Israel would be solved.

New immigrants are plunged suddenly into a society in a state of rapid urbanization and economic growth. Their ruthless encounter with the models of life of a technical environment has

[5] J. Klatzmann, *op. cit.*, p. 247.

many consequences that complicate the government's task. In particular, *olim* newly arrived from Asia and North Africa, ideologically and politically unprepared, immediately develop new needs when they come in contact with Israeli comfort. They immediately want things they had never even heard of, as an older immigrant told me. In their *moshavim* they dream about the city, shop windows and entertainments, and what they believe to be an easier, better life. And when they leave the *moshav* and swarm into a teeming suburb near Tel Aviv or Haifa and find a more or less permanent job, they think themselves happy.[6]

THE INVASION OF MASS CULTURE

The extraordinarily rapid multiplication of movie houses and movie attendance is only one of the signs of the penetration of Israel by mass culture.[7] Since there is no systematic study of the origins and categories of films distributed in Israel, I can only record my impression that American films are dominant, and are often mediocre in quality, including those of the sex and crime school. There is some cheap Israeli movie production, and French films of the type made for the general public are also shown, although quality films are not excluded. In February 1963, one of the biggest movie houses in Jerusalem was showing *Les Liaisons dangereuses*, not unsuccessfully.

As for radio (in 1965 Israel had 500,000 licensed sets), the directors of Kol Israel, faced with such a heterogeneous public, can hardly be blamed for leaning heavily on the mass-culture models of the West, particularly North America, or filling out

[6] A. Meister, *op. cit.*, pp. 105–106.

[7] Cf. *Statistical Abstract of Israel*, 1966. Between 1951–52 and 1965–66 the number of movie houses increased from 125 to 303, the number of seats from 79,500 to 186,774, and the number of attendances from 21.8 million to 50.3 million. Sociological studies of the mass media agree that movie attendances decline with the spread of television, except among the young, and in considering these figures it must be borne in mind that the cinema in Israel has not yet been faced with competition from television.

their programs with variety material and "light music" inter-larded with commercials. They would be justified in maintaining that it is their duty to satisfy the tastes and inclinations of a public increasingly dominated by "oriental" immigrants who lack basic education and their families and children in the *moshavim*, where the mass media provide the only cultural nourishment. One of these *moshavnikim*, a recent immigrant, said in this connection: "Before we had electricity, we thought they did not read because they had no light. Now they have it, but they listen to the radio."[8]

I am not, of course, overlooking the fact that admirable institutions of higher culture[9] have been established in Israel. There are famous theatrical companies, such as the Habimah, which in 1961–62 played to 460,000 spectators, and the Ohel Company, formerly a workers' theater, which during the same period gave 387 performances, seen by 235,000 people. The Chamber Theater (Cameri), established in 1944, was similarly successful, and the excellent Israeli Philharmonic Orchestra, whose concert hall at Tel Aviv seats 3000, has 25,000 sub-scribers, which, in proportion to the size of the population, is unequaled anywhere, even in such "musical" countries as Germany or Holland. I am also well aware that Israel has many museums, and artists' villages near Haifa and at Sfad.

But higher culture can nowhere put up an effective barrier against mass culture unbridled and unchecked. In Israel the task is peculiarly difficult. The models of mass culture are consumed, not only by the relatively privileged sectors of the population—immigrants of long standing and *sabras* who are the offspring of the *yishuv* and as a whole are well adapted to the technical environment of Israeli society—but also by the masses of "oriental" immigrants, recently uprooted from their native communities, who, with the exception of weak traditions that are on the point of disappearance, have no defense against the

---

[8] A. Meister, *op. cit.*, p. 100.

[9] For purposes of convenience I am taking the three levels (higher, medium and lower or crude) used by many American sociologists in their study of mass culture.

ascendancy of these models. Religion, which is declining among the young, is not, broadly speaking, sufficiently deeply felt to be able to counter the imperious and toxic effect of the mass media. The new *moshavim*, largely populated by these immigrants of recent date, put up only fitful resistance to the influences of the society by which they are surrounded and rapidly penetrated.

Not even the oldest *moshavim* or the most self-contained and independent *kibbutzim* are immune, whether they like it or not, to gradual penetration by the tentacles of the "other society." The liberalizing trend mentioned earlier must be regarded in the light of this permanent and irresistible pressure. Israeli society is opening itself up to the multiplication and, in some sectors of the economy, abundance of modern products and amenities, and it is because of this "normalization" that the attitudes of the *haverim* as consumers are changing.[10] New habits, the private bathroom, the radio set, the record player, "necessities" that were unthinkable in the *halutz* period, have now been legitimized by all the federations, and, no doubt, a television set, a motorcycle, or even a small private car will soon become necessities in the *kibbutzim* too. The young people of the *kibbutzim* are exposed to the influences of western mass culture (selectively, according to their level of education) by the radio, records and films. Many *kibbutzim* have formed film clubs, which show films, generally of good quality, for the benefit of their members.

Work has been done on the penetration of mass culture in some "underdeveloped" countries,[11] and it would be interesting

[10] The development of standards and patterns of private consumption in the *kibbutzim* has undoubtedly been influenced by the progress of urbanization. *Cf.* Eva Rosenfeld, "Institutional Change in the *Kibbutz*," *op. cit.*

[11] UNESCO, "Les moyens d'information dans les pays en voie de développement," *Études et documents d'information*, No. 33, 1961, and various studies published by *Communications*, Éditions du Seuil, Paris. *Cf.* No. 1 (1962), B. Sternberg-Sarel, "La radio en Afrique noire d'expression française"; No. 2 (1963), Claude Brémond, "Les communications de masse dans les pays en voie de développement"; No. 3 (1964), Claude Bataillon, "Communications de masse et vie urbaine au Mexique." A research team from the Bureau of Applied Social

to compare the findings with those in Israel. There is one factor that can be regarded as negligible in Israel, although it is by no means negligible among its Arab neighbors: local cultural traditions. These tend with varying degrees of success to acquire a new lease on life through the channels of mass communication. But, apart from some moribund sub-cultures to which I have already referred and will refer again, there are no "local cultural traditions" in the Israeli community, which is continually enriched and modified by new contributions.

On the contrary, the dominant world-wide mass culture (whose origin is North American and whose effects penetrate even the Iron Curtain) exercises in Israel a multiple influence that is the more effective because it does not have to overcome the resistance of a traditional culture. The only force capable of putting up a delaying action against it is the associations of persons of the same national origin founded by immigrants from Europe (particularly Russians, Poles, Rumanians and Germans).[12] These form a cultural sub-group, so to speak, but disintegrate as the survivors die off and their *sabra* children and grandchildren move to the forefront of the social scene.

Account must to be sure be taken of the moral imperatives, bans and taboos that restrict means of expression in communities in which the individual remains subject to traditional values and norms of a cultural, ethical or religious nature. In Israel such bans or taboos may derive either from orthodox Judaism (whose hold on youth seems, however, to be pretty weak; it was not, for example, able to impose a selection of films that would conform to its directives), or from the pioneer ideology, whose influence is declining with the disappearance of the first gen-

---

Research (Columbia University, New York) in 1950–51 studied societies "in transition" between "traditional" and "modern" in six Middle Eastern countries: Egypt, Syria, Lebanon, Jordan, Turkey and Persia. The report summing up the conclusions was ably written by David Lerner and published as *The Passing of Traditional Society; Modernizing the Middle East* (Free Press of Glencoe, 1958), and is a document of exceptional interest for purposes of comparison with Israel.

12 The prototype of these is the *Landsmannschaften*. Similar associations have recently been formed by "oriental" immigrants.

eration of *halutzim*. Here again Israeli society is in a weak position to resist mass culture.

Finally, there is yet another factor: the formation of an uneducated, unskilled urban proletariat, cut off from its cultural roots and particularly receptive to the mass media. This applies, broadly speaking, to the whole of the recent influx of North Africans (Algerians, Tunisians and especially Moroccans). Here the uprooting, either of individuals or of whole families, is not compensated for by their religious faith, which often takes the form of observances practiced too formally and superficially to be able to resist the pressures of a rapidly industrialized society. What I have said in this connection of the new *moshavnikim* of "oriental" origin is still truer of the workers in many urban areas and in the new towns, whose only distractions are the radio and the cinema. The only hope of gradually competing with the mass culture that is all too often absorbed in its crudest and most inferior form is free, universal education for the young, adapted to different age groups and ethnic origins, and the establishment of municipal cultural societies and institutions. These will make the young better educated than their parents, and hence better able to resist. Whichever way you turn in Israel, you come across the urgent need for a huge educational effort.

Under these circumstances it is understandable that Israeli leaders have hesitated, and are still hesitating, about establishing a television service.[13] Unless rigorous control, "enlightened despotism," is exercised to make television exclusively educational, it is likely to accelerate irreversibly the spread of a degraded mass culture.

In the universities and the *kibbutzim* I met a number of people who consider that mass culture is already one of the

[13] Proposals debated by the Knesset several times, and again in February and March 1964, have included only the establishment of an educational television service. The opposition, as well as certain circles in the Mapai to whom Ben-Gurion's authoritarian leadership was disquieting, were, however, more fearful of putting a new weapon into the government's hands than of the effects of mass culture on a "developing" society.

gravest threats to keeping Israeli society "different" and preserving the original principles of which it might be the em-
bodiment and example. These people blame the proliferation
of newspapers and magazines that give as much space to scandal
and gossip about film stars as their opposite numbers in Rome,
Paris or New York. As in the West, mass culture is blamed
for the irresponsibility of youth and its indifference to collectivism; it is also, of course, blamed for the appearance in the
towns of juvenile delinquency, which was previously unknown.
Very few seek an explanation in the heart of the new Israeli
society, in which both the idealism of the pioneers and orthodox
Judaism have no substance for the majority of young people,
and those in authority in politics and education, thought and
action—in other words, the older generation—have allowed a void
to arise that their children try to fill as best they can. This
brings us back again to the crisis of values.

Israel at the present time is faced with a phenomenon that
differs from and transcends mere post-war psychology. Is the
young state going through a period of relaxation, a kind of
tactical withdrawal, so to speak, a transient phase before new
tensions and new struggles, which will be accepted, or even
willed, by a whole enthusiastic nation sustained by a messianic
vocation and advancing toward an ideal of justice and peace? Or
are these the preliminary symptoms of a struggle between the
"chosen people" and the new technical environment of the twentieth century?

Will Israel, after almost miraculous successes, winning its
independence through determination, heroism and self-sacrifice,
succumb to the process of daily, subtle infiltration? I am thinking
of the sort of specter that haunts the minds of humanist philosophers in the United States and elsewhere. Homer, Aeschylus,
Plato, Virgil, Dante, Shakespeare and other geniuses closer to
our own time, whose work has survived dark or catastrophic
periods of history and recurrent destruction and barbarism, may
not survive the adaptations, manipulations and distortions of
today's mass culture, still less tomorrow's. Should one similarly
fear that the "Jewish people," having survived more than three

thousand years of tribulations, persecutions and massacres, may not survive the multiform erosion of the century of comic strips, television, Sputniks and cheap magazines?

A struggle of particular significance is in progress in this strip of Palestine. Like others in our time, it is subject to many unforeseeable circumstances and hazards, and, in the eyes of an unbeliever, the outcome is not foreordained. No pleasure is to be taken in the paradox, but it is legitimate to believe that the Israelis today have one piece of great good fortune that keeps some of them in a state of healthy tension and prevents many others from going to pieces under the manifold impact of "normalizing" and softening influences. Z., a poet and a prophet, caustically summed it up for me on one of our sabbath walks. "The dirtiest trick that the Arabs could play on the Jews at the present time," he said, "would be to make peace with them."

6

The Second Israel

In the course of these pages we have several times been brought face to face with the realities of the "second" Israel, created by the influx of "oriental" immigrants from Asia and Africa who have entered the country since the establishment of the state.[1] In 1948 about 80 per cent of the Israeli population was of European origin, except for a few thousand of American origin. In 1966 more than 60 per cent, *sabras* included, were "orientals."

These immigrants differed greatly from those who settled in Israel before 1948. They came from "development" areas of the Arab world and from communities of very varying degrees of culture. Nowadays, generally speaking, they do the least sought-after and least well-paid work in Israel. Is the "ethnic" dividing line also a social dividing line? The "second" Israel is second in order of time (hence the title of this chapter). Is it also second in status, both psychological and moral, and in the place accorded to it in the economy and institutions of the country? Is it true, as certain observers claim, that the chief, if not the exclusive, beneficiaries of the progress whose signs I have noted are the veterans of the first *aliyot* and their children,

[1] It is customary in Israel to distinguish "western" Jews of European or American origin from "oriental" Jews. The latter include not only Yemenis, Iraqis, Persians and Syrians, but also Egyptians, Libyans, Tunisians, Algerians and Moroccans, as if the last group came from "east" of Israel. I have retained the term as a matter of convenience. It is no longer appropriate to differentiate these two very broad categories of immigrants by referring to them as Ashkenazim (Jews who observe the German-east European rite) or Sephardim (those who observe the Spanish-Portuguese rite).

most of them Ashkenazim? Are there really "two Israels" today? How grave are the difficulties of "fusing the communities" manifest from Dan to Eilat? Are they insoluble in present conditions?

CONTRASTS

The first Israel was primarily of European origin. The first *aliya* (1882–1903) consisted of young people, including many students, from Russia, Poland and Rumania, and these were the pioneers of Jewish settlement in Palestine. The second *aliya* (1904–14) consisted principally of immigrants from Russia, who established the first *kvutzot* (Degania, 1910) and created the *halutz* labor ideology. The third (1919–23), after the Balfour declaration[2] and the end of the First World War, was 45 per cent immigrants from Russia, and 30 per cent from Poland. Most of them were Zionists and socialists, and it was from them that the founders of the Histadrut were recruited in 1920; Ben-Gurion became general secretary in 1921. The fourth *aliya* (1924–31) differed from its predecessors and was much less idealistic. It consisted chiefly of petty bourgeois, who would no doubt have emigrated to the United States if its doors had not been closed to them. This influx was again almost exclusively European: half from Poland, a fifth from Russia, and another fifth from the rest of Europe. The fifth *aliya* (1932–38) was even less Zionist and less drawn toward "pioneer" ideals; it was the result of the Nazi persecutions in Germany and anti-Semitism in Poland and Rumania. It should be noted that, although this was the period of the Great Depression in America and most of Europe, relative prosperity prevailed in Palestine, particularly from 1932 to 1935. The sixth and last *aliya* before the proclamation of the state (1939–48) was provoked by the

---

[2] The Balfour declaration, made on November 2, 1917, led to the establishment of a Jewish national home in Palestine under the British mandate which lasted until the establishment of the state of Israel (May 15, 1948).

Nazis' systematic extermination of Jews in all the territories under their control. This immigration often took place in dramatic circumstances, which, since the mandatory power had laid down a rigorous policy of restricting entry, had to be clandestine. Nevertheless, 153,000 immigrants from Poland (25 per cent), Rumania (19 per cent), Germany (12 per cent), Czechoslovakia (9 per cent) and Hungary (6 per cent) entered the country, two-fifths of them illegally. Of the 92,000 who were officially registered, only 13,000 came from Asia (Yemen, Turkey, Iraq). It was during this period that shiploads of refugees, whole families often including grandparents and children, who had reached the threshold of safety and liberty, were guarded day and night by British sentries and finally sent away from the shores of Palestine.

All these *aliyot* were from countries that had already set out on the path of industrialization. They included—and this applied especially to the first, second, third and fifth waves—many educated and often highly cultivated men, members of the liberal professions or at least skilled workmen (tailors, cabinetmakers, etc.), who could readily readapt to the conditions of a society approaching the point of economic "take-off." It was the first three waves that provided most of the leaders of Israeli socialism and the founders of the *kibbutzim*, the Histadrut and and the labor parties, the great *vatikim* like Ben-Gurion (who immigrated in 1912), Chaim Weizmann, Ben-Zvi, and the "veterans" against whose prolonged tutelage the "young Turks"—notably Moshe Dayan and Shimon Peres (who incidentally differ greatly from each other and have still younger personalities already crowding on their heels)—are in revolt. The fifth *aliya*, consisting largely of middle-class Jews from Germany, made up for its lack of idealism by introducing technical knowledge and often even capital; these were the "Yekkes," so called because, being town dwellers, they wore *Jäcke* (jackets), unlike the working clothes worn by earlier settlers; they were regarded with some mistrust by the idealistic settlers and pioneers of the *yishuv*, most of whom came from Russia and Poland.

On the whole, all these pre-1948 European immigrants succeeded in adapting themselves more or less rapidly and made good in whatever their field of activity.

Simultaneously, with the achievement of independence, the proclamation of the Law of the Return was promulgated which gave every Jew the right—and even the duty, according to some Israelis, in whose eyes the Diaspora has since been a shocking anomaly—to immigrate to Israel and assume Israeli citizenship without any formality whatever. The law was based on religious, humanitarian, economic and security considerations. There were passages in the Bible in which the prophets foretold the reunion of the Jewish people in the Holy Land; the law was also intended to provide a home for the survivors of the great massacre and the victims of an ever-renascent anti-Semitism, which was apparently as "eternal" as the Jewish people itself; to secure the manpower necessary for the exploitation of the country and its rapid development; and finally to protect the population of the frontier regions and establish a powerful army to meet the Arab threat.

Thus, after the foundation of the state, particularly between 1948–51 and 1955–59, new waves of immigrants entered the country of whom only a minority (46.9 per cent) came from Europe and America, while the majority (53.1 per cent) came from Asia and Africa[3]; during the period from 1919 to May 15, 1948, the proportions had been 89.6 and 10.4 per cent; 1963, they were 30.7 and 69.3 per cent. The principal contingents from Asia (28.6 per cent) came from Iraq, Yemen, Turkey and Persia, from Africa (24.6 per cent), from the Maghreb—chiefly Morocco and Tunisia—and from Libya. Since 1948 the Jewish communities in the Muslim states, fleeing to Israel from countries in which they had lived for thousands of years, have been almost completely broken up; the Syrian, Iraqi, Yemeni,

---

[3] These figures have been calculated for the period May 15, 1948 to May 21, 1961 (cf. State of Israel, Central Statistical Service, *Demographic Characteristics of the Population*, I, p. xxi).

Libyan and Egyptian communities, for instance, have practically ceased to exist.

The two groups of *aliyot* that between them have made up the present population of Israel have little in common, even in religious feeling and observance. The "orientals" all came from countries where the dominant population was Arab, and Zionism was too young to have exercised any influence even among their educated elite. In the Middle Ages and up to the sixteenth century, these communities, particularly in North Africa, produced a brilliant culture, famous men of learning and poets. Then, cut off from the Ashkenazim, who after the emancipation, except those who were isolated or isolated themselves in the ghettos like the Hasidic communities in eastern Europe, kept pace with intellectual, social and technical progress in Europe, they shared for centuries the poverty, backwardness, slow rhythm of life and lack of aptitude (or interest in) "ascending social mobility" characteristic of the Arabs in whose midst they lived.

The Asian communities included a minimal number of technically qualified personnel and members of the liberal professions. The latter were far more numerous among the Jews of North Africa, but they did not choose to go to Israel; educated Algerians went to France, where they could expect an easier life and material advantages that Israel could not provide. I frequently saw signs of the resentment this has caused among many Israelis. For example, in January 1963, a mock trial of Algerian Jewry was held in Jerusalem in the presence of a large audience. Prosecution witnesses accused it, sometimes with passion, of having disappointed the hopes placed in it by the state of Israel. For the defense a number of young Algerians, including a former member of the Algiers bar, stated their feeling of being misunderstood and sometimes discriminated against, and their difficulties in adapting psychologically and vocationally to Israel.

Most of the "oriental" immigrants were farm workers, small traders, shopkeepers or peddlers—strangers to modern techniques, unskilled, unused to western ways of thought, even illiterate. They had no understanding of or preparation for the ideals and pioneer institutions of Israeli socialism. Consequently they adapted themselves far less quickly than the western immigrants, chiefly from Poland and Rumania, who arrived in the country between 1948 and 1957 had.

AN OVERSIMPLIFIED EXPLANATION

Whatever some North African Jews may say to explain their difficulties, disappointments or setbacks, this contrast is not to be explained by attributing deliberate discrimination against the "orientals"—in schooling, housing, jobs, for instance—to the authorities, the *vatikim*, or the "first" Israel in general.[4] What happened in fact was that Israel, which had opened its gates to all Jews of whatever origin, including the aged, the infirm and the sick, received an influx of immigrants ill-adapted to its needs and institutions who arrived at a time when the country was beginning to recover from a long period of chaos. These immigrants were lifted bodily out of a society in a state of transition and dumped in another at a different stage of development that was being totally transformed. The conditions that were offered them (*shikunim*, work, wage scales, etc.) were often unsuited to the size, way of life and cultural traditions of "oriental" families.[5] From the outset a huge educational effort was obviously the only hope of integrating them within a reasonable period, giving them equality of opportunity, protecting them against the risk of "Levantinization" and bringing about a real fusion of the two Israels.

A friend whose duties led him to accompany groups of immigrants from Morocco to Haifa in recent years described to me the scenes, worthy of a medieval fairground, that took

[4] Judith T. Shuval ("Emerging Patterns of Ethnic Strain in Israel," *Social Forces*, May 1962, p. 38), observes in this connection that prejudice in Israel shows itself most often inside an informal social group.

[5] For the difficulties of adaptation of certain types of "oriental" families in the 1950–53 period *cf.* S. N. Eisenstadt, *op. cit.*, Ch. VI, pp. 139–225.

place at the harbor station in Marseilles among the ragged, pitiful crowds with their belongings wrapped in old newspapers. These were the same immigrants, or their neighbors and relatives from the same North African *mellahs*, whom I saw and spoke to a few months later in the *shikunim* at Katamon, near Jerusalem, or those at Afuleh, Ashdod or Kiryat Gat. Their original condition does not excuse the mistakes and misunderstandings in dealing with them, but it throws light on the complexity of the problems the Israeli leaders have to face.

It is easy and tempting to the foreign observer to give a simple and cruel explanation of the questions with which this chapter opened: The *vatikim*, most of whom are Ashkenazim, are the men in possession. They "exploit" the newcomers, who form an "underdeveloped" substratum from which most manual laborers and subordinate employees are recruited, and they keep them at the bottom of the scale by their status and wage rates. The *vatikim* occupy all the key positions (beginning with the Ministries and the Histadrut), and it is they who are the beneficiaries of economic growth; and they accept the fact that the great mass of "orientals" in Israel now play the part of a colonial proletariat, shutting their eyes to the real situation or obscuring it with phony explanations. They cried scandal when a journalist, Kalman Katznelson, tore aside the veil in an arrogant and hate-filled pamphlet, *The Ashkenazi Revolution* (Tel Aviv, 1964). They themselves have in fact repudiated the principles of the now-outworn ideology of the Zionist pioneers, just as the egalitarianism of their classless, originally agricultural society has been undermined by the progress of industrialization. Side by side with the development of a pluralist economy, a hierarchy of technicians has appeared who fight tooth and nail to maintain their status and increase their salaries and privileges under the umbrella of a capitalist sector dominated by the upstarts of the "first" Israel.

I have already indicated how oversimplified and mistaken this analysis is, and I will later substantiate this. But first let me refer to my notebooks, for some observations that are in place here.

SOME HUMAN ENCOUNTERS

On the morning after my first arrival in Jerusalem I went into a barbershop kept by a Moroccan in the charming, flower-filled quarter of Rehavia, where the Hebrew University had put me up. He complained of his living quarters (although he had passed the *ma'abara* stage) and said that he earned too little to keep his large family. The promises that "they" had given him (in regard to working and living conditions) had not been kept. "They" considered Moroccans "blacks."[6]

The French-speaking North Africans to whom I spoke were delighted at the opportunity to use the language. The "they" they spoke of referred sometimes to the representatives of the Zionist agencies and movements, sometimes to the Israeli authorities and sometimes to the Ashkenazim ("the masters of the country," my barber called them) regarded *en bloc* as a single entity. In cafés, buses or at the gates of factories or docks I met a number of "angry" Algerians, Tunisians and Moroccans. N., a fitter in the copper mines at Timna, near Eilat, was married to a Tunisian by whom he had four children. He had hearing trouble caused by the noisy machinery. Instead of being appointed foreman (which "they" had promised him), he had been moved to a less well-paid job, and the job he had been "promised" had been given to an Ashkenazi who had only just been taken on. The Histadrut was of little help to him. It is difficult to judge the validity of such complaints, but the feeling of being cold-shouldered, unfairly treated, secretly discriminated against, is widespread among the Jews from North Africa. G.B., a good-looking, intelligent Algerian aged about forty, employed as a bookkeeper in the port of Z., was not an "angry" man, but calm and apparently resigned, although he believes he was twice the victim of grave injustice

[6] This is a reference to the term *chahor* ("black"), which North African Jews regard as insulting.

when he was passed over for the post of chief accountant. F.H., a Moroccan, assistant to the manager of a provincial branch of the National Bank of Israel, claimed that in spite of his services and merits he had been passed over promotion in favor of younger and less competent colleagues, naturally of European extraction.

In several big restaurants I noted the unanimity of the western headwaiters and chefs (of German origin) in running down their subordinates, the "oriental" waiters and kitchen assistants, whom they jealously kept to their subordinate tasks. On one occasion when I was a guest at a big hotel at Tel Aviv I felt obliged to intervene on behalf of a Tunisian waiter who was being disgracefully bullied by the big, square-shouldered headwaiter, an Israeli of German appearance, for having actually dared to take an order from a customer who was in a hurry.

I am well aware of the doubtful value of such chance observations, and I recall that several times I had the feeling that some North Africans were attributing to systematic Ashkenazi prejudice against them disappointments and setbacks due to their own (temporary) lack of adaptation. (Some North Africans are so convinced of the existence of this prejudice that they tell prospective employers they come from the south of France.) Nevertheless their persecution complex is real, and is kept alive by the image of themselves as idle, incompetent and incurably uncivilized that is often attributed to them by Westerners and "interiorized" by them in accordance with the process subtly analyzed by George H. Mead in a classical study.[7] And since a sufficient number of systematic studies[8] of the psychological aspects of these tensions is lacking, I have been

[7] *Mind, Self and Society*, University of Chicago Press, 1947, and in particular pp. 135-226.

[8] I have already quoted that of Judith Shuval. The work of Doris Donath, of the National Center of Scientific Research (Paris), who has spent several years studying the problems arising from the lack of adaptation of North African (and in particular Moroccan) immigrants will fill an important gap.

unable to ignore my personal impressions of this delicate subject.

These were by no means all unfavorable. There were many signs that the Israeli crucible is having a favorable effect on North African immigrants. In contrast to the bitterness of N., I recall the happy face of the young Algerian worker at the Timna mines who sat next to me in the little Arkia (internal air service) aircraft from Eilat to Tel Aviv, where he was taking his aged mother, dressed in the traditional black, to help her prepare for a visit to France. He was on a three-months trial period, after which he had every expectation of being promoted to foreman, and he did not believe in discrimination. "If you work hard and are not in too much of a hurry, you have every chance of making good," he said. (The most frequent complaint against the new immigrants made by the *vatikim* is that they expect too much and are in too much of a hurry.[9]) When he got his promotion he would be earning I£550 a month, which was good pay. Another who was satisfied was a young man who came from Meknès in 1954 and was employed by the Jewish Agency at Jerusalem. He had decent living quarters, he told me, and enough to keep his wife and two children on in comfort, besides helping his parents. He had had no trouble with the Ashkenazim. We had a long, frank talk. He was satisfied, although he suffered from a wound that was still bleeding. As we sat in a bar at Rehov Yafo in front of two big glasses of orange juice, which is very cheap in Israel, he took a photograph from his wallet; it was of his younger brother, who was killed in 1956 in Operation Sinai. "The poor fellow was much handsomer and more intelligent than I," he said.

Other jottings in my notebook refer to the young. The education of the children of "oriental" immigrants presents a for-

[9] A story about some Yemenis brought to Israel by "Operation Flying Carpet" bears on this question. "What?" they exclaimed to a bus conductor. "We were brought here for nothing by air, and now you expect us to pay the fare on a bus?"

midable problem, and existing resources (schools, teachers, boarding schools, syllabuses, means of influencing the family environment) are far from sufficient or adequate. Nevertheless, good results are already observable. At the Maritime Museum at Eilat one morning I mingled with a group of pupils from an agricultural school near Haifa who had been brought across the Negev to the Red Sea. The boys and girls traveled in trucks, in charge of an Italian agricultural expert, who was both serious and enthusiastic, and slept in the open air. They wore their working clothes—the small, brightly colored cloth caps that are to be seen everywhere in the Israeli countryside and heavy boots—and some carried rifles (they traveled along frontier roads, which are always dangerous). Many were North African, mostly from Morocco, and came from very poor families. Some had come to Israel alone with the youth *aliya*. Their school gave them both general education, with intensive instruction in Hebrew, and a theoretical and practical training in agriculture. The young Moroccans seemed relaxed and happy. Thanks to this school, they said, they were getting free secondary education.[10] Their ambition was to become agricultural specialists and their dream to be sent as "experts" to the countries of Black Africa. Others would be going to *moshavim* or *kibbutzim*. Several of the girls wanted to be nurses. For these young people born in the squalid *mellahs* of North Africa the *aliya* had been a blessing. Israel was turning them into educated citizens. If this process can become general, in a few decades the problems of the "second" Israel will be near solution.

In industry I came across frequent examples of young North Africans who had adapted successfully. The regional council of Beit Shean is a marketing headquarters for agricultural products—citrus fruits, dates, dried alfalfa and cotton. Boys and girls recently arrived from Morocco work there, and I made

[10] With the exception of schools associated with *kibbutzim* or *moshavim*, secondary schools in Israel charge tuition. Scholarships are granted on the basis of tests at the end of elementary school. They are freely available to western and "oriental" children alike, but this is a grave mistake, to which I shall return later.

a point of observing them in the poultry "factory," which is very modern and mechanized; chickens and turkeys are bled in conformity with the dietary laws and plucked by conveyor-belt methods that are a small-scale replica of those used in the United States. The manager, A.B., a *haver* of German origin from a religious *kibbutz* in the neighborhood, said that, in spite of the low cultural level of these young people on their arrival (he told me they had to be taught how to use such modern devices as douches and lavatories), after a year they had learned operations requiring concentration and precision and had attained a satisfactory level of output.

What are needed to solve the problem of the communities and integrate these North African immigrants into the state are large-scale administrative measures, a vast public health and educational system, and the provision of housing and jobs. To accelerate the process and make it as effective as possible, the greatest need is knowledge; knowledge of the images of each other (varying with different ethnic origins, age and social and occupational categories) that the two groups, "orientals" and Westerners, have formed and the consequent distortions. A huge campaign is required to spread knowledge among the older-established Israeli population about the North African immigrants, the history of their communities, their living conditions among the Muslims, their traditions and way of life. This would help to correct views that, by a now-familiar process of interaction,[11] help to keep alive shortcomings attributed to the "orientals" and thus to prolong tensions. Among Ashkenazi office workers, servants, taxi drivers, etc., I frequently encountered an image of the North Africans that depicted them as idle, apathetic, malingering, stubborn, undisciplined, uninterested in correcting their mistakes or learning from their seniors, and insistent on being immediately given wages and living conditions they had never even imagined existed in their country of origin. It was surprising to find these generalizations repeated

[11] Gordon W. Allport, *The Nature of Prejudice*, Cambridge, Massachusetts, 1954.

in scarcely more sophisticated form in educated circles, even by
brilliant academics able to embellish them with learned theories,
such as the psychologist S., or the economist W., who denounced North African youth as "very dissolute" and responsible for "new-wave" behavior in urban areas. I had difficulty
getting W. to agree that a far greater problem was involved—
the general crisis of values affecting the second and third generation of *sabras.*

DIFFICULTIES OF INTEGRATION

My impressions have been confirmed by studies carried out
under the auspices of the Israeli Institute of Applied Social
Research. Judith Shuval has demonstrated the tensions arising
from relations between ethnic groups, and the principal fields
in which these manifest themselves.[12] If Allport's celebrated
definition is accepted,[13] it appears from Shuval's investigation,
carried out between 1950 and 1959, that prejudice against
"orientals" increased during that period and was concentrated on
the North African group, particularly the Moroccans. The proportion of individuals who admitted this prejudice rose from
5 per cent in 1950 to 19 per cent in 1953 and 34 per cent
in 1959. These percentages are almost certainly too low, for
people dislike offending prevailing standards and openly express-
ing hostility to an ethnic group as such. In each group a withdrawal into itself was noted, especially in social relations outside
working hours; the "European" and "North African"[14] groups

[12] Judith Shuval, "Class and Ethnic Correlates of Casual Neighboring,"
American Sociological Review, August 1956; "Patterns of Inter-Group Tension
and Affinity," *International Social Science Bulletin* (UNESCO), 1956, No. 1;
Immigrants on the Threshold, Free Press of Glencoe, New York, 1964; and in
particular the article previously quoted, "Emerging Patterns of Ethnic Strain in
Israel," *Social Forces,* May 1962.

[13] G. W. Allport, *op. cit.,* p. 9: "An antipathy based on an erroneous and rigid
generalization . . . applied to a group considered *en bloc* or to an individual
because he is a member of that group."

[14] The 1959 inquiry distinguished between Jews of North African origin
and those from the Near East (Asians).

had practically no social contact with each other. More serious, a similar phenomenon was taking place in the schools, on both sides. The "expectations" of "oriental" children created prejudice on their part, and they tended to repulse the western children who wanted to mingle with them. As for the adults, they tended to accept the stereotype of their group spread by "Europeans" and emphasized their rejection of and hostility to other North Africans.[15] This is the well-known phenomenon of "self-hatred," demonstrating the existence of the prejudice of which it is an interior reflection among the group that is its object. Another significant fact is the satisfaction many "orientals" feel in making use of the services of the Kupat Holim, which gives them the feeling of being treated completely without discrimination and on a basis of full equality (i.e. in conformity with one of their principal expectations when they came to Israel).[16]

It is, of course, natural and inevitable that a certain proportion of expectations should be disappointed. Setbacks and failures are inseparable from immigration, which involves transplantation and acculturation. To Jews (and particularly "oriental" Jews) an *aliya* involves multiple and intense expectations, and it is the most likely of all types of immigration to lead to acute disappointment; the higher the climb, the more painful the fall. Disappointment sometimes leads to the "emigration of immigrants," and in other cases to permanent, chronic inadaptability, which must not be overlooked in enumerating the problems of the "second" Israel.[17]

Among the unadapted, the failures, the "disappointed," there

[15] Thirty-three per cent of the North Africans in the sample of 1511 persons stated that they did not want to have North Africans as neighbors.

[16] Inquiry in progress 1964–65 conducted by the Israeli Institute of Applied Social Research into the attitude of "oriental" immigrants to the medical services of the Kupat Holim and the causes of the excessive use that they tend to make of them.

[17] "Between 1948 and 1960, of 967,748 new immigrants 122,453 recognized the failure of their experiment after a trial period and left the country" (A. Chouraqui, *L'État d'Israël*, P.U.F., Paris, 1962, p. 74). *Cf.* also J. Klatzmann, *op. cit.*, statistical appendix, p. 276.

are, first of all, those who came too old and too late. There are some of these in all new societies. The "return" to Israel cannot succeed in every case. It involves hazards and struggles in which a whole complex of qualities and motivations are at work. The success of the experiment depends on what the immigrant leaves behind—his way of life in the Diaspora, his degree of assimilation, and the strength and quality of his traditions—and what he finds on arrival. The combination of these factors explains to a great extent the ability of groups, and of individuals within them, to fulfill social roles different from those that they fulfilled in their country of origin.[18]

A detail worth noting in passing is that the most pessimistic opinions about relations between Westerners and "orientals" and the chances of merging the two communities that I heard were expressed by Ashkenazim who had not succeeded in Israel. They described the North African young as "completely wild . . . they have stopped being Jews, and they don't know what they are." The individual who talked to me in this bitter fashion, in very good French (but without witnesses), is employed at the reception desk in a big hotel at Haifa, a very modest job, so he told me, for one who, "yielding to Israeli propaganda," had given up his job as commercial manager of a textile factory in Budapest.

[18] In 1956 S. N. Eisenstadt and J. Ben David noted as a principal characteristic of the new type of immigrant a lesser degree of adaptability to new social and cultural roles ("Assimilation culturelle et tensions en Israël," *Bulletin internationale des sciences sociales*, VIII, 1, 1956, p. 71): "No group, or hardly any shows the aspiration so often observed in the *yishuv* to carry out a complete social and economic transformation and create a new society and a new culture." The process of active adaptation to the new Israeli environment differs in different groups, however. It is relatively most vigorous among Bulgarians, Yugoslavs and Yemenis, and weakest among immigrants from post-Nazi Europe (who desire a restoration of the conditions to which they were accustomed before 1939) and North Africans. These last, having lived for the most part in an economically backward civilization, "have a traditionalist conception of Jewish nationality." They wish to preserve their traditions and customs, while freeing themselves from their previous semi-servitude and gaining access to a fuller and freer life; hence their reputation for "asking for too much."

The difficulties in the way of integrating the "orientals" to which the work of Israeli sociologists draws attention are to a great extent explained by the cultural differences between the two principal communities, which are themselves divided up into sub-cultures. These appear strikingly at the time of the great festivals of Pesach (Passover), Shavouoth (Pentecost) and Sukkot (Tabernacles). I was in Jerusalem in May 1964, at the time of Shavouoth, an enormous, noisy, motley fair centered on Mount Zion. It is a veritable place of pilgrimage; there is no alternative to climbing the celebrated hill on foot, for vehicles are banned from the approaches by the police. Shavouoth is primarily a festival of the "oriental" Jews, and it is they who sing, shout, eat, drink (without getting drunk) and dance not far from the presumed tomb of David, the site of the palaces of the Davidian kings, of the Last Supper, and the bathing pool of Suleiman the Magnificent. The crowd on the hill is divided into families, clans, whole tribes. They come from all the *moshavim* and villages in the mountains of Judaea and from as far as Ramla and Tel Aviv, and they eat squatting on the ground in circles, the matrons, wearing brightly colored scarves, producing food from the yellow plastic babies' baths they use to transport it. To the orthodox, Shavouoth has three meanings. Historically it celebrates the arrival at Mount Sinai; religiously it recalls the giving of the Law; and agriculturally it is the festival of the first fruits. For lack of those mentioned in Deuteronomy—grapes and pomegranates, olives and honey—the pilgrims of 1964 brought all the vegetables and fruits produced by their *moshav*, which they offered to the Almighty by joyously consuming them. All the nations of Asia and North Africa were represented here, I was told by V., who guided me through the astonishing throng. Suddenly two young Iraqis detached themselves from a group in front of us, made room for themselves, and began dancing to the rhythm of a drum, supported by the rhythmical cries of their families. A few pairs of Westerners, dignified and out of breath, a party of Russian Orthodox priests with shiny beards and long hair, a few radiant, tousled nuns, and one or two tourists armed with cameras, struck a discordant note in the midst of the exuberant East. In the passages and caves leading to the monument that marks the alleged tomb of David, the multitude of candles lit by the pilgrims had turned into a huge barrage of flame and smoke that sent us hurrying back to the surface and the pure warmth of the sun at its zenith. A little later, on our way down the hill, our path was blocked for a time by a throng of new arrivals who came swarming up the steep road and the steps to reach the festival by the stroke of noon. The East gave itself wholeheartedly, jubilantly and naïvely to the festival. The jackets of the *Yekkes* stood out like motionless dark blobs against the whirling, colorful mass. The spectacle helped me to understand certain aspects of the problems we are considering here.

POPULATION STRUCTURE

Statistical, particularly demographic, information makes it possible to place the preceding observations in their social context and better explain the realities of the "second" Israel, which are so often obscured by emotion and distorted by personal reactions.[19]

The essential fact from which one must start is the radical transformation of the demographic structure of the country since the war of independence. The overwhelming majority of the population when the state was established consisted of immigrants who, from the first to the sixth *aliya*, were Westerners coming chiefly (89.6 per cent) from eastern and central Eu-

---

[19] In the pages that follow, in addition to information supplied by the Central Statistical Office in Jerusalem, I have made extensive use of the solidly documented lecture delivered by André Chouraqui to the Cercle pour la Fusion des Communautés, "Réflexions sur les structures demographiques de l'État d'Israël" (1962), an extract from which he was kind enough to supply, as well as his article "Israël au carrefour de l'Orient et de l'Occident," in *Tiers-Monde*, October–December 1962. I will refer to these as C1 and C2 respectively.

rope (Russia, Poland, Rumania, Hungary, Germany) and in some cases from America. Today, as previously noted, more than 60 per cent of the Israeli population originated in Asia or Africa,[20] and, other things being equal, in fifteen years' time, in view of the "age pyramid," this figure will increase to 80 per cent.[21]

The situation stands out still more clearly if one distinguishes three groups in the Jewish population of Israel,[22] each forming approximately one-third of the total: (1) The Westerners (34 per cent) whose average age is forty-four (in other words, of every 100 Israelis of European or American origin about one-half have statistically passed the age of reproduction). This group has little chance in the foreseeable future of being noticeably increased by new *aliyot*, which could come in substantial numbers only from the United States or the Soviet Union. (2) The "orientals" (32 per cent), whose average age is twenty-six. Their birth rate, particularly that of the North Africans, is one of the highest in the world, although it has been decreasing slightly for some years, a sign of acculturation to Israeli society. The average number of children per family is 4.9, as against 3.2 in western families, and the population explosion among them is the more rapid since their mortality rate now equals that of the older inhabitants, which is very low as a result of progress in public health and improvement of medical services. (3) *Sabras* (34 per cent), whose average age in March 1962 was eight years.[23] At that date it was already calculated that the proportion of *sabras* of "oriental" origin to those of western origin was at least seven to three. Because of the "oriental" birth rate and the drying-up of western immigration,

[20] Between 1952 and 1954, 78 per cent of immigrants came from Asia or Africa; from 1954 to May 21, 1961, the percentage was 57.7. (General Census of the Population, Central Statistical Service, Jerusalem, 1963.)

[21] C2, p. 670.

[22] According to the census of May 22, 1961, this numbered 1,932,357, and there was a minority of 247,135 Arabs and Druses. On January 1, 1966, the Jewish population was 2,299,100.

[23] C1, p. 2.

the imbalance between the two groups can only increase in favor of the former.[24]

The size of the families founded by *sabras* shows the growing influence of "orientals" on the country's population structure. If social, economic and psychological conditions remain unchanged, the size of families in the second "oriental" generation will approach the average of the "underdeveloped" population of their countries of origin in Africa and Asia. This development is already creating acute and sometimes dramatic problems in Israel. When the census was taken on December 31, 1961, there were only 1400 western homes consisting of nine or more persons, but there were 15,200 such homes among the "orientals."[25]

The steps originally taken to assure equality of conditions (size of living quarters, wages, social-security benefits) fail to assure equality of opportunity in education or work to members of an "oriental" family. Take, for instance, the hypothetical case of two identical two-room flats in a *shikun* given ten years ago to two young couples, one western and the other "oriental." Originally there was theoretical equality between them. But today the two Westerners will probably have two or three children at most, while the "orientals" will probably have six and may have as many as twelve, and may in addition be giving shelter to grandparents, an uncle, a woman cousin, etc., in conformity with the family structure of the Jewish communities of Africa or Asia.[26] Equality has been changed into tremendous inequality in living conditions, educational opportunities, intellectual development and promotion in the social scale, accen-

[24] Average fertility of women of European origin is 1.9, while that of women coming from Asia and Africa is 6.1 (press conference of the Central Statistical Office, Jerusalem, August 14, 1963).

[25] C1, p. 4.

[26] In his study of the problems of integrating "oriental" immigrants from the days of the *yishuv* to 1953, S. N. Eisenstadt showed how the different types of traditional family influence the absorption rate of their members (*op. cit.*, Ch. IV, pp. 90–104, and Ch. VI, pp. 143–168).

tuated by the fact that Israeli legislation provides only very small allowances for large families.

This *de facto* inequality recurs in the employment structure.[27] The "orientals" are the most underemployed group in the society (about one-third work for only part of the year) and their employment is the least stable (the average time they remain in a job is two and a half years in comparison with five and a half years for Westerners). To be convincing, however, these figures should be interpreted in relation to the immigrants' date of immigration, which is sometimes very recent. Some of them have simply not yet had time to show stability of employment. Most "orientals" (56.7 per cent) are employed in industry, agriculture and construction (public works and building), while the corresponding figures for Westerners and *sabras* are 42.3 and 38.1 per cent. In the distribution of employment in the public services and certain liberal professions the contrast is even more striking. Only 5.4 per cent of senior officials and 31 per cent of "technicians" (doctors, teachers, journalists, skilled social workers, etc.) are "orientals."

In short, "orientals" have a distinctly lower income per home than Westerners and have to support a much bigger family on it. When social and cultural conditions otherwise remain the same, these differences tend to be accentuated.[28]

EDUCATION FOR SURVIVAL

Obviously the only solution to the problems of the "second" Israel is education in the broadest possible sense of the term, including influencing the family environment. Unfortunately Israeli achievements in the field of national education, in spite

[27] C1, pp. 5–7.

[28] This process is a reminder that the frontier of the Third World now passes through the small state of Israel. A similar development has been noted on a large scale in economic relations between developed and underdeveloped countries. The poorer tend to grow richer while the latter grow even poorer (*Cf.* my *Problèmes d'Amérique latine*, II, Gallimard, Paris, 1961, pp. 133–134.

of the extra attention and funds recently devoted to these problems, are less impressive than those in agriculture, industry or national defense.

Soundings made at various levels of the educational system at the end of 1961 produced alarming results.[29] At that time the "orientals" provided 55 per cent of the children beginning elementary school, 40 per cent of those in the last year at elementary school and only 27 per cent of those who gained their certificate of elementary education. Higher up the educational scale these proportions continue to decline, and decline rapidly. The "orientals" provided 25 per cent of those beginning secondary school, 13 per cent of those completing it, and only 5 per cent of those beginning higher education. Of a total of 10,000 students who were going to the Hebrew University, the Bar Ilan University, the Weizmann Institute and the Technion at Haifa[30] only 500 were "orientals." Also many of them, often for both economic and psychological reasons, abandon their studies. In 1961, of a national total of 9824 students, 1726 took university degrees, but only thirty-five of these (2 per cent) were "orientals." In the face of such a shocking disproportion, it is fair to say that the cultural integration of the "second" Israel has hardly begun.

Are sufficient resources devoted to the task? The education estimates for 1963 were I£200 million of a total budget of I£2800 million, or about 7 per cent, a pretty high proportion if the requirements of national defense are taken into account. But only 2 per cent of the additional estimates (in relation to 1962) were devoted to reducing the gap between the two communities. School attendance is insufficient; 13 per cent of chil-

[29] C1, p. 8.
[30] The Hebrew University, which until 1948 was on Mount Scopus, has built a new university city at Givat Ram on the edges of Jerusalem, and has a branch at Tel Aviv. The Bar Ilan University, which bears the name of a famous rabbi, has a religious background and is situated at Ramat Gan, a suburb of Tel Aviv, and has been richly endowed by American and Canadian patrons. The Weizmann Institute is at Rehovot. The total number of students rose in 1966 to 21,150, but the proportion of "orientals" has hardly changed.

dren below the age of fourteen have never been to school.[31] The Ministry of Education, deciding that the children of *sabras* of "oriental" origin needed no preferential treatment, decided to concentrate its efforts on the children of recent immigrants. The shortage of teachers remains a serious obstacle. Teaching, which is hard work for poor pay, has little attraction for the children of the *vatikim*; the pioneering spirit of the young, however strong it may be elsewhere, does not turn in that direction. A leading article in the *Jerusalem Post* for September 6, 1963 noted bitterly that it was high time for the pioneer youth movements to realize that the population itself, and not just its soil, was an object of national service.

The Israeli school, its staff, syllabuses, teachers' training and examination system, were devised by *halutzim* of European origin for their own children. In such schools equality of "oriental" and western children is a myth. What are required are nursery schools to which young "orientals" can be sent before their fifth year, and an adequate number of primary schools at which children would spend the whole day, in order to remove them from a family environment and living conditions that are unfavorable to learning. But at the same time care must be taken to avoid cutting them off from their environment. Educationalists familiar with these problems fear that the new trend, under the pretext of avoiding "segregation" and differential treatment, ignores the values and cultural traditions of the "orientals." The present trend imposes a kind of bargain on the most gifted of them. It is as if they were told: "Turn yourselves into Ashkenazim, and we shall give you a good position in *our* society." What is generally lacking at present is understanding and respect for the "other side."[32] The provision of more suitable

[31] Central Statistical Office, statement of August 14, 1963.

[32] Certain recent and still limited projects (1964) show some progress in this respect; the educational experiment called the Beersheba project, for instance. There are also programs combining general education with vocational training in the new schools in five "development towns" which will be attended chiefly by young "orientals." Steps have also been taken to facilitate young "orientals" entrance to secondary schools. Scholarships are awarded by examination, and lower marks are required of them than of their western comrades.

textbooks, increasing the number of secondary boarding schools, more aid for buying books and other educational requirements, free education at all levels, including the granting of scholarships for higher studies, all are good and necessary. But they will be dangerous if they are put into practice by the "first" Israel in a spirit of selfishness and domination. The integration of the "second" Israel requires raising it to a higher level as a whole, not distilling out of it an elite alienated from its community of origin, which would consequently be incapable of actively cooperating. To recent "oriental" immigrants, the economic and technical development of a *moshav* is a much more effective means of integration than the intellectual and social advancement of a handful of selected individuals. The *moshav*, whose organization and activities correspond to the aspirations, tastes and capacities of many "orientals," has an educational function that must not be overlooked.[33]

These problems imply grave dangers to the country, to which both Israeli and foreign observers draw attention. The economic future, security and very existence of the young state depend on the effort it makes during the next few years to educate *all* its citizens. The establishment of the state and its first economic and military successes, with the aid of investments from abroad, were achieved by the men provided by successive *aliyot* since the beginning of the century. "The present system results in a grave loss of elites, since the selection is made from only part of the population. Men who might render great services in leading positions remained restricted to subordinate positions. The economic development of the country will surely suffer from this. . . . Centurion tanks are a security factor for the immediate future, but for the more distant future the school

[33] These reflections owe a great deal to talks with Haim Adler of the Hebrew University, a specialist in the sociology of education, to whom I here express my thanks. Dov Weintraub, who is well known for his work on the *moshavim*, rightly emphasizes the considerable role that their organization in regional units makes them capable of playing in integrating the immigrants of the "second" Israel; for both economic and psychological reasons the *kibbutzim* could not undertake this task on such a large or effective scale.

and the university represent much more important security factors."[34]

The waste of brains in our increasingly scientific and technical world is worse than a crime, it is a blunder—and a particularly grave blunder for developing countries. Numerically the western community, from which students and leading figures in all fields are almost exclusively recruited, is steadily decreasing in relation to the Israeli population as a whole. Unless an energetic and adequate effort is made in favor of the "orientals," the proportion of qualified people will decline too. In the last resort it has been superiority of the average cultural level that has been responsible for Israel's economic successes, and for the military advantage it has so far enjoyed over the Arabs. But if the cultural level of Israel stagnates while that of its enemies gradually rises, the days of its independence will be numbered. Integrating the "orientals" as rapidly as possible means among other things increasing the number of citizens capable of effectively handling modern weapons. Could the funds necessary for this integration be obtained by launching a press campaign under the slogan, "Education is also national defense"?

For that to be done, the country's leaders would themselves have to be convinced of the necessity of investing huge sums for the benefit of the "oriental" communities, and they would have to be supported by public opinion. Ben-Gurion is certainly aware of the gravity of the situation, but, absorbed by the imperatives of defense, harassed by the internal divisions of the Mapai, obsessed by the consequences of the Lavon affair, he has not succeeded in imparting the necessary psychological shock to the Israeli population. Most Israelis did not seem to me to be very worried by the problems of the "second" Israel, or even very much aware of its innumerable repercussions on the life of the young nation, except, of course, the militant elite of the *kibbutzim*, who co-operate closely with the youth *aliya* in receiving young children and bringing them up side by side

[34] J. Klatzmann, *op. cit.*, p. 259.

with their own. Elsewhere, in the "other society" in urban areas, people do not seem deeply concerned at the inequality of the communities. The new bourgeoisie adapts itself very well to the way in which the fruits of growing prosperity are at present divided. Each vocational group tries to improve its own status, and the heroes of former struggles who raise their voices to denounce these evils and perils are rare. As for the young "western" *sabras*, they show little enthusiasm for working in the development towns among the new immigrants. It is a difficult and no less ungrateful task than reclamation of the marshes was in the old days. What is required is a renewal of the old idealism, a re-creation and readaptation of the *halutz* ideology. The lack of it leaves a gaping void.

Many people console themselves with the thought of the healing power of time. There is nothing new, they say, under the Palestine sun. I often heard present tensions between communities compared with earlier ones. The Russians who came with the first *aliyot* are said to have looked askance at the Poles, and the Hungarians and Lithuanians pulled long faces at the *Yekkes* of the thirties. "This famous 'oriental' problem is simply a question of assimilation, an affair of one or two generations," a factory manager said to me. This lazy optimism is belied by the facts. In the absence of carefully considered, concerted, large-scale action the material and moral gap between the two communities in income, living conditions, qualifications and mentality can only deepen.

The "second" Israel is now launching a formidable challenge to the first.[35] Having done all in its power to put its experience and its best educational and technical minds to work to aid developing countries in Black Africa, Latin America and Asia

[35] The challenge is the more formidable in that immigration in 1963 was the largest the country had known since 1958. Immediately upon becoming Prime Minister, Levi Eshkol drew attention to the fact that, "as a consequence of difficult conditions in their countries of origin, immigrants now required more care and social services than preceding *aliyot*." (Statement to the executive of the Jewish Agency, July 8, 1963.)

—as much out of national interest as out of idealism—it is unthinkable that Israel should leave unaided its own Third World which it magnanimously received within its narrow frontiers.

7

The Religious Problem

Religion was for a long time one of the main components of the Jewish personality—in the eyes of the religious the only essential one.[1] This implies a way of life, which should affect all the acts of daily life. Hence the simultaneously social and national character of religious problems in Israel. The founders of the state, though for the most part Zionists and socialists who were detached from religion, nevertheless, from complex motives in which heart and mind, loyalty to traditions and political necessities, mingled, talked of the Return in a lofty Biblical context. The proclamation on May 14, 1948 of a Jewish state in Palestine called Israel invoked the spirit of the prophets and the protection of Almighty God, and appealed to the Jews of the whole world to rally to it in order to achieve the millenary promises.

THE LAND OF THE BIBLE

To religious Jews regarded as a whole, overlooking their differences, the return of Israel to the Holy Land is not the advent of the kingdom of heaven announced by the prophets. To the strictest of them, represented in Jerusalem by the ultra-orthodox community of the Natorei Karta, the "guardians of the city," the state of Israel, the immense majority of whose citizens vio-

---

[1] The *mitzvot* were observed by the vast majority of members of Jewish communities until about 1750 and the beginnings of the emancipation movement.

late sacred laws to a lesser or greater extent, has nothing whatever to do with the promises of the scriptures, or rather, it is a shocking negation of them which these intransigents totally reject at all levels. To others, who are more moderate as well as more numerous, there is a mystic tie between the land of Israel and the "Jewish people" which the foundation of the state has strikingly revived, although it was never completely severed. "As soon as I set foot on the soil of Palestine," A.R., a Tunisian intellectual, said to me, "I felt myself to be re-Judaized. Ever since the time of Abraham there have always been Jews in Palestine. The return to the Holy Land is a human return. It is not yet the divine fulfillment, but it *may* pave the way to it." From this point of view spiritual progress, seen in the messianic perspective of the scriptures, goes hand in hand with national and social progress and is involved in the epic of agricultural and industrial renascence, the reconquest of the country by tractors and by arms carried out by the *halutzim*, who were for the most part socialists and atheists.

The founders of Israel, faced with a situation that had no equivalent in the annals of human societies, found themselves in a dilemma. They could either establish a theocratic state, submitting social and private life to the Mosaic law, or, as Theodor Herzl, the prophet of the Jewish national state, demanded,[2] they could separate church and state, religious practice and civil law, following the pattern of the great twentieth-century democracies.

In practice, the confusion and even chaos of religious opinions in the small state of Israel are such that the leaders have had to maneuver and adopt a policy of compromise.

In appearance there is a unifying factor—the Bible. Religious Israelis, wishing to convince the world (or themselves) that their country is a land of living faith, like to emphasize the role

[2] "Shall we then end up with a theocracy? No. If faith keeps us united, science makes us free. Consequently we shall not permit the development of theocratic caprices on the part of our ecclesiastics. We shall keep them in their temples, just as we shall keep our professional soldiers in their barracks" (*L'État juif*, Rubin Mass, Jerusalem, 1946, p. 94).

played in it by study and knowledge of the Bible. But there are an infinite number of ways of reading and drawing nourishment from the Bible. It is true that, as the doctors of the law formerly required, the Bible is taught to all children from the age of five upward in all Israeli schools; a verse is explained and commented on every morning, even in non-religious state schools. It is also true that the Bible is history in Israel, and that children can relive it at every step. Distances are so small that on their group excursions they can easily visit the sites of the towns of King Solomon, Hazor, Megiddo, Etzion-Gever, near Eilat. They can study on the spot the strategy by which the Philistines defeated King Saul on the flanks of Mount Gilboa, or that of David at grips with the Amalekites.[3]

It is true many important dates in the religious calendar are observed, not only by the religious, but also in the labor-movement *kibbutzim*, even those of Hashomer Hatzair. Nevertheless, the interpretation that is put upon Pentecost or Tabernacles at these institutions, and the ceremonies and dances for which these holidays are the occasion, have preserved only a symbolic envelope of faith. Except in the religious *kibbutzim*, they are not accompanied by prayer, and they tend to recall pagan festivals dedicated to the cult of nature, harvest festivals or fertility rites.

The pupils of a school belonging to an atheist *kibbutz* can comment on the same verse from Deuteronomy as their comrades in a secondary *yeshiva* without the coincidence signifying a moral tie or community of inspiration. Ben-Gurion has throughout his life been passionately interested in Jewish history, and when he was Prime Minister fortnightly meetings of a Biblical study group were held in his house in Ben-Maimon Street in Jerusalem, only a few hundred yards away from the ghettos of Mea Shearim, where other Jews, who consider him

---

[3] It is distressing, however, when Biblical memories are excessively exploited for the benefit of tourists. The service station on the road from Tel Aviv to Jerusalem called "Samson's Inn," or "Lot's Wife's Café" near Sodom, are no better advertisements for the Old Testament than are Lacryma Christi or the Bank of the Holy Spirit for the New.

a limb of Satan, might be poring over the same text in an entirely different spirit. Every Jew, of course, feels more or less concerned with the Bible, which, apart from its sacredness to the religious, is also the only document on his origins and ancient history. In that sense it is of the most varied interest to many Israelis. It would be very instructive at the present time to make a study of the extent, quality and type of interest taken in the Bible by *sabras* between the ages of fifteen and twenty in different ethnic groups and occupational environments. But in the present political climate such a project would certainly rouse the opposition of the Ministry of Religious Affairs, reinforced by that of the Chief Rabbinate.[4] On the basis of known facts,[5] in the absence of the information that such a study would provide, it is hazardous (i.e. mystical, not realistic) to appeal to the "explosive value of the Bible," to use an expression dear to the religious, as a basis for attributing a messianic future to the "Jewish people" in Israel.

ATTITUDES TO RELIGION

The state of Israel inherited this confused situation from the Diaspora. In 1939, on the eve of its worst ordeals, Judaism was in a state of crisis. On the one hand there was the reform movement, which declared Judaism to be an undogmatic religion and the Torah a piece of inspired law-giving in which everyone could seek and find his own rules for living, adapted to the requirements of modern society and modern thought. On the other there was the counter-reform movement of orthodox

[4] The Ministry of Religious Affairs is in the hands of the National Religious Party (Mizrahi-Hapoel-Hamizrahi), and the Minister, Zerach Warhaftig, takes a very firm stand.

[5] If one takes the whole population of the country, there seems to be a negative correlation between level of education and strict religious practice. This is evident among those who have completed—or not completed—elementary education, and is still more marked among students. *Cf.* A. Antonovsky, "Israeli Political-Social Attitudes," *Ammot*, 1963, No. 6 (original in Hebrew, mimeographed English translation).

Judaism. The struggles between the two were fierce and sometimes implacable, even going as far as denunciations to the Russian or German authorities or refusals of religious burial. There
were all sorts of intermediary trends and factions between the
two extremes. These internal divisions and schisms served only
to encourage the young to detach themselves from their traditions, were conducive to indifference or actual hostility toward
religion and encouraged assimilation. There was every sign that
religious Judaism was fatally sick.

The extermination of six million Jews by the Nazis and the
destruction of all the great centers of Jewish religious life in the
countries occupied by them were followed, a few years later, by
the creation of the state of Israel; and there was nothing surprising in the fact that the religious regarded this rebirth from
the abyss as a sign from heaven, the dawn of messianic times.
But, in spite of the Return, religious Judaism has not overcome
its divisions, and it displays them before the eyes of a population that, under the bracing influences of the Israeli crucible
and a society in full economic growth, has to a large extent
abandoned its traditional beliefs and ways of life.

It is always difficult to make positive statements about the
depth of religious feeling. In Israel one hears the most varied
opinions, depending on to whom one is talking. The orthodox
point out that this tiny state, with a Jewish population of two
million, had more than four thousand synagogues and places of
worship in 1964, nearly four hundred rabbis paid by the state
and approved by the Chief Rabbinate (there are two Chief
Rabbis, one for the Ashkenazim and the one for the Sephardim), and an enormous number of religious councils and committees throughout the country working for a religious revival.
They point to the large number of students (about six thousand) at the *yeshivot*, which are both theological faculties and
rabbinical seminaries, and they claim that for some years past
there has been a revival of religious practices among young
people at the universities.

The agnostics reply by pointing to the unimpressive performance of the three religious parties in elections. At the

general election of November 2, 1965, they secured no more than 14 per cent of the total vote. Moreover, the platform of the more important of the three, the National Religious Party, merely states the aims of a moderate clericalism, inspired by a kind of religious Zionism, that enables it to be represented in the cabinet side by side with three socialist and lay labor parties[6] and to obtain substantial advantages in civil legislation and education in return for supporting the government. It is also pointed out that the "orientals," whose numbers are continually growing, practice a more moderate, tolerant, perhaps more easygoing form of religion than the Ashkenazim. Laymen add that the orthodox will in the future have to look to a different kind of voter to support them in their intolerance. Did Ben-Gurion and his team take this situation into account? With the country perpetually exposed to the Arab threat, did they wish to assure a maximum of moral unity among the people and above all to avoid the specter of a *Kulturkampf*, which is threatened from so many quarters for different reasons? And may not another factor, and perhaps a vital one, be that the support of the religious parties[7] in the Knesset has been essential to successive coalition governments since 1949?

The chief, and no doubt one of the few dependable sources of information about the range of attitude toward religion in Israel, is Aaron Antonovsky's study. The variety and intensity of the reactions it provoked confirmed its interests.[8]

[6] The Mapai, the Achdut Ha'avoda and the Mapam, the Herut, the liberals, the Agudat Israel, the Communists, and the Rafi (detached from the Mapai by Ben-Gurion) are in opposition.

[7] After the formation of the fourth Ben-Gurion cabinet (December 23, 1952) the Agudat Israel, the most obdurate of the religious parties, was in opposition.

[8] Cf. *Ammot*, 1963, Nos. 6 and 7. Antonovsky is one of the team directed by Louis Guttman at the Israeli Institute of Applied Social Research. His work is part of an important project being carried out in eleven countries by the Institute for International Social Research, Princeton, New Jersey. Questions about religion in Israel and its relations with the state were added to the international questionnaire. Included in the survey were a representative sample (1170 individuals) of the adult Jewish population outside the *kibbutzim* and a special sample (300 individuals) of the adult *kibbutz* population.

A first question, deliberately couched in simple terms accessible to everyone, was put to individuals in a personal interview, and they were asked to choose between four answers:

Do you observe the religious tradition?

(a) I definitely observe all its commandments.

(b) I observe religious commandments for the most part.

(c) I observe traditions to some extent.

(d) I am not at all observant, completely secular.

Fifteen per cent chose Answer (a) and another 15 per cent chose (b). Thus it seems that 30 per cent of the Jewish population can with good reason be described as religious.[9] The biggest group (46 per cent) chose Answer (c). This, it should be noted, includes people whose ties with religion are very loose and casual, those, for instance, who go to synagogue only once or twice a year, at Rosh Hashana and Yom Kippur. Those who declared themselves totally non-observant numbered 24 per cent, a high proportion if the affective "force of inertia" of traditions in Jewish families is borne in mind. As was to be expected, this was the dominant group among *kibbutznikim*, 76 per cent of whom declared themselves to be non-observant, while 14 per cent still kept up some religious observances (Answer (c)). Only the 30 members of the religious *kibbutz* who were questioned chose Answers (a) or (b).

The second question was more political: Should the government see to it that public life is conducted in accordance with Jewish religious tradition? Here again there were four answers to choose among:

(a) Definitely yes.

(b) Probably yes.

(c) Probably not.

(d) Definitely not.

A feature of the second group of replies compared with the first was the tendency toward polarization. The anti-clerical

[9] This figure coincides with the proportion of schoolchildren whose parents wish them to have religious instruction (A. Chouraqui, *L'État d'Israël, op. cit.*, p. 88).

group (Answer (d), 37 per cent) was now the largest, and it
was followed by the pro-clerical group (Answer (a), 23 per
cent). The less positive anti-clericals and pro-clericals constituted 16 and 20 per cent respectively. If the replies to the same
questions put to *kibbutznikim* are also taken into account, it
appears that a distinct majority of Israelis are opposed to a religious hold on public life. Another conclusion emerges from an
analysis of the answers to both questions. The "consistent"
anti-clericals (i.e. those who adopt an anti-religious position on
both) number 49 per cent, while the "consistent" pro-clericals
(those who took a pro-clerical stand on both) number 22 per
cent. As for those whose attitude was "hesitant" (or "sophisticated"), 19 per cent of those who took no or little part in
religious observances were in favor of a public life that accorded
with religious traditions, while 6 per cent of observers or near-
observers were opposed to it.

Antonovsky carried his investigation further by introducing
five variables into his statistical analysis: occupation of head of
the family, level of education, country of birth, date of immigration, social class with which the interviewee identified himself.[10]

I will not go into details here, but merely indicate that they
provide a warning against generalizations. It is not correct, for
instance, to say that "orientals" are religious or that *sabras* are
irreligious. In the absence of "absolute" figures, however, the
conclusions are significant. So far as ethnic origin is concerned,
the North Africans (53 per cent) are the most religious, closely
followed by the Asians (44 per cent).[11] The groups of European origin and the *sabras* were much less religious (the figure
varied from 18 to 28 per cent). As for occupation, unskilled
workers are by far the most religious group (47 per cent), while
"professional men" and technicians, the managers and middle

[10] This part of the inquiry was inspired by the work of Richard Centers,
The Psychology of Social Classes, Princeton University Press, 1949.

[11] Bearing in mind that the religious practices of the "orientals" differ from
those of the orthodox Ashkenazim, as previously pointed out, Antonovsky considered those who answered (a) or (b) to the first question to be religious.

ranks in industry and commerce, were at the other extreme (15 to 20 per cent). Farmers, skilled workers, small businessmen and lower-grade white-collar workers were in between (28 to 32 per cent). The correlation between level of education and "religiousness" was distinctly negative: 48 per cent of those who did not complete their elementary schooling were religious, as against 29 per cent of those who did. At higher educational levels the percentage varied from 16 to 20 per cent, depending on the length of the individual's education. Those with some university education, even if they did not complete it, were by far the most hostile to religious intervention in public life. So far as social class was concerned, the higher people placed themselves in the social scale, the less likely they were to be religious. Among those who identified themselves with the "upper," "upper middle," "middle," "working" or "lower" class, the religious constituted respectively 22, 25, 35 and 46 per cent. On the second question, the spread was similar, though a little less distinct. Finally, in comparison with the other variables, date of immigration was a less important factor; *sabras* and pre-1951 immigrants are less religious (from 20 to 31 per cent), and post-1951 immigrants are more (from 40 to 41 per cent). This factor also played no part in the attitude toward clericalism.

These findings, solidly based though they may be, offer of course only partial evidence that will have to be checked against the results of other studies of other samples. The religious immigration, with which we shall deal later, which has introduced into the country some orthodox or Hassidic communities from the United States and Canada under the leadership of their rabbis, cannot affect the total picture of the distribution of attitudes that emerges from both election results and sociological investigations. The correspondence columns of the newspapers offer a cross-section of public opinion every day. The "Junior Forum" in the *Jerusalem Post* is especially interesting in this respect, for here the religious and the irreligious, the pro-clericals and the advocates of separation of synagogue and state, set against each other with the fire of youth. The former argue that the historical right of Israelis to live in Palestine derives essentially from their loyalty to the Torah; "losing our religion means losing our right to live in the Promised Land." Young liberals concede that anyone who wants to live in the Promised Land must tolerate the orthodox, but there must be no religious coercion by them, to which the reply is that honoring their forefathers who professed and suffered for their religion means accepting their heritage, and cherishing their memory involves preserving religion as the basis of the constitution: "Jewish survival through the millenniums is a miracle that can be explained only by religion."

In addition to these idealistic arguments, some have the frankness to use others that weigh heavily in government decisions. It is pointed out that money from American Jews is vital to Israel, and that this source would dry up if Israel became a secular state.

At the other extreme, statements are made, sometimes in violent terms, illustrating the disaffection of the young from the religious practices of the orthodox. "Young people hate the synagogue as it exists in Israel today." The outdated atmosphere, the old men praying as they did in the ghettos of the Diaspora, "drives the young away." Some plead for the conservative cult, or the liberal cult, which are said to be "capable of offering something new and attractive to the young." Many deplore the intolerance of the orthodox, their pettifogging interpretation of the *mitzvot*, sabbath observance or the dietary laws, or the sometimes dramatic consequences of the application in the twentieth century of age-old laws on marriage, divorce, the woman who is *aguna*[12] and the matriarchal law according to which the decision whether an individual is Jewish or not depends on whether his mother was a Jewess.

In contrast to those to whom the sole *raison d'être* of Israel

[12] According to Talmudic law, a woman who has not obtained a deed of repudiation written by her husband and approved by the rabbi is *aguna*; that is to say, she cannot have a second religious marriage ceremony. See below, p. 186.

and, in the last resort, its right to existence depend on its loyalty to tradition, are those who argue that "if our people suffered so much for fifteen centuries, it is because we differed from others. Therefore all differences must be eliminated and our state must be organized like others." This means that the synagogue should have the same rights in Israel, no more and no less, as those enjoyed by the Catholic Church in France or the Anglican Church in Britain.[13]

These youthful opinions show that dissatisfactions and differences are not confined to adults. They also illustrate the sociological findings mentioned above. In particular, they show that many young people, even among those who remain attached to tradition as a result of family influence, resent the hold of orthodox Judaism on public life and even its conception of ritual observances.

A THEOCRATIC STATE?

Most Israelis (including those who feel that the privileges of the orthodox minority are justified on historical grounds) admit that the political influence of the religious parties is out of proportion to their following in the country and their representation in the Knesset. In spite of massive and repeated votes in favor of lay institutions, Israel has in many respects become the theocratic state that Herzl repudiated in advance. No work is done, of course, on the fast and feast days in the religious calendar, and the dietary laws have legally to be observed in the army, the schools, university dining rooms and even on El Al aircraft and the Israeli ships of the Zim line that cross oceans and connect continents. Also—and this is the subject of endless

[13] These opinions are quoted from the Young People's Forum published weekly by the *Jerusalem Post*, and more particularly from the Junior Forum (J.P.W., June 19, 1964), consisting of long extracts from secondary school-children's essays (written at the Hugin School, Haifa) on whether religious reform in Israel was necessary or not.

controversies and difficulties to which I shall return—civil marriage is not officially recognized in Israel, though the Supreme Court, consisting of nine lay judges sitting in Jerusalem, has recently several times called on the civil authorities (the Ministry of the Interior) to register civil marriages.

The law of 1955, which granted the religious authorities full jurisdiction over marriage and divorce and which is still in force, makes civil marriages and mixed marriages impossible and keeps alive ancient rabbinical rules that can lead to personal tragedies, such as preventing a "Cohen"[14] from marrying a divorced woman or putting a childless widow under the tutelage of her brother-in-law until he renounces his right to marry her, that is to say, to exercise his right of levirate. The authority of the rabbinical courts goes even farther because, if those concerned desire it, they can deal with cases of succession just as the civil courts can. The judge-rabbis (*dayanim*) enjoy a status equivalent to that of civil judges. Religious schools of all levels up to the *yeshivot* are subsidized by the state and protected by the Ministry of Religious Affairs, whose responsibilities include not only legal tutelage of rabbinical communities in the courts, but also the religious registration of marriage and divorces and observance of the dietary laws and the sabbath.

Here perhaps some personal observations are in order.

The synagogue (in the sense of the leaders of orthodox Judaism, in spite of their divisions) has not ultimately benefited by establishing close links with political parties. True, it has extended its hold on daily life, marriage and divorce, education, religious practices (*bar-mitzva*, the dietary laws, ritual slaughter, sabbath observance, etc.). But in the eyes of many middle-of-the-road Israelis, it has paid for this by loss of spiritual prestige. I often heard it said, not only in the universities, but also by businessmen, officials and workers, that "religion in our country

---

[14] "Cohanim," descended from a Biblical family of sacrificial priests of whom the patriarch was Aaron, the brother of Moses, do not necessarily bear the name of Cohen.

is politics." (An alternative version was that "religion in our country is big business," in connection with the attitude of the Chief Rabbinate in the matter of the Marbek slaughterhouses, which I will discuss later.) When important votes come up in the Knesset, compromises and deals between the religious parties and the government are everyday occurrences. The government assures its survival by concessions that demoralize public opinion and accentuate public discomfort. Current legislation, which is an inextricable mixture of secular and state religion, gives orthodoxy the advantage of exercising a diffuse social pressure that encourages a formalism devoid of all *kavana* (the concentration of mind and purity of heart without which religious practices are devoid of spiritual value). It empties religious laws and commandments of the substance that Israelis still attached to religious traditions—who are numerous, as the studies already mentioned show—would put into them if they observed them with complete freedom.

This is true with the *bar-mitzva* that many people impose on their sons because "one has to." I accompanied G.L. of the Hebrew University to Heichal Shlomo, the seat of the Chief Rabbinate in Jerusalem, a majestic edifice built by a wealthy family of British industrialists, the Wolfsons, whose name is displayed at the entrance in a fashion that makes it impossible for any visitor to remain unaware of their piety and generosity. G.L., a freethinker, went to the "Datican"[15] with his son to arrange with the cantors for the occasion on which, in accordance with tradition, the boy would himself conduct part of the service. "Why do you observe this practice?" I asked my colleague. "Because everyone does," he replied, and added, "Besides, it can't do him any harm." G.L. allows no rabbinical intervention in his family life except on "special occasions." He is not even one of the "seasonally devout," to use a term introduced by Gabriel Le Bras in his typology of those who practice Catholicism in France. In non-orthodox circles in Jeru-

---

[15] *Dati* in Hebrew means "religious." Hence the name "Datican" given to the seat of the "Jewish papacy" in Jerusalem.

salem I heard parents complain that, in spite of the number of synagogues, there was none that was suitable for their children.[16]

The most unpopular clerical intervention is the state's non-recognition of civil marriage, which in practice makes it impossible to marry without the rabbinical blessing and prevents marriages between Jews and non-Jews. While staying at the Hebrew University, I came across three young Christian-Jewish couples who, being unable to marry in Israel, were proposing to go to Cyprus as soon as they could afford it. People in Israel were going to Nicosia to get married (though the troubles in the island have made this much more difficult) just as people in the United States go to Reno to get a divorce. On my visits to factories I was accompanied by a representative of the Histadrut, a man of Scandinavian origin; at the time of his immigration he had innocently disclosed that he was a *Cohen* on his mother's side, not realizing that this meant that he could not marry his fiancée, who had been divorced.

The anomalies of rabbinical law in these fields are innumerable, and their pettifogging application provides daily material for the Israeli press and topics of controversy for its readers. A Jew, for instance, who has married a non-Jewess in Cyprus can go through another marriage ceremony with a Jewess in Israel before a rabbi in whose eyes his first marriage is non-existent, but if he does so he will be liable to civil prosecution for bigamy.

The situation is complicated by the fact that the rabbinate refuses to accept as a convert a non-Jewish woman whose motive is simply to marry a Jew. If she honestly admits this, she suffers for it; if she is a good liar (and the rabbi enters into the game), after one or two years spent in acquiring a religious

[16] In 1964 there were two liberal synagogues in Jerusalem and six in all Israel. The Chief Rabbinate does not recognize liberal (or "reformed") rabbis and prevents them from conducting marriages, etc. or holding official office. This strictness is not peculiar to the orthodox in Israel. The associations of orthodox rabbis in the United States and Canada decided in February 1964 to refuse non-orthodox Jews the right to use the title of rabbi.

education (which is practically never required with the same degree of thoroughness of brides-to-be of Jewish extraction) and, of course, after a ritual bath in the presence of three rabbis,[17] she will be able to get married. It is quicker to go to Cyprus, even if later the children are not considered to be legally Jewish. In the Hashomer Hatzair *kibbutzim* a movement is now afoot to encourage young couples to do without a religious ceremony and have "natural children" in order to force the government to introduce civil marriage.

Strict application of orthodox rules also creates innumerable difficulties and agonizing conflicts in the matter of divorce. Mosaic law (Deuteronomy 24:1) provides for divorce in the case of grave incompatability, and a whole tractate of the Talmud (the *Gittin*) is devoted to the rules governing the *gett*, a simple act of repudiation that can be declared valid by rabbis acting simultaneously as judges, notaries and court officials. A first difficulty may arise from the question of the rabbi's competence. The validity of the *gett* depends on the authority the rabbi enjoys, and there have been several cases in recent years of women immigrants who had been divorced in the United States and become Israeli citizens who were prevented from marrying again by the Chief Rabbinate because their *gett* had been granted by conservative rabbis in New York or Pittsburgh. Another source of difficulty, and sometimes of unpleasant maneuvers and even of blackmail, is the traditional rule that a divorce is valid only if a letter of repudiation is written by the husband; this, of course, depends entirely on his good will in the matter. A woman who is *aguna*, not "repudiated" by her husband but abandoned by him, cannot have a second religious marriage. So far only liberal rabbis, after making a final attempt to reconcile the couple, are willing to grant a certificate of dissolution

---

[17] Ben-Gurion caused a fine scandal in June, 1964 in connection with this ritual bathing. As a result of his intervention, a bitter controversy arose between the orthodox and non-orthodox on the question of whether the proselyte, under the rabbis' eyes, should enter the ritual bath naked or whether she wear something; a new version of Susanna and the elders.

of marriage[18]—but this has no validity in the eyes of the orthodox.

Court decisions, in particular the sensational Supreme Court decision of February 22, 1963, which greatly upset the synagogue, have called on the Ministry of the Interior[19] to register civil marriages, arguing that there should be no penalization of young couples who marry in disregard of religious laws, which in other fields are transgressed by a majority of the Jewish population of Israel. But orthodox officialdom is deaf in that ear; it used to enter on identity cards the words "married not in accordance with the laws of Israel." However, as a result of lay protests, the Ministry of the Interior forbade this by its circular of May 28, 1963.

These concessions provide a way out for young people who can afford the fare to Cyprus. But a government with a socialist majority keeps alive clerical legislation of which the majority of Israelis disapprove because it fears that repealing it would start a *Kulturkampf*, encourage the isolation of the religious section of the population, which tends toward a kind of embittered self-segregation, and, as we have mentioned before, alienate an influential section of American Jewry and dry up its generosity. Such results, leaders of the Mapai assured me, would be paying too high a price, whatever the ethical and political value of such a measure might be. They hope that time will reduce the price, and they count on the liberalism of the new "oriental" immigrants, most of whom are Sephardim. "The Sephardim are not fanatics; they are the Protestants of Judaism," Y., a representative of the Mapai in the Knesset, said to me. "The fanatics, who wish to impose their way of life and religion on others, are always Ashkenazim." Those who take this line are betting on the growing demographic importance of the "second" Israel, which, when it becomes the overwhelming majority, will bring down the scales on the side of tolerance. The argument is not without sub-

---

[18] A. Zaoui, *L'Enseignement libéral du judaïsme*, Paris, 1961, p. 121.

[19] The Ministry of the Interior is in the hands of the National Religious Party. The Supreme Court has several times made the same appeal in relation to mixed marriages in Cyprus.

stance and deserves consideration.[20] Its weakness is that it puts
the problem in a perspective quite different from that of the
orthodox whose dominant and overriding preoccupation, after
the cataclysm of 1940–45, is to keep alive at least one last enclave
of pure and unadulterated Judaism as the guarantee of a future
renascence. These intransigent old men, these doctors of the
law who seem to belong to another world, live in fear that the
delicate mechanism of the ancient system, whose guardian they
are, will collapse, like a wall whose foundations are taken away,
if the slightest change is made in it.

KASHRUT AND CASUISTRY

This fear at least partially explains other aspects of the clerical
hold on Israeli society, whose effects are less serious than those
mentioned above but more widespread and more irritating in
daily life. I refer to their surveillance of the *kashrut*, the dietary
laws, which originated in the laws of Moses and were elaborated
in the *Hulin*, a section of the Talmud. It would be easy to make
a sizable anthology of new "Jewish stories" arising out of the
application and interpretation of these rules in present-day Israel.
Kosher restaurants and hotels (i.e. the vast majority) live under
the permanent threat of kitchen checks carried out without
warning by inspectors employed by the orthodox rabbinate,
which alone can grant the precious *kashrut* certificate attached

[20] In this matter the Histadrut takes a cautious line, dictated by its multiple
functions and the variety of groups that it represents and knows how to handle.
It is believed at the "White Kremlin" at Tel Aviv that the vast majority of
workers are opposed to rabbinical intervention in public life, and that a national
referendum among them would call for a separation of synagogue and state.
Mixed marriages would be agreed to, but without enthusiasm. Even in non-
religious circles there is believed to be a more or less conscious concern for
preserving the "Jewish people." "Fortunately," a member of the central bureau
said to me frankly, "the Histadrut is in a comfortable position. It is not obliged
to take sides in these quarrels and has no intention of compromising itself for
no good purpose. It is up to our members freely to make up their own minds
on this question."

to the door of the establishment. This involves observance of the Biblical and Talmudic prescriptions concerning the distinction between "clean" and "unclean" animals, ritual slaughter (*shehita*), the curing of meat, and the separation of milk from meat.[21] Strict observance of this last affects not only the choice of food, but also its preparation, since it requires the separation of cooking vessels and utensils.

Hypocrisy is as ingenious in getting around these rules as their application is niggling. In a big hotel in Jerusalem I had a long talk, to my great advantage, with the headwaiter, Joseph, a quick-witted Moroccan of distinction in his calling. Realizing that he was dealing with a Frenchman who had little inclination toward dietetic strictness, he suggested that I go up to the snack bar on the first floor, where (as there was a different kitchen, different crockery and different utensils) I would be able to end my meal with cheese or ice cream. In a kosher boardinghouse, kept by Ashkenazim of Polish origin, the waitress was perfectly willing to serve forbidden food to customers, but only in the absence of witnesses.

A bitter and interminable dispute between the government and the Chief Rabbinate, packed with tragi-comic incident and casuistical arguments the details of which I will not repeat, took place between 1962 and 1964 on the question of whether the *Shalom*, a luxurious new liner built at Saint-Nazaire for the Zim line, which is subsidized by the state, was to offer its passengers a choice between kosher and *treifa* cooking. The press published thousands of letters on the subject, from both Israelis and Americans. Some thought it would be commercially absurd to lose international custom by forcing passengers to submit to constraints that corresponded to neither their beliefs nor their tastes. Others expressed horror at the idea of a ship flying the Star of David—Israel's ambassador on the oceans of the world—

[21] This rests on the principle, three times repeated in the Torah (Exodus 23:19 and 34:26; Deuteronomy, 14:21): "Thou shalt not cook a kid in its mother's milk." Animals whose flesh is "pure" and permitted are ruminants with cloven hoofs (which excludes, among others, the pig, the horse and the rabbit). Permitted fish have scales and fins (which excludes all shellfish).

provocatively defying the basic, sacred laws of Judaism. Their indignation was often flavored with other arguments. If there were two different restaurants on board, would not observing Jews feel themselves segregated, "as in a ghetto"? And was there not, after all, a kosher *haute cuisine*, which was not inferior to any in the world? The Chief Rabbinate, supported by its allies in the government and helped above all by Warhaftig, the Minister of Religious Affairs, threatened not only to deprive the *Shalom* of her *kashrut* certificate, but to withdraw it from all vessels of the Zim line. The directors thought they had found a way out by applying for a certificate to an association of conservative rabbis in the United States, but the obstinacy and threats of retaliation made by the synagogue, the intervention of American extremists[22] and the hesitant attitude of a divided government forced them eventually to capitulate. Some resigned. Orthodoxy triumphed. No kid is cooked in its mother's milk on the *Shalom* on the Haifa–New York run, but, thanks to the ingenuity of Israeli cooks, its cosmopolitan passengers are able to eat "cream" ices after the meat course. The cream is artificial.

My friend Joseph, the Moroccan headwaiter, had a way out. The thing to do, he said, would be to send for French chefs, who would invent attractive kosher dishes adapted to the taste of an international clientele.[23] "But it will be difficult because of the American Jews," he said. "At home they eat pork and lobster, but here they are worse than the rabbis." I am grateful to Joseph for having revealed to me so soon after my arrival this highly important practical aspect of the religious problem. One

[22] Rabbi Soloveitchik, of Boston, one of the leaders of orthodoxy in the United States, declared himself ready to proclaim a boycott (*herem*) of all the vessels of the Zim line, and even of El Al, the Israeli airline, unless the proposal to supply non-kosher food on the *Shalom* were abandoned. At the same time, on December 22, 1963, Chief Rabbi Nissim presented the Zim line with an ultimatum: unless the latter conformed within a fortnight the *kashrut* certificate would be withdrawn from all its ships.

[23] Joseph's idea was carried out, at any rate in the ships of the Zim line. The *J.P.W.* reported on October 9, 1964 that M. Raymond Oliver had arrived at Haifa at the invitation of the Zim line with a party of six French chefs to teach his Israeli colleagues the secrets of *haute cuisine* strictly adapted to the dietary laws.

of the reasons for the strictness in regard to the *kashrut* certificate is consideration for the susceptibilities of American Jews, whose contribution to Israel is of primary importance in the tourist as well as other economic spheres. A big restaurant or luxury hotel cannot run the risk of losing its *kashrut* label. The attitude of many American Jews is curious. Joseph was perfectly right. They seem to travel to Israel to find an image of the country that includes observance of the dietary laws, although at home, as surveys have confirmed, many or even most of them hardly ever or never observe those laws.

A letter to the *Jerusalem Post* (January 31, 1964), written by S. A. Weinstock, of New York, is worth quoting in this connection. He said that he regarded the letters the newspaper received from certain of its American readers lavishing advice to Israel on the subject of religious observance as one of its least pleasing features. Their common theme was urging Israel to adopt a line in better accordance with the supposed imperatives of the Torah and orthodoxy. They even went so far as to add that if their recommendations (on such matters as sabbath observance, Christian missions, cooking in the *Shalom*, etc.) were ignored, their dissatisfaction would be expressed in economic terms.

It was sad, he continued, to see religious Jews using the same threat against Israel—economic sanctions—as the Arab states. Many of us believe that American democracy would be threatened to its foundations if the separation between church and state were abolished. Nevertheless, here were American Jews insisting that the United States remain a secular state while Israel should be a religious one, although they preferred living in the former. In other words, they put pressure on Israel to make it adopt a kind of life they did not want for themselves.

There are, to be sure, non-kosher restaurants in every town in Israel, and one is apt to see well-known faces in them—leading officials and members of the academic profession. Most of these establishments do not have windows leading on to the street, but are situated in an apartment or in some discreet blind alley.

Non-observant Israelis seemed to me to frequent them without a bad conscience, enjoying the double satisfaction of defying rabbinical controls and savoring forbidden dishes.

SAVING THE CHOSEN PEOPLE

Sabbath observance is obligatory. The Torah regards the sabbath, as it does circumcision, as a sign of the alliance between Jehovah and His people. It twice invokes death by stoning as the penalty for profaning it by work (Exodus 31:14 and 35:2).

Strict observance of an orthodox sabbath would require the stopping of all work from the moment when the first star appears in the sky on Friday evening until the same time the next evening. No cooking could be done, a plate could not even be warmed, and one could not travel in any kind of vehicle, use an electric switch or answer the telephone. Hence the innumerable stories about *shabbes-goyim*, non-Jews whose paid help is taken advantage of for indispensable tasks on the sabbath day, though this strategem is specifically forbidden by the fourth commandment, which says "Neither thy manservant, nor thy maidservant, nor the stranger within thy gates . . ." This also raises some difficulties in agricultural work in the religious *kibbutzim*, where ingenious arrangements are made to ensure the automatic starting and stopping of certain operations.

It is difficult to get about in Israeli towns during the sabbath, but less noticeably so in Tel Aviv and Haifa than in Jerusalem. Even in the Holy City, however, the observances are inevitably declining, provided one does not approach Mea Shearim and provoke the anger of the Natorei Karta. If one is unwise enough to go there in a car on a Saturday, one risks a Biblical stoning from the "Guardians of the City."

Sabbath incidents, such as the demonstrations by the "Activists of the Torah" against Christian missions,[24] or the affair of

---

[24] The "Activists of the Torah," who insist on not being confused with the Natorei Karta, were formed soon after the establishment of the state to maintain and further religious belief among immigrants, chiefly by ensuring that

the Marbek slaughterhouses, reveal the deep division in Israeli opinion and the inconsistencies of government policy in religious matters. In March 1963, when students of a *yeshiva* stoned some buses that were working on the sabbath at Kfar Ata, above Haifa, the Minister of Religious Affairs promptly sent them his congratulations for having defended the *status quo* and protested "against the violation of existing religious rules." Meanwhile some of the young demonstrators had been arrested for creating a disturbance on the public highway. There was indignation among laymen at a minister's encouraging violation of the law. There are violations and Violation, laws and Law. The following September, when the Activists of the Torah organized a march to the sound of the *shofar* in protest against the schools set up by various Christian communities in the principal towns, most of their fellow citizens disapproved. Yet the Activists' arguments were capable of striking a responsive chord in the heart of anyone who has preserved some attachment to the "Jewish people": "For centuries we tried to preserve our beliefs and our law. We tried not to lose a single soul. Today, after the massacre of six million Jews by people who called themselves Christians, we must do all in our power to avoid losing any more. More than ever we need every one of our people."[25] The anxiety of the survivors of the chosen people appears here again, this time directed at the activities of the missionaries, those "fishers of souls."

When Chief Rabbi Unterman campaigns against the success of the Marbek slaughterhouses, which, thanks to their modern equipment, are able to undercut the slaughterhouses controlled

---

their children receive a religious education. They proclaim their respect for Christian schools and missions in Israel to the extent that these address themselves to Christians, but they are categorically opposed to their offering needy immigrants inducements such as money, clothing, food or free education for the purpose of getting them to send their children to Christian schools, which they fear may be the first step to conversion. They want legislation: (a) to forbid missions to offer Jewish families material advantages to attract their children, and (b) to forbid conversion from one religion to another before the age of eighteen.

[25] Letter to *J.P.W.*, December 27, 1963.

by the local rabbis, he protests that his motive is not only to protect the public against the establishment of a monopoly, but is also essentially religious, to assure the ritual purity of the *shehita*, though the general public does not see how this is threatened on the short journey between Kiryat Malachi and Tel Aviv. But it does see orthodoxy fighting to defend a valuable source of revenue.

The Marbek slaughterhouses are run by co-operatives, including *moshavim* and *kibbutzim* affiliated to the two religious parties. Their meat, which is indisputably kosher, sells at prices from 7 to 15 per cent lower than those of the local slaughter-houses under the control, and to the pecuniary advantage of, the religious authorities of Tel Aviv, and has been well received by the population. The Chief Rabbinate withdrew their *kashrut* certificate, arguing that there was an infringement of the ancient principle of Jewish law that "all meat that has been lost from sight (even for a short time) must be considered *taref*." As in the *Shalom* affair, there have been endless repercussions. After an appeal by Marbek, the Supreme Court in June 1964 called on the Chief Rabbinate to justify its opposition.

Israeli opinion is profoundly divided. The heads of the synagogue feel the crushing responsibility of having to save and keep alive the last relics of pure and unadulterated Judaism that escaped the great massacre, and in the service of that aim they recoil neither from compromises with their enemies nor from fanatical intolerance. The non-religious consider that in agreeing to these compromises they have made great sacrifices in the interests of national unity, and that in return it is now the duty of the religious parties publicly and categorically to disavow the fanatics for the same interests. The right of non-believing Jews to live their own life can be assured only by the tolerance of the orthodox. But, to the latter, tolerance is not merely scandalous (are they to tolerate violation of the Torah by Jews in the Holy Land?), it is also a kind of suicide, forging the instruments of their own destruction—and on this last point it is by no means certain that they are entirely wrong.

Behind a statement made to the first assembly of the Chief

Rabbinate by one of the few spiritual masters of contemporary Judaism, Chief Rabbi Abraham Isaac Kook, there may perhaps have been a hope of finding, not a basis of agreement (for the extremists in the two camps do not talk the same language or live in the same world), but a *modus vivendi*. He called on religious Jews to make a clear distinction between laws, which are unalterable, and rules, which it is permissible "in all liberty to change and correct with the people's assent."[26] But was this not equivalent to admitting the necessity (and possibility) of holding a kind of new Sanhedrin to adapt the ancient texts to the young society of Israel? So far, in spite of the recommendations of the revered Chief Rabbi, the synagogue has not followed them up. The necessities of economic life have, however, imposed modifications on the *halacha* (rules of everyday life). Continuous shifts have had to be introduced in some industries, for instance. Thus at a Histadrut chemical factory near Haifa work, which goes on night and day on a three-shift basis, is interrupted neither for the sabbath nor during Yom Kippur. Workers who object to working on the sabbath (in particular Iraqis) are not required to do so.

The divisions inside Judaism further complicate the problem. The diversity of the communities of the Diaspora has been reproduced in Israel; each community betrays its different origins, cultural traits, style of religious life, conception of the synagogue service. Visiting the Jerusalem synagogues, Sha'arei Hassed, Nachalat Achim, Kyriat Moshe (named after Sir Moses Montefiore, a benefactor of Zionism) and, of course, Mea Shearim, one feels one is passing from one country, one period, one social environment, one civilization to another. The synagogues of the Persian, Iraqi and Yemeni Jews in particular provide a striking contrast to the bourgeois synagogues in the handsome residential quarters of Rehavia and Talbieh. The range is still further widened at Tel Aviv, the holy city of Sfad, and the new towns of Beersheba, Kiryat Gat and Eilat. But the Chief Rabbinate's attitude to this diversity is marked by its uncompro-

[26] *Revue de la Pensée juive*, April 1950, No. 3, p. 133.

mising suspicion of liberal or "reformed" Judaism. In its eyes reform, which it calls "excessive" reform, is, together with assimilation and mixed marriage, a grave danger to Jewish communities throughout the world. In Israel orthodoxy is able to impose its exclusiveness on the representatives of the government and even on the head of the state. When the Minister of Religious Affairs was invited to attend the official opening of the School of Biblical and Archaeological Studies in Jerusalem in March 1963, he declined the invitation because the building contained a liberal synagogue. What was more surprising, and more serious, was that President Ben-Zvi did the same.

Even the two-headed summit of the clerical hierarchy, which is shared by an Ashkenazi Chief Rabbi and a Sephardi Chief Rabbi, is not immune to squabbles. After the death in 1960 of the Ashkenazi Chief Rabbi Herzog, the post remained vacant because of the stalling tactics of the National Religious Party and the Mapai, each of which feared the selection of a candidate not to its liking. Finally, on March 17, 1964, Chief Rabbi Unterman of Tel Aviv, a veteran of seventy-eight, just managed to squeeze in (by sixty votes to fifty-seven) against the younger, popular Chief Rabbi of the army, Shlomo Goren, who was the moderate candidate. The preceding protracted haggling between the Mapai and the National Religious Party did not add to the spiritual prestige of these elections in the eyes of the Israeli public.

THE LAST MYSTIC STRONGHOLD

The orthodoxy that combines jealous protection of the law with political tactics is itself condemned root and branch by the extremists, who refuse all compromise with the state. The Natorei Karta do not recognize the Chief Rabbinate, which responds by forbidding its *zaddikim* all recognition and official responsibilities. This adds another touch of variety to a picture already swarming with contrasts. The Hasidic and Mitnagdim communities (which were themselves once violently opposed[27]) live in isolation in their bastion of Mea Shearim, a few hundred yards from the frontiers of Jordan and the Old City. Their very intransigence gives them an importance entirely disproportionate to their numbers by throwing a kind of indirect light on certain aspects of religious and national problems.

During my visits to Poland before 1939 I often went to the quarters in which Hassidim lived. My first visit to Mea Shearim was a shock. I felt as if by some miracle of space and time I had been projected back twenty-five years into a ghetto in Warsaw, Czestochowa or Bialystok. There were the same people and the same streets, the same traditional clothing, the same round hats bordered with fur, the same bearded old men walking slowly and talking to small boys on either side of them who wore *kipot* on their heads and ringlets, and whose slender frames were completely covered in kaftans, breeches and long black socks in spite of the heat. A young man in a light kaftan with golden reflections in it, no doubt a *kolel*, was returning from the synagogue, followed at a respectful distance by his wife (young and very unfeminine in spite of her braided wig), and he turned every now and then to make sure that she was duly following her lord and master. I had already seen this dilapidated market, these shops in which cobblers or tailors were working in the semi-darkness, at Lodz or Lwow. Suddenly there was a summer storm, and I took refuge in the nearest shop, which was wide open to the street and full of worm-eaten furniture, books, secondhand copies of the Torah covered in ancient dust, *tallethim, menoroth, tefillin* and other cult objects. The downpour continued, and I discovered that I was not alone. An old man was sitting behind a desk at the back of the shop, poring over a book. Was it one of the innumerable selections from the Talmud, a discussion of the occult interpretation of the Law, a page from the

[27] The Mitnagdim, continuing the tradition of the Talmudic rabbis, reacted against the neo-mysticism of the Hasidim in the eighteenth century. But a century later both united against the common threats of the "Enlightenment" (the Haskala) movement, irreligion and "reform."

Book of Splendor? He did not notice me when I walked in, and when I went out he did not even raise his head.

Sha'arei Hassed, only a few yards from Rehavia, with its modern villas and flourishing gardens, is an outpost of the ghettos of Jerusalem. Cross the road, and you are in a different world. I was accompanied by a friend who had a pious upbringing in Hungary and knew the ways of the Mitnagdim. During the hours that we spent in their synagogue (as during those we spent on other sabbaths in those of the Natorei Karta) we felt ourselves to be quickly welcomed and, so to speak, accepted. Many of the men, old and young, were *sabras* whose families had been long established in Israel but had nevertheless preserved intact the traditions of communities in Galicia or Lithuania. They prayed swaying their heads and bodies, chanting verses and responses with fervor and exaltation, some of them actually in a kind of frenzy. I shall never forget one little man, still quite young, covered from head to foot in clothes as black as his beard and round felt hat, in accordance with the Mitnagdim custom, and the way he went blue in the face as he bawled a prayer to the accompaniment of convulsive bodily movements. Near him was a long desk occupied by some shabbily dressed adolescents, like him communicating with the Almighty and hardly less agitated than he. Sitting apart in one corner, two young *kolels* in kaftans were engaged in animated discussion, in Yiddish of course; to them, using Hebrew except for prayers and studying the sacred texts is a shocking thing.

But a service at Sha'arei Hassed is like an oasis compared with the tumult that prevails in the Natorei Karta synagogue in Mea Shearim. This involves all generations, from the aged to small boys hardly able to walk, who creep among the congregation's legs, play and suck oranges while the *zaddik*, his back turned to the commotion, his head and shoulders covered with his silver-embroidered *tallet*, calmly reads and chants in front of his desk on the right of the Ark of the Covenant, from which emerge the scrolls of the Law, which, at the end of the service, he carries around while the congregation press about him to kiss his garments. To the Natorei Karta and other Hasidic sects their *zaddik* is an adored master, a miracle worker, a mystic guide. Nevertheless, each one of them is his equal by reason of prayer and the presence of the divine in the least act of everyday life. In the midst of a sacrilegious people whom they regard as Jewish only in name, they wish to be a reminder and a forerunner of the "people of priests and makers of sacrifices" prophesied by the Torah who would await the Messiah. They were the first to stone tourists' and diplomats' cars near the Mandelbaum Gate. They refuse to pay taxes, refuse to serve in the armed forces, some refuse even to use the stamps issued by the state of Israel, which they regard as an impious challenge to the city of which they are the "guardians."

It is easy for the non-believer to become ironic toward such behavior, as many Israelis are and as the western, agnostic Jew is tempted to be. If one wants to understand Israel, however, it is more useful to place these men and what they stand for in the tradition of Judaism and try to penetrate the meaning of their total repudiation of the Jewish state.

To the Hassidim, in accordance with the teaching of their master, Baal Shem Tov, there is a divine spark in everything, in every sentient being, in every event. "Classic Hasidism," Gershom Scholem writes, "was not the product of any kind of theory, or of any cabalist doctrine, but of direct and spontaneous religious experience"; and he adds that to the Hassidim "a ray coming from the essence of God is present and perceptible everywhere and at every moment."[28] This presence forms the basis of the prayer that each daily act can be; and the prayer of the pious man, whether in the bosom of his family or at a synagogue service or solemn ceremony, is joy. More particularly, the essence of the sabbath is joy; the fervor of the religious rekindles the spark and makes it rise to God. "Each one of us can thus be a mediator who by means of his joy returns the world to Him who is all joy."[29]

[28] *Major Trends in Jewish Mysticism*, Schocken Books, New York, third edition, 1954.
[29] Edmond Fleg, *Revue de la Pensée juive*, January 1950, No. 2, p. 81.

Prayer, with its swaying and convulsive movements of the whole body sometimes to the point of frenzy, is to the Hassid a means, not only of raising himself toward God, but also of bringing God down to earth, penetrating oneself with Him and making of Him "a living God and friend with whom one sings, dances, discusses and even argues."[30] This is the explanation of the exaltation, tumult and apparent chaos that reign in the synagogues of the Natorei Karta, who are both embittered, anachronistic protectors of a mystic treasure and upholders of a tradition they hold to be a sacred trust, the only living pledge in Israel of the messianic promise and of redemption.

The Natorei Karta exaggerate some things to the point of caricature, but they are nonetheless in line with the Hasidic tradition, seeking salvation in the total unity of a life in which prayer, whether visibly or not, is omnipresent. I was much struck by the importance Martin Buber attached to it. "Hasidism has not ceased to have a message for mankind even today."[31] Buber was disturbed by the growing dichotomy in the life of many of our contemporaries, between work that had ceased to be the center of gravity of life and was done without interest, and a disorderly leisure that was without meaning or equilibrium. Hasidism, he said, was a reminder of the unity necessary to human life.

It seems to me that the Jewish religion offers the believer two possible (and not mutually exclusive) paths to follow: communion with God and communion with the world. Hasidism has resolutely taken the former. But, its critics say, it prevents communion with the world (particularly in its most extreme and individualist forms, such as those of the Natorei Karta), and it places itself outside the great universal "Davidian" stream of Judaism which opens itself to the world. The Hasidic communities' repudiation of the new Israel is withdrawn, es-

---

[30] André Zaoui, *Revue de la Pensée juive*, April 1951, pp. 134–135.

[31] This statement, as well as the thoughts that follow, were noted down during a conversation with Martin Buber at his house at Talbieh in Jerusalem on February 21, 1963.

capism in time and space, congealment in despair rather than joy.

The characteristic features of Hasidism quoted by Gershom Scholem make it possible to understand the forms it has taken in the state of Israel. The development and daily life of the community are centered on the personality of its religious guide, the *zaddik* or *maggid*. What gives him his prestige is not his learning, as is the case with the traditional Talmudic rabbi, who is a doctor of the law, but the life that he leads.[32] Martin Buber said that the Hasidism of Baal Shem Tov "is cabalism that has developed into an ethic."[33] It developed among threatened and isolated Jewish communities living in spiritual autarky in Poland and the Ukraine who felt the need to center on a saintly, venerated figure the religious hopes, the messianism, all the impulses that proliferate in Jews of this type, that is to say, men fashioned in heart and mind by centuries of very special physical and moral, economic and social conditions. It is understandable that Hasidism should have developed a kind of "mystic personality cult" whose maintenance requires both a hostile outside world and the warmth of the ghetto. The Natorei Karta have assured themselves of both by their total rejection of Israeli society and their reconstitution for their own use of the environment and image of the ghetto, although nothing obliged them to do so and a powerful stream all around them was actually moving in the diametrically opposite direction. The "Guardians of the City" are also the guardians of the ghetto, in whose absence Hasidism would probably fade away and disintegrate into the ordinary forms of religion as practiced in Israel.

There is another, final aspect of the pathetic "no" of the Natorei Karta, who are consistent in their illogic. The long, black coats they wear, the small boys in kaftans and long black stockings that deprive their bodies of air and sun, the men in their fur-rimmed hats, the women in shawls, living under the

---

[32] G. Scholem, *op. cit.*, pp. 343–344.
[33] *Die Chassidischen Bücher*, Hellerau, 1928.

Palestine sun as if the climate were that of Galicia or the
Ukraine, are a defiance of the twentieth-century race for pleasure, the hedonism that is making rapid strides in Israel, a
challenge to the throngs hurrying to the lakes and beaches of
the Promised Land. The defiance is senseless, of course, as senseless as their acts of violence on the sabbath, their threats to
kill in the Biblical manner, the stoning of cars that daily and
inevitably multiply on the roads of Israel, even (and particularly) on the day of rest ordered by the Almighty. Spinoza,
another Jew (although he was cursed by the synagogue), said
that true joy must be accompanied by satisfaction of the senses,
the pleasures of dress and the adornment of everyday life, by
aesthetic pleasures—music and drama—and even by "games that
exercise the body": "A wise man will use things and take as
much pleasure in them as he can (without continuing to the
point of satiety, which is no longer taking pleasure in them),"[34]
he said. A large part of Israeli society is already moving as fast
as it can toward abundance and beyond it, to the search for
pleasure characteristic of the masses of our time in all industrialized societies. How are they to be stopped and prevented
from crossing the line laid down by the sage in his *Ethics?* And
where would a new humanism worthy of mankind in the plenitude of its vocation draw that line? Can the abrupt, *a priori*
rejection of the race for happiness proclaimed by the Hassidim
of Jerusalem in the name of spiritual life as they conceive it
be their "message" to the modern world and to Israel in particular?

Can this last mystic square closing its ranks around its *zaddik-
kim* hope for reinforcements or, if not reinforcements, allies?
Religious immigrants, often Hassidim, have been coming to
Israel under the guidance of their rabbis ever since *aliyot* began, and since the foundation of the state they have continued
to do so. Most of them have been Americans, although
their numbers have been few.[35] Unlike other *olim*, these people

---

[34] *Ethics*, IV, 45, scholium.
[35] Since 1948 not more than 15,000 Americans and Canadians have settled
permanently in Israel.

were neither driven there by persecution nor had as their aim to escape poverty or to be able to live an easier life. They came in the hope of a fully Jewish life for themselves and their families and of an affirmation and development of their Judaism.

Many were members of Hassidic communities. One of the best known was Rabbi Yekutiel Halberstamm, the descendant of a celebrated line of Hassidic rabbis at Cluj (or Klausenburg) in Transylvania. After escaping the great massacre, he emigrated to Brooklyn after the war, where he rapidly established his authority over a large congregation. But mass society and American prosperity, which form a dangerous environment for the cohesion and purity of faith of such communities, were disturbing to him, so he led his flock to Israel. With the aid of the Jewish Agency, he settled near Netanya, where his community at Kiryat Sang now numbers more than two thousand. It includes a *yeshiva*, many of whose students are from the United States, a home for orphans and children from broken families, and a house of retreat. Like many Hassidim, the residents of Kiryat Sang are skilled at diamond-polishing, from which they derive their livelihood. Their rabbi, a practical man, is building a hotel for tourists, who will have the opportunity of holidaying in a special environment (this is the sort of idea that would never occur to the *zaddik* of Mea Shearim). He also has other projects, including building one hundred dwellings for the reception of the rearguard of his Brooklyn congregation.

Among other recent immigrations of religious communities have been that of Rabbi Hananiah Teitelbaum (of Sassow), the founder of Kiryat Yismah Moshe—where one thousand dwellings are projected—and that of Rabbi Samuel Ehrenfeld, whose Mitnagdim congregation is to be installed at Kiryat Mattersdorf, named after the town in Hungary from which he came; it will have a synagogue and a *yeshiva*, of course, three hundred dwellings and a number of factories, one for the manufacture of polyester.

Can this immigration of communities led by Hasidic or orthodox rabbis, financed by wealthy Americans or Canadians and supported by religious groups in Israel, change the underlying realities of the problems that I have been trying to state? The reinforcements they provide are small in number and alien to the Israeli culture that is coming into being, and they are static, particularist and conservative. Most of these rabbis are aged men born in the ghettos of central and eastern Europe, vigorous and typical defenders of the traditions, some nuclei of which they have managed to insert into the Israeli tissue. But they bring with them nothing adapted to the spiritual needs that have arisen in the new conditions in which the population of Israel lives. If it is true, as some believers said to me, that there is a "thirst for God" in the country, above all among the young, these are not the masters who can assuage that thirst. I scrutinized their faces at the laying of the foundation stone at Kiryat Yismah Moshe. These solemn, venerable old men, traditional from head to foot, are not the type to revive the spirit of the Bible in the twentieth century, reconcile to Judaism the atheist pioneers or social justice, kindle a new messianic and prophetic flame or recall the indifferent popular masses to God.

In the big cities of America they feared their flocks would be "assimilated by prosperity," and they will not be able to prevent this for long from happening, at any rate to many of them, in the Israeli society that is now on the way to normalization. In the minds of these religious immigrants the only way of living a really Jewish life and assuring the "Jewishness" of themselves and their children was to live in Israel. But before they die they will discover for themselves or, if they do not, their children certainly will, that this was a vain hope, and that the new Palestine, that of today and still more that of tomorrow, has grave dangers in store for them.

THE REIGN OF ORTHODOXY

The efforts of orthodoxy to ensure survival in an unfavorable environment are largely concentrated on education. It is estimated that rudimentary religious instruction is given at 40 per cent of the elementary schools in Israel. Many new *yeshivot* are being built. In 1948 there were seventy; by 1964 the number had risen to nearly two hundred, having a total of about twelve thousand students and divided into several categories: *ktana*, for those between fourteen and eighteen; *gdola*, which are equivalent to theological faculties; and *kolalim*, for married men over the age of twenty-two, entirely devoted to the examination of the inexhaustible ocean of sacred texts and commentaries. There is also a kind of *yeshiva* secondary school, which sets out to combine study of the Torah with secondary lay education. Harmonizing the scientific and technological spirit of the "second twentieth century" with a body of rules several thousand years old is a formidable task. Is it practicable if the latter are considered sacred and untouchable? However that may be, applications for admission to these establishments exceed the number of places that they have to offer. Skeptics point out that this is perhaps not exclusively due to religious motivations. The *yeshivot* have received lavish endowments from the United States and Britain that enable them to offer free board and lodging to their pupils, and many families are not insensible to the advantages of this in a country in which fees for secondary education vary from I£430 to I£570 yearly, and the number of scholarships is very inadequate. Students at the big *yeshivot* which train rabbis for work in Israel as well as in the Diaspora are exempt from military service.

The system of religious educational establishments covers the whole country, all the way to the south and its development towns. Two new secondary *yeshivot* have been built, one near Ashdod and the other at Beersheba. The Bnei Akiva movement has seventeen *yeshivot*, some of which are attached to religious *kibbutzim* or *moshavim* and combine sacred studies with agricultural training. Another variety are the "vocational *yeshivot*" run in collaboration with the O.R.T. (a Jewish organization with headquarters at Geneva that promotes vocational training of the young in the Diaspora and in Israel).

The Bar Ilan University, at Ramat Gan, Tel Aviv, is worthy of special mention. It had eighty students when it was established in 1954, nearly 1400 in 1965, and a predicted "ceiling" of 6000. Its aim is to provide a synthesis of science and religion. "As a religious institution, the Bar Ilan University attaches special importance to the sacred teachings of Judaism," the Introduction to the 1963–64 syllabus reads. "It considers that one of its chief aims is to revere and defend these principles, to form men and women of wide culture, scientists and researchers who will achieve an integration of the wisdom of the Torah with modern knowledge in other fields."

A preliminary knowledge of the Talmud is required of all students except non-Jews. Religious studies, or "Judaica," constitute a quarter of the curriculum required for the B.A. degree, which consequently takes four years instead of three. The validity of the degrees conferred by Bar Ilan, or at any rate its doctor's degrees, has been disputed in high places—an instance of Israeli academic jealousy,[36] a kind of infantile malady, accentuated in this case by the Hebrew University "laymen's" mistrust of an institution suspected of clericalism. The Bar Ilan University can congratulate itself on having won the battle. With two ministers, both members of the National Religious Party, Shapiro and Warhaftig, on its committee of patronage, it has powerful support.

It has no less valuable friendships in the English-speaking world. A document distributed by its public relations committee says that its financing is chiefly assured by generous individuals in America, Canada and Britain who appreciate the needs of education in a developing nation, and that it also receives aid from the Israeli government and the Jewish Agency. The many patrons who have lent their names to faculties, laboratories, clinics, cultural centers, libraries, etc., and even to the synagogue at Ramat Gan, have indeed been generous. The huge and flourishing campus at Bar Ilan is richly equipped from every point of view, and the luxury is unusual and slightly oppressive.

[36] The issue became public in June 1964, revealing to the Israeli public a deplorable squabble between the Hebrew University of Jerusalem and the young university at Tel Aviv. Cf. documents published by J.P.W., June 19, 1964. The new home of the University of Tel Aviv at Ramat Aviv was officially opened on November 4, 1964.

In spite of all these institutions, however, orthodoxy is unsatisfied and worried. It feels that religion is misunderstood, indeed caricatured, by the image that the ordinary Israeli has of it. To the man in the street it looks like nothing but a lot of bans and restrictions on his liberties, leading to a succession of incidents that he regards as shocking. The reason for this, the orthodox say, is that he does not understand the deep reasons for them. Orthodoxy would like to reach the average, middle-of-the-road Israeli whose position is between that of the extremists and who knows nothing of the whys and wherefores of the rites and the commandments. Recognizing that it has so far failed to reach him, and that this is a grave setback, it has set in hand a huge program of adult religious education at all levels at Yad Harav Maimon, covering all aspects of Judaism from the Bible to the Talmud, from history to the literature of the "Jewish people," which is intended to reach all the living cells of Israeli society, even the centers of its economic life. It is less clear on how these are to be reached. The founding of the institution was celebrated on June 10, 1964, in the presence of President Shazar, chief rabbis and ministers, and was honored by an introductory lecture by Ben-Gurion.

Thus orthodoxy today reigns over the official religious life of Israel. Its representatives, most of them products of central and eastern European *yeshivot*, assure the training of new rabbis in accordance with immutable traditions. (However, in religious circles I heard people deploring the lack of rabbinical schools that provide a training adapted to scientific progress and the social developments of our time. In the opinion of these critics, this lack illustrates one of the major aspects of the crisis of orthodox Judaism and dangerously compromises its future.) Two religious parties, over and above their differences, are associated with it. Representatives of deviant trends (both liberal and conservative) have only a minimal influence in the new state, and the Chief Rabbinate does all in its power to repress them. Unorthodox rabbis who try to establish themselves have great difficulty (if they succeed at all) in finding places where they can conduct services; they are excluded from civil responsibilities and rabbinical committees and courts. In some cases the validity of decisions made by them in the Diaspora concerning marriage and divorce is not recognized, and their right to bear the title of rabbi is sometimes denied. I had an unforgettable discussion on the basic problems of Judaism with Z., an exceptionally cultured and intelligent man whom I met in an office in a large town in Israel where he was employed as a clerk. Not until we parted did he reveal his identity to me. He was a non-orthodox rabbi of Hungarian origin and (as I subsequently discovered) had fought in the resistance and risen to senior rank. He now makes a living as best he can. He was among those who communicated to me the deepest and noblest thoughts about Judaism—its present difficulties and its future. How many other men of high quality have been similarly shelved in Israel? An orthodox student told me that the conservative movement was a "cocktail, adapted to the taste of American Jews, that had no chance in Israel." As for the liberal reform movement, born in Germany, "it leads to the destruction of Jewish life, it is the sister of assimilation."

. . . AND ITS PRECARIOUSNESS

But orthodoxy's reign is precarious. A change in the government coalition would be sufficient to bring it to an end. Unification of the three labor parties, which would enable the government to dispense with the support of the National Religious Party and put it in opposition, would ring the knell of the privileges orthodoxy has enjoyed since 1948.

It appreciates the danger, and defends its positions with the greater stubbornness. It cannot ignore the fact that, quite apart from the various trends we have noted, its relations with the Jewish population as a whole have deteriorated in recent years. So far it has succeeded in preventing the establishment in the country of the conservative and liberal movements, but an important section of public opinion tolerates its yoke with increasing impatience. Conflict is latent, and the situation is explosive, as is shown by the violence of the periodic debates on religious problems in the Knesset. That of May 25, 1964, on a report by the Minister of Religious Affairs on his departmental activities, for example, was tumultuous.

The conflict has deep roots. The paradox of the state of Israel is that it is both "non-Jewish" and intolerant. The chief criticisms of orthodoxy are its monopoly in marriages and divorces and its desire to impose its ideas and practices on all the Jews in Israel, many of whom have by no means abandoned their traditions and beliefs but want a rabbinate with broader and more modern views, particularly for the young. In a Haifa factory an Egyptian foreman who still kept up the observances (he did not work on the sabbath) said to me: "How do you expect us to manage nowadays with rules made by the Kings and Judges?" There is a growing body of opinion, among both Ashkenazim and Sephardim, in favor of a separation of synagogue and state, which, many of its advocates claim, would be in the interests of both. There is also a great deal of discussion in intellectual circles and in the press on whether or not there should be a "reform," and whether or not a Sanhedrin should be called. But the first question to be asked is whether these things are possible. Can Judaism be reformed?

The solution of current religious problems, and even the future of the Jewish religion, depends on these essentially theological questions. I discussed them with historians and sociologists, some of them recognized authorities, holding different views about religion. I alone am responsible for the brief reflections that follow.

The so-called reform movement from the eighteenth century and the emancipation onward did not lead to any deep-seated, real reform. It arose too late, after the Enlightenment, when religion was under attack by rationalism, and led to the contraction and withdrawal into its shell that is one of the principal weaknesses of modern Jewish orthodoxy. In relation to the Talmudic tradition the pseudo-reform was more a disintegration than a renovation leading to a purified and simplified religion. This is as true of the conservative movement as it is of liberal Judaism. A real reformation, if it is to succeed, must discover a new source of authority; in the case of Protestantism this was the use of the Bible in its original purity as a weapon against Rome. "The Jewish religion," K.J. said to me, "is a Catholic Church without Protestantism; it has not found an alternative source of authority that will enable it to reform and readapt itself to the spiritual needs of the Jew in modern society. A few modifications of the *halacha* rules cannot be considered a reformation." But can Judaism, with its 3000-year-old structure and spirit, find a source of authority that will impose itself on all believing Jews, both in Israel and in the Diaspora, and thus bring about a real reform?

There is a great deal of discussion in Israel about holding a Sanhedrin, and I have read learned discussions of the history and role of that institution as described in the Mishna and the Gemara. A modern Sanhedrin could not, of course, be satisfied with being a mere court of justice, but would have to be a kind of ecumenical council competent to reconsider the whole of the *halacha* and, as Chief Rabbi Kook suggested, distinguish between immutable laws and rules capable of being modified or perhaps dropped. But, even supposing that the orthodox in Israel and the Diaspora were willing to face the risk of holding such a council, it would consist only of the orthodox, interested in the defense and preservation of the system. In other words, in the absence of a radical change of heart among its leaders, it would be incapable of the wide and audacious vision without which a genuine reformation is unthinkable. Besides, it would constitute a source of authority only to the orthodox, and non-orthodox believers, in Israel and in the Diaspora, would not consider themselves bound by its decisions. I met no one in Israel who regarded a Sanhedrin as a possible solution of the religious problem, except on a very long-term view, at the end of a very long road that has still to be traveled.

Tradition plays a huge role in orthodox Judaism, so huge that it constitutes another major obstacle in the path of reform. The Talmud, or rather the Talmuds, the Jerusalem version and the Babylonian, fill about five thousand octavo volumes. The Mishna, compiled in the second century of our era by Rabbi Judah the Holy, consists of sixty-three tractates concerning doctrine and practices. To the orthodox the Talmud and the Mishna are sacred. Everything, absolutely everything, has been discussed in them, and in the course of generations upon generations of rabbis the discussions led to commentaries, which themselves have become sacred. Indeed, everything has been discussed in them, including, apparently, the roundness of the earth, atomic theory and, according to certain interpreters of cryptic passages, radio, television and space travel. In our own time more manuscripts have been discovered in libraries and museums, and recently still more have been found in the desert borders of the Dead Sea. At the Talmudic Institute attached to the Emet Rabbi Herzog Academy in Jerusalem one can find two hundred variant readings for a single page of the "official" text (Vilna, 1880–86) offering the reader numerous versions, all equally valid and corresponding to different schools of thought. The Talmud is a sea of traditions into which every doctor of the law since the destruction of the Second Temple has taken a plunge and chanced his arm in the hope of finding a new path, which, if his learning and faith are sufficient to merit it, will itself become sacred. But, as Gershom Scholem points out, in the eyes of Judaism the true tradition is a purely human creation. Tradition "is a living contact in which man seizes the ancient truth and links himself with it over and above the generations in a dialogue of giving and taking."[37]

What authority is there inside Judaism bold enough to lay

---

[37] Die Tradition "ist die lebendige Berührung, in der der Mensch die uralte Wahrheit ergreift und über alle Geschlechter hin in der Zwiesprache des Gebens und Nehmens sich mit ihr verbindet." G. Scholem, "Tradition und Kommentar als religiöse Kategorien im Judentum," in Der Mensch, Führer und Geführter im Werk, edited by Adolf Portmann, Rhein-Verlag, Zurich, 1963, p. 47.

hands on a tradition thus constituted and thus regarded, and solid enough to have its decisions accepted by believers greatly divided among themselves? Is not the reformation of such a formidable tradition a superhuman task?

Liberal Judaism has tried to "modernize" the Jewish religion by differentiating between the *literal* observance of rites and practices, according to the interpretation at the closing of the Talmud (sixth century A.D.), and the *spirit* that inspired them. It has gone a long way in that direction and no longer attaches "fundamental importance" to respect for either the dietary laws or those of the sabbath. "The essential is to preserve the spirit of the Torah and to observe practices within the limits of the possible."[38]

To this the orthodox reply is that Judaism is *essentially* bound to a system of practices and a way of life. My friend A.R. said to me in Jerusalem: "A believing Jew cannot appeal to salvation by faith, as a Christian can. Jewish life is co-substantial with Jewish religion. Our religion is without dogmas, and without the practices that constitute it it is nothing. Abolishing or even modifying the *mitzvot* means emptying our religion of its content and destroying it." A young British rabbi, "angry" with orthodoxy but nevertheless hostile to the "over-reform" of liberal Judaism, indicated the borderline that he refuses to cross in a phrase that seems to me invaluable for understanding the Jewish religion. He said: "There are depths in the human spirit which only ritual can reach."[39]

These reflections enable one to understand the resignation of certain religious Jews who, having gone to Israel to lead a fully Jewish life, are reduced to seeking personal salvation, each for himself, in ritual observance and in his own family stronghold. Must it be admitted, as one of them cruelly said, that "if there is no reformation of the Jewish religion, it is because there cannot be one"?

[38] A. Zaoui, *L'Enseignement libéral du judaïsme, op. cit.,* p. 81.
[39] Rabbi Louis Jacobs in *J.P.W.,* May 29, 1964.

THE RELIGIOUS *KIBBUTZIM*

There are barely a dozen religious *kibbutzim*, which is not many. The Hadati federation, founded in 1930 and affiliated to the National Religious Party, consists of about 3500 people, families included. But what do numbers matter if there is a nucleus here of real faith, open to the world and deriving living nourishment from it, radiating, or capable of radiating, influence far and wide? I met students and teachers who talked about them with warmth. "I ought to be in a religious *kibbutz*," A.R., an assistant in a university library, sadly confided to me. "One day my wife and I will settle in one for our children's sake. That is where the most satisfying and coherent conception of the Jewish religion is to be found."

The visits that I paid to some of them, and the talks that I had with some of their best-qualified spokesmen, gave me the impression that the image of them that exists in many minds in the "outside world" is a highly idealized one. The men whom I met in them were of rare moral quality, and their faith did not obscure their clear-sightedness. Far from embellishing the real state of affairs, they talked with complete frankness, not concealing the difficulties and weaknesses of their movement. They are well aware that without objectivity there is no chance of overcoming them.

The religious *kibbutzim* do not constitute a nucleus from which a great spiritual revival can come. All those I spoke to, over and above their differences of temperament and the varying degrees of confidence or anxiety that they felt, painted the same broad picture.

In the first place, the economic problems of a religious *kibbutz* do not in general differ from those of a socialist *kibbutz* belonging to the Artzi or the Meuhad. Most of them nowadays are well-organized, successful and profitable concerns. But, like the others, they had a hard struggle, which for a long time absorbed the greater part of their energies, before this was achieved. At

S.H., in the valley of Beit Shean, when the difficulties of the heroic period had been overcome, the *kibbutz* paid off its debts and now enjoys a substantial income. What is to be done with the money? The *haverim* live in comfortable, modern, air-conditioned houses—real bourgeois homes. The Torah and the Talmud teach sobriety and moderation. The *kibbutz* is now surrounded by and cannot isolate itself from a society making rapid economic progress. "The religious *kibbutz*," A.B. said to me, "is following the trend. It is a little way behind, but still it is following it." As in other *kibbutzim*, collectivist principles are threatened. There are difficulties in recruiting new members. The most gifted of the young people who pass through the Nahal or the Dati *kibbutz* youth movements choose to become *yeshiva* students; like many of their comrades belonging to the Hashomer Hatzair, they seem to feel that the *kibbutz* offers an insufficient field for their aspirations. This adverse selection is particularly serious to the religious *kibbutzim*. The best material goes into the traditional theological grooves and is wasted in bookish study and the endless examination of sacred texts, far from the mainstream of modern life and the knowledge by which it can be understood and mastered. Thus the hope of religious idealists that young "rabbi prophets" capable of reawakening their generation will arise out of the religious *kibbutzim* seems vain.

For a long time *haverim* in the religious *kibbutzim* were absorbed by economic problems. Will their relative prosperity make them available for an active religious life? It is too early to tell. Some of them periodically attend a *yeshiva* for a period of six months at a time. But there is no sign at present in the religious *kibbutzim* of any original movement not in conformity with orthodoxy. The *haverim* often do without a rabbi, conduct services and meticulously observe all the festivals in the liturgical calendar by themselves, but there their boldness ends. It seemed to me that, apart from a few strong personalities and original minds (such as Eliezer Goldman at Sde Eliahu), the *haverim* in religious *kibbutzim* are believing Jews who have found an answer to their personal needs in these communities, leading a pious working life and bringing up their children in accordance with their faith. They are men who have found a retreat rather than militant believers with a sense of "radiating" mission, convinced that their life is the true one and that they must help others to share it.

How is one to explain this withdrawal into their shell of the religious *kibbutzim*, this abandonment of the prophetic vocation attributed to them by intellectual idealists? The answer seems to me to be briefly as follows: In the first place, the pressure of daily work, the struggle to ensure the success and profitability of the *kibbutz* for a long time absorbed the energy of its members and even in some cases exhausted them. Second, the religious *kibbutz* movement was born under the spiritual leadership of men of the quality of Rabbi Kook, but they had no successors of the same stature. "The rabbis," G.E. said to me, "have lost all creative power in the field of the *halacha*. Most of them are mere specialists with a narrow outlook." Third, and this is a factor that underlies all the others, the religious *kibbutz* movement has been affected by the withdrawal into itself of Israeli orthodoxy in general. It failed to find in itself the moral strength necessary to oppose this trend, the historical reasons for which are obvious, but the importance of which cannot be overemphasized. The extermination of a third of the world's Jewish population, the destruction of the principal centers of its religious life and its elites, have created an obsession among the survivors to maintain and protect what has been saved. The purity of the miraculously reassembled survivors of the chosen people and its law must at all costs be preserved. Hence the fear of the world, the fear of contact with reality, the withdrawal, the contraction of a religious life, the narrow horizon of which is deplored by many believers. The religious *kibbutzim* share in this anxiety, which penetrates both heart and mind. I shall not easily forget my encounter in Ben Yehuda Street at Tel Aviv with S.E., who goes there weekly to teach at a *yeshiva*, the sad eyes under his *kipah* as he glided furtively through the tumult of this other world like a drop of oil floating on the surface of a torrent, seeming not to see it, hurrying toward the bus that would take him back to his retreat, his monastery.

REARGUARD ACTION

A religious situation so complex and so little understood is the subject of the most conflicting opinions among the people at large. Believers assert in spite of everything the messianic and universal vocation of the "Jewish people," which will cause all the nations of the world to turn to the Holy City. In their view, the moral crisis, aggravated by orthodox mistakes and sectarianism, is the sign of a "thirst for God," which new spiritual springs will arise from the soil of Israel and the sacred books to assuage. Rationalist observers regard the phenomenon as part of an irreversible trend, a historical necessity bound up with economic growth in a society subject to acute pressures from both within and without. On the one hand there is unshakable faith in the chosen people, and on the other this provocative view of a sociologist: "There is no people on earth less religious than the people of Israel."

There is another factor that throws light on the religious problem in Israel. The twentieth-century heirs of the prophetic spirit, the men who tried to put into practice the ideals of social justice, the Zionist and socialist pioneers, the *halutzim* and those who followed in their wake, have for the most part worked outside and apart from the religious movements and parties, which have never made any serious effort to join them. The existence of about a dozen religious *kibbutzim* and about sixty religious *moshavim*, whose members are often "anti-clerical," does not change the picture as a whole. The synagogue, unlike the Catholic Church, has no active, social wing.

Both official orthodoxy and the mystical sects seem to wish to preserve their purity from all contact with the builders, whose aims nevertheless have indisputable moral value and coincide with millenary spiritual impulses. The danger of this breach has been seen by Chief Rabbi Kook, who was strong enough to denounce the errors of his friends. "The workers who repair the breaches in the house of Israel are workers in the house of the Lord," he said. Does the moral quality of the men (even if they were non-observers) who struggled and faced setbacks and disappointments to give Israel its basic institutions deserve to be considered alien to the spirituality of the Israeli people? Are not those who proclaim their determination to make Israel a nation "different from the others" the best (and perhaps at the present time the only) workers for a messianic future?

In other words, in the religious world of Israel there is no such thing as social Judaism. The absence of such a movement among the religious youth of the country is surprising; one would have supposed that there would be those among them who desired to impart a new spirit to religion, seeking to adapt it and link it to the search for social justice in the modern world, thus rejoining the great universal and prophetic tradition. It was not in Israel that I heard it said that the Holy Land must become a hive of activity for "missionary rabbis who would bring the workers in the towns and the fields back to the faith of their forefathers."[40] It was a French philosopher who penned this warning to the religious Jews of Israel, this denunciation of their withdrawal into themselves: "The kingdom of God is not of another world. But neither can it be established around an isolated man or group who preserve *halacha* for themselves and fear polluting it by contact with the masses of a nation who have become atheist."[41]

The kingdom of God is of this world. To a believing Jew, humanity is progressing irreversibly toward messianic times; some even believe that with the Return and the creation of the state of Israel those times have already begun. Others ask how a nation can be messianic. Is it not a contradiction in terms? A nation, particularly if its territory is minute and threat-

[40] André Zaoui, *Revue de la Pensée juive*, April 1951.
[41] André Neher, *Revue de la Pensée juive*, October 1950.

ened, inevitably accepts means (more and more lethal weapons, for instance, and secret services) that have nothing to do with any universal vocation.

But believers already see in certain projects undertaken by the state the first signs of fulfillment of the promise. The Israeli expert missions sent to various countries of the Third World, particularly in Black Africa, are said to be a ray of light, the beginning of universalism, an attempt to achieve peace and brotherhood, which, together with social justice, become the aim of history in messianic times. Unlike the wealthy great powers, Israel cannot at the present time supply the Third World with arms, money, expensive equipment, but it sends men capable of transmitting the spirit of the Nahal and the experience of its pioneers. This is also a useful card in Israel's military and diplomatic strategy to combat its encirclement by the Arab states.

These projections of faith into the future do not change present realities. The orthodox see the threat of extinction hanging over the survivors of the "Jewish people." Its most dangerous aspects, in their view, are assimilation by an industrialized, hedonist, atheist society; the disintegration of its defenses, its laws and traditions, by an unchecked reformation; and finally the irreparable evil of mixed marriages. There are variations in attitude toward the maintenance of observances and building up the communities' defenses, but all, from the intransigents to the moderates, agree on the categorical imperative of religious marriage, doing away with which would mean losing control of mixed marriages and permitting them to multiply. For there to be progress toward the messianic age the "Jewish people" must survive. Today, as after the destruction of the Second Temple by Titus in the first century of the Christian era, the "sole thought" of the rabbis is "to save the remnants of authenticity of a people and a tradition which run the risk of disappearing."[42]

Hence the withdrawal of the synagogue into a position so

[42] A. Chouraqui, *Histoire du judaïsme, op. cit.*, p. 58.

cramped in relation to the vast spheres into which its great doctors and mystics once launched themselves; hence the obsession with protecting the "Jewish people" from biological contamination by Gentiles and the cunning assaults of their missionaries; hence the particularism that so often degenerates into sectarianism, the absorption in means that obscure ends. "We have rabbis; what we need are prophets," H.J. said to me at the end of our talk, accompanying me to the entrance of his *kibbutz* under a June sky thick with stars; the bright light of the Milky Way seemed to reinforce the song of the crickets. It was a Biblical night, a night of shepherds and prophets. . . . The rabbis want to save what can yet be saved. The religious are fighting a rearguard action. But is not attack the best defense? Instead of fearfully withdrawing from a monstrous century, is not Jewish spirituality's best and only chance to plunge into it, face its realities, take part in the adventure of humanity at grips with technology and help it to emerge from the struggle victorious and free, having achieved justice and fraternity together with abundance?

8

Jews and the State of Israel

In all these religious quarrels one constantly comes across the notion of the "Jewish people," which is used very differently in different circumstances and environments. To explore its content, let us examine more closely the relations between Jewishness, by which I mean the sense of belonging to Judaism, or, to use the terminology of the psychologists, Jewish "self-identification," and Israeli citizenship, and between Jewishness in the Diaspora and in the state of Israel. I will also try to clarify the notion by observing the attitude toward it adopted by political leaders; Zionists; the orthodox, to whom the uniqueness and permanence of the "Jewish people" are an article of faith; nationalist *sabras*; and Jews of the Diaspora, assimilated to a greater or lesser extent in countries where their families have been established sometimes for centuries.

First of all, let us recall some figures. According to estimates made by the Jewish World Congress, in 1939 there were about 16 million Jews in the world.[1] The European catastrophe reduced the number to about 10 million in 1945, but by 1966 it had risen again to about 13 and a half million. This rapid increase in twenty years was chiefly due to the high birth rate among North African and Asian Jews.

At the end of 1965, according to the *American Jewish Year-*

[1] *The Jewish Communities of the World*, 1963. Attempts to obtain accurate figures have failed (or have not even been undertaken) in countries in which the persistence of anti-Semitism makes Jews nervous of official census-taking; this is the case in the Soviet Union. Estimates by experts do not always agree. All we are concerned with here is the order of magnitude; and what seem to be reasonable estimates have been used in round numbers.

book 1966, more than 12 million Jews were divided approximately as follows among these countries:

United States	5,720,000
Soviet Union	2,486,000[2]
Israel	2,299,000
France	520,000
United Kingdom	450,000
Argentina	450,000
Canada	275,000[3]
Brazil	130,000
Rumania	120,000
South Africa	116,000
Morocco	70,000[4]
Tunisia	23,000[4]
Algeria	3,000

Large communities in Muslim countries, such as Morocco (250,000 in 1947), Iraq (120,000), Egypt (80,000), Yemen (50,000), Tunisia (120,000), Algeria (150,000 in 1960), Libya (36,000) and Syria (30,000) have either substantially diminished or practically disappeared. Most Algerian Jews came to swell the French community, raising it to third place in the Diaspora, although it is still far behind the communities in the United States and the Soviet Union. Before the war 58 per cent of Jews lived in Europe; today only 30 per cent (of whom the vast majority are in the Soviet Union) do, as against 48 per cent in the Americas.

A fundamental fact emerges from these figures. Israel, which its leaders increasingly consider to be the center of world Judaism, is the home of not quite 17 per cent of the world Jewish population. In the eyes of many Israelis this is a shocking and

[2] This is a minimum figure and, in the opinion of some specialists, much too low. But can Soviet Jews who conceal their origin at the time of the census because of the anti-Semitic environment be considered as still belonging to the "Jewish people"?

[3] Canada is the only country in the Western Hemisphere in which the census specifically lists the number of Jews; hence it is exceptionally accurate.

[4] The exodus of Jews from Morocco and Tunisia continued after the beginning of 1963, the date of the census quoted here.

even scandalous situation. What are all those Jews doing in the *galut* ("exile"), where they are more or less unwanted and unintegrated and "do not belong any more" (as I often heard people say in Israel), while the state of Israel awaits them, appeals to them and needs them to exploit its resources fully, to defend it against its enemies and to assure its prosperity, survival and salvation as well as their own? In the course of an address to Jewish youth in Paris Levi Eshkol observed bitterly, "There are half a million Jews in this country, but you would have to search the beautiful streets of Paris with a lantern to discover any Jews ready to leave in an *aliya* to help to construct the homeland."[5]

JEWISHNESS AND ISRAELITY

Does Israel address its forcible appeal to the Diaspora in the name of the new nation and its economic, political and military imperatives, or in the name of the "Jewish people" whose center it claims to be? Unfortunately little research has been done on the Jewish consciousness of Israeli citizens and their sense of belonging to a "Jewish people." An interesting study by Simon N. Herman tackles the problem indirectly, through the reactions of groups of American Jewish students staying in Israel and working with the population.[6] These students, most of whom had preserved links with Judaism, came in the often strong expectation of finding common ties between themselves and the

[5] *Jerusalem Post*, July 3, 1964.

[6] "American Jewish Students in Israel," *Jewish Social Studies*, January 1962, from which the passages in quotation marks have been taken. S. N. Herman, in collaboration with Erling Schild, had previously studied the reactions of American Jewish students in Israel from other points of view: "Ethnic Role Conflict in a Cross-Cultural Situation," *Human Relations*, No. 3, 1960; "Context for the Study of Cross-Cultural Education," *The Journal of Social Psychology*, No. 52, 1960. The concept of "ego-identity" was elaborated by Herman on the basis of the work of E. H. Erikson, who defines it as the "gradual integration of all the identifications" (*Childhood and Society*, Norton, New York, 1950).

inhabitants of Israel, who in their eyes formed a part of the "Jewish people." Considering their Jewishness to be the very substance of these ties, which would immediately unite them with the Israelis, they emphasized them, in the expectation of thus accelerating their acceptance by Israeli society, to which some of them were thinking of emigrating. But "they were very disappointed in finding the Israeli *sabras* less Jewish than they wanted and expected them to be" (p. 13).

Confronted with so many people from such different countries and cultures, their image of the "Israeli" became more sophisticated, and they grew increasingly aware of its contrasts. "Before coming to Israel," one of them wrote, "I thought that all Jews formed only a single people. Now I doubt it." The indifference of many Israelis to religion was bitterly resented by American religious students. In general they were disappointed by the Israelis' "Jewishness" and inability to understand the problems of Jews in the Diaspora, and they ended by making a distinction between the land of Israel, with all its affective aura, and its inhabitants. "In regard to Israel, I feel 'us'; in regard to the Israelis, I feel 'them'" (p. 15).

Their stereotype of the Israelis became less favorable. What they appreciated in them was their "character," "energy," "pioneering qualities" rather than their Jewishness. Their own experience revealed to them the dissociation between Jewishness and "Israelity."

The young Americans, understandably enough, gradually came to feel that their own Jewishness was based, not, as they had previously supposed, on similarity, but on interdependence[7] of destiny. Their visit to Israel certainly weakened their feeling that Jews, as such and irrespective of their origin, were their kith and kin (p. 26, Table VIII).

A new and important study of the problems of "Jewish iden-

---

[7] To use Kurt Lewin's classic definition. *Cf.* his article "Bringing Up the Jewish Child" in *Resolving Social Conflicts*, New York, 1948. He elaborated the distinction between interdependence and similarity factors in a previous article (reprinted in *Field Theory in Social Science*, New York, 1951, pp. 130–154).

tity" among Israeli secondary schoolchildren and students is
in progress under the direction of S. N. Herman and with the
support of the Institute of Contemporary Judaism. A preliminary stage will try to pin down the very vague concept of
"identity" by examining the relationship between "Jewishness"
and "Israelity." Are these two notions congruent in Israel, or is
there a sharp dividing line between them? When they are congruent, to what extent and by what sections of Israeli youth
are they felt to be consonant or dissonant? Does consonance
or dissonance have the bigger impact? Identity can bring together, but it can also divide. In the United States, Jewish
identity divides a minority from everyone else (Christians, Negroes, Puerto Ricans, etc.), while in Israel it marks off a majority
wishing to live "a normal life" from minorities (Arabs, Druses,
etc.). In my talks with *sabra* students I often heard them use
the phrase "normal life," and it seemed to me to be significant of the aspirations of many of them. A people's "being
normal" meant "being itself," "developing according to its own
laws," "living its life as other majorities do in other countries."

On the basis of known facts drawn from scientific studies
and current observation, Jewishness and Israelity seem, at the
present time at any rate, not to be congruent ideas among the
majority of *sabras*. Their self-identification with the Jews of the
Diaspora (in the first place with the tourists who visit Israel),
their sense of belonging to a unique community called the
"Jewish people," is weak. It is certainly much more marked
among the *vatikim*, particularly if they are Ashkenazim. On the
other hand, the *sabras'* sense of belonging to an Israeli community is strong and, as previously noted, is sometimes expressed with a certain provocativeness or aggression.

The reactions noted during the several months of the Eichmann trial in 1961 revealed very varied expressions of "Jewish
consciousness" among the Israeli population, depending on the
individual's origin, age and experiences.[8] What the *sabras*

8 S. N. Herman, Y. Peres, E. Yuchtman, *op. cit.*

learned on that occasion about the extermination of the Jews between 1940 and 1945 seems to have confirmed or accentuated their sense of non-congruence between Jewishness and Israelity. Having been brought up in complete liberty as citizens of a state that had established itself by fighting, possessed a strong army and was primarily preoccupied with its own security, they regarded self-defense as an elementary duty, and they felt themselves to be very different from the Jews who "had let their throats be cut like sheep." Their attitude to the victims of the great massacre was a mixture of pity, incomprehension and remoteness. Some even considered that, apart from the activities of some partisan groups and the Warsaw ghetto revolt, the whole thing was an inglorious episode in Jewish history.

Israeli youth's attitude to Jews in the Diaspora, the weakness of both their feeling of interdependence with them and their "Jewish consciousness," has caused concern among members of the government, judges of the Supreme Court and educationists. Levi Eshkol, addressing the second world Jewish youth congress on August 4, 1963, sounded the leitmotiv of Israel's political philosophy when he said: "Jewish life throughout the world will reach its full significance when Israel becomes its home and its center." He then added: "This appeal is also addressed to young people growing up in Israel. I know that this feeling cannot arise spontaneously; we will have to make immense efforts to inculcate into Israeli youth the sense of being part and parcel of the Jewish people." The Prime Minister did not conceal the arduousness of the task. In order to build up their "Jewish consciousness" and give them a sense of interdependence, young people would have to be familiarized with the Jewish past in the Diaspora, the dramatic history of its communities and the various phases of anti-Semitism. In September 1963, the government decided to make these compulsory subjects in secondary schools, as the Minister of Education, Zolmann Aranne, announced at a press conference on September 2, and to give a bigger place in the syllabus to lessons inculcating "Jewish consciousness." Before this change in the school syllabus, a marked change had already taken place in the presentation of the events of 1940–45. It was less and less frequently described as the "holocaust," suggesting the wholesale slaughter of "passive victims." The Yad Vashem monument is now everywhere described as a "memorial dedicated to the martyrs and heroes," and often the order of those words is reversed. Exhibitions and pamphlets offer schoolchildren a "true picture of the Jews of Europe," in which they are represented as having died in combat or in prayer, but "all without fear, conscious of the significance of their martyrdom."[9]

Judaism has been characterized since its beginnings by a dialogue between particularism and universalism, with the emphasis varying from one to the other. God's special alliance with His people was associated with a universal vocation, the proclamation of a single God and a messianic future for all mankind. We have seen the anxieties and pressures that have led to the withdrawal into itself of religion in Israel today. The young state, for no less compelling reasons, has had to forge the material and moral means to assure its survival; its sometimes overaccentuated nationalism is a bastion, an instrument of self-defense. It is an absurd and bitter paradox that, while the messianic ideology attributes to it the mission of "bringing peace to the world," the state itself, based on force, has to assure its own survival by force. It has to train its young people, not for an apostolate of universal brotherhood for all eternity, but for the immediate future and its own immediate interests, has to inculcate into them a spirit of national and military self-confidence by teaching them the most lethal techniques of combat. So it is not surprising that young religious idealists, newly disembarked from the Diaspora and imbued with the standards of a traditional education, and young *sabras* should have some difficulty in understanding one another.

[9] A. L. Kubovy, chairman of the Yad Vashem Council, *Yad Vashem Bulletin*, December 1962, pp. 4–5.

THE MISADVENTURE OF ZIONISM

The preceding reflections help to explain the background of the disrepute into which the Zionist movement has fallen with Israeli leaders and the long history of mutual complaints, misunderstandings and disputes between the two.

The Zionists found it difficult to acknowledge the state of Israel as the center of world Judaism, and even today not all Zionist associations have acknowledged it. Nahum Goldmann, the president of the World Jewish Congress and the World Zionist Organization, still thought it necessary in March 1963 to urge Zionists to try to make the communities of the Diaspora realize what the "centrality" of Israel meant.[10]

"Israel is the center of Jewish life and the source of the main values on which the communities in the Diaspora will live spiritually," he said. "Acceptance of the 'centrality' of Israel is certainly not yet fully shared by all the Jews of the world, and in particular is not shared by many in the United States who generously help with funds. The Zionist movement in the United States has failed to fulfill its task." On the other hand, he added, the World Zionist Organization would be unable to ensure the co-operation of the Jewish people with the state of Israel unless it received the latter's full support: "This is not criticism of just the government or the Prime Minister [then Ben-Gurion]—it goes deeper, and concerns a large part of Israeli public opinion, and especially Israeli youth."

The Zionist Organization of America, one of the most important in the United States, held its sixty-sixth annual convention in Israel, and Israeli press comment on that occasion— particularly two articles in *Jerusalem Post Weekly* for July 19,

[10] J.P.W., March 29, 1963. A year later, Goldmann, who had long been the leading figure in the Zionist world, made a striking gesture of personal acknowledgment by landing at Tel Aviv airport with immigrant's papers.

1963—throws light on the public opinion that Goldmann had in mind.

The articles declared that, while the vital role played by American Zionism in the establishment of Israel would not be forgotten, it was more important to seek goals for future cooperation than to wrangle over the credit for past achievements. They expressed disappointment and dissatisfaction at the failure of the American Zionist leadership, with isolated exceptions, to come to Israel and take part in the project they had helped to set in motion, and at the failure of the movement actively to encourage and support immigration from the United States. "Indeed, the ten thousand American Jewish settlers in Israel seem to lend support to the Israeli view of American Zionism." Gifts of dollars, the buying of Israeli bonds, direct investment in Israeli industry, the support of land reclamation and resettlement projects "have come to appear less the wholehearted participation of committed brothers than apologetic charity." These are hard words, which call to mind the once-famous definition of a Zionist as a Jew who wanted to send another Jew to Palestine with a third Jew's money. And the basic complaint is constantly reiterated. What the Israelis, headed by Ben-Gurion, a severe critic of American Zionism, want is a massive *aliya* from the United States, an *aliya* not only of capital, but of men. The United States has certainly sent a great deal of capital and a good many tourists, who come to spend a few days, or sometimes weeks, in the country, looking for traditions, rites and a spirit from which most of them have become estranged. The Israelis ask for more than that. "Zionism can be taught in America, but it can be learned only in Israel," Ben-Gurion told the leaders of the Zionist Organization of America in Tel Aviv on July 14, 1963. The huge American community, two and a half times bigger than the Jewish community in Israel, seems to the Israelis a shocking anomaly. It is this feeling that accounts for a great many of the continual misunderstandings that arise between them and American Jews.

It would not be enough for Zionism merely to recognize Israel's "centrality" to the Jews of the Diaspora; in order to have an *aliya,* a wholesale immigration to Israel from the United States, there would have to be a revolution in the situation and mentality of American Jews, the vast majority of whom belong to the middle classes and, in the absence of religious motivation, can feel no temptation to uproot themselves and settle in Israel.

Nevertheless the Z.O.A. convention had promised to encourage immigration to Israel by American Jews and to prepare for it through the "conquest of American Jewish communities." A network of day schools would provide them with a Jewish education centered on Israel and the teaching of Hebrew.

Thus the "centrality" of Israel is a fundamental principle, closely linked to that of the "unity of the Jewish people." American Zionists admit that this double principle is not generally accepted by Jews in the United States, who might well point out, as Nahum Goldmann does, that it is not accepted by the new generations of *sabras* either. Nevertheless Israelis stand by their position; public opinion seems to correspond to Ben-Gurion's feelings on the matter, which he has expressed very forcibly, notably in April 1963, on the occasion of the twentieth anniversary of the Warsaw ghetto uprising, where he declared that the only way Jews could prevent more massacres was to "cease to be a people depending on the mercy of others"; only a great gathering-in of the exiles would make Israel a sure and powerful shield for them. "Hatred of Jews will not vanish," he said, "until the majority of our people are reunited in their original home and until that home is secure."

These words sum up the Israeli leaders' aspirations: massive immigration, the end of anti-Semitism, the security of Israel and, simultaneously, of the Jewish people of the Diaspora. One sees why they are unalterably opposed to the maintenance in other parts of the world of large Jewish communities, which, in their opinion, should play only a loyal supporting role to Israel, "the powerful link that unites Jews throughout the world," as Ben-Gurion put it in the same speech.

One also sees why everything affecting Jews in the Soviet Union is a matter of passionate interest and concern to the government and people of Israel. The press constantly draws attention to their condition and their cultural and religious problems. This immense potential source of immigration, exceeding in size the whole Jewish population of Israel, is practically inaccessible to Zionist propaganda. Jewish emigration is forbidden by the Soviet government, which in recent times has repeatedly confirmed its total veto in the matter. There is said to be a continual clandestine emigration, the exact size of which is, of course, impossible to establish, but it is probably only a trickle. Yet all the Israelis can do is denounce the manifestations of the anti-Semitism that is still violent in Russia and cause diplomatic steps to be taken and protests to be made, generally through the American Zionist organizations, but also in the committees of the United Nations. A massive *aliya* by Russian Jews would have incalculable political, economic and military consequences for Israel. I even heard it said that, in the event of a marked liberalization of the Soviet regime, the security of Israel might one day depend on a decision by the Kremlin—a very tenuous hope at present, it seems to me, and likely to remain so for a long time to come.

THE AMERICAN-JEWISH CONSCIENCE

Ben-Gurion's indictment of American Zionism and Israeli criticisms of American Jews are based on the belief that a large-scale *aliya* by the latter is a possibility in the not too distant future—a belief that corresponds more to wishful thinking than to the facts. The only sociological study of the question was, to the best of my belief, one made in 1952 by Marshall Sklare and Marc Vosk in a small industrial town in New Jersey (given the fictitious name of Riverton).[11] The town has 130,000 inhabitants, of whom 6500 are Jews. Adults were asked if they would like to live in Israel; only 7 per cent said yes, and few of them, in the opinion of the interviewers, had any

[11] *The Riverton Study*, published by the American Jewish Committee, 1957.

real intention of doing anything about it. Asked what they felt about a possible *aliya* for their children, 8 per cent were in favor, 59 per cent against, and 33 per cent replied that it was a matter for the young people to decide for themselves. This seems to indicate that, in promoting "Israel-centered" Jewish education the Zionists can look forward to encourage sporadic emigration to Israel by young Americans, but a mass movement appears unlikely. Moreover, religious young people who go to Israel in order to live a "fully Jewish" life there are those most likely to be disappointed.

The general conclusions drawn from that investigation are still valid. It is not by chance that immigration from the United States to Israel had been so negligible in proportion to the number of Jews in America (about 10,000 of a total of 5,500,000, or 0.18 per cent). American visitors to Israel are told *ad nauseam* that their place is not in the United States, that sooner or later they will be the victims of racial persecution there, and that they should come and live in Israel. But impartial observers of the United States know that anti-Semitism, where it exists, is on the whole mild (the violent anti-Semitism of Negroes in certain big towns must be regarded in the total context of the American Negro problem), and believe that, in the absence of a radical change in the economic and political conditions of the country into which they are increasingly integrated, the chances of a large-scale American *aliya* are minimal. This is the view of Paul Lazarsfeld, among other authoritative observers. The C.O.M.O.I. (Committee on Man-Power Opportunities in Israel, an organization run by the Ministry of Labor and the Jewish Agency) experiment, by which responsible positions in Israeli industry, suitable to their qualifications, are given to technicians, who are provided with high salaries and comfortable quarters, has been far from successful, that is to say, it has not been followed in a large number of cases by permanent settlement.

According to an official statement made by the Israeli immigration services (January 10, 1967) 50 per cent of the immigrants coming from the United States have, since the creation of the State, returned to their country of origin: Among them, recently, was a high proportion of skilled non-manual personnel who were unable to find openings in the Israeli economy.

An American Jew has to have strong non-economic motives of a moral or spiritual nature to make up his mind to emigrate. Some eminent scholars I met at the Hebrew University had such motives; they indeed "chose Israel," but they are exceptions. Let me quote this passage from a typical and, it seems to me, sensible letter written by a New York schoolteacher after his second stay in Israel.[12] "All too many Israelis have a woefully ignorant knowledge of the life of United States Jews," he wrote. "It *may* happen (though I doubt it) that what happened in Hitlerite Germany may yet occur in America, but playing the prophet is a matter of conjecture, while life in the present-day United States is a matter of fact. United States Jews are not living under widespread and repressive anti-Semitism. As one result of this, few United States Jews are going to emigrate to Israel, and for Israelis to harp on this is nonsensical."

The emigration from Israel to the United States is, in fact, far greater than that in the opposite direction. In 1961 the Israeli consulate in New York registered 3935 applications by Israelis who wished to emigrate, 2441 of them to the United States. In the same year Canada announced that more than 3000 Israelis had applied for Canadian nationality. Many *sabras* who leave Israel do not at the time intend to settle abroad permanently. They come to the United States as students or on official or private business and remain there; others arrive as tourists and marry. Most of them say they were induced to remain by the greater opportunities available in America, the prospects of quicker advancement and a more rewarding career, and the comforts and conveniences of the American way of life—all motives that are shocking and horrifying to the *vatikim* in their native country. Some of them talk of returning to Israel, but never do so. "Israelis in the U.S.A. are lost to Israel" was the title of a well-documented article that aroused

[12] *J.P.W.*, April 19, 1963.

violent controversy between the "realists" and the "idealists" in Israel (*cf. Jerusalem Post Weekly*, May 22, 1964, and the June 1964 numbers of that journal).

The likelihood of an American-Jewish *aliya* is further reduced by the decline in "Jewish consciousness" among American Jews. Religiousness is declining among Jewish students in the United States much more rapidly than among their Protestant and, particularly, their Catholic counterparts. Among adults the "return to religion" is mostly an empty shell. It has been said of American Jews, not without reason, that the less they pray the more synagogues they build, and the laxer their observance of the *kashrut* the more abundant the kosher products on the shelves of the supermarkets. The study of mixed marriages leads toward the same conclusions. Erich Rosenthal's work on the subject[13] caused a sensation. Even those who dispute the application of his conclusions to the United States as a whole do not deny the rapid growth of mixed marriage in the third generation (i.e. the second born in the country). According to Rosenthal, the children of at least 70 per cent of mixed marriages are lost to the Jewish community. Among members of the third generation who receive a university education the rate of mixed marriages is double that of the rest; in Washington, for instance, it rises from 17.9 to 37 per cent. The picture as a whole is gloomy. As suggested in a penetrating article by C. Bezalel Sherman,[14] the American Jew tends to make his "Jewishness" an aspect of his "Americanism." A curious piece of evidence of this trend is provided by the "Jewish funeral scandal," denounced by Rabbi Samuel Dresner in his 1963 book *The Jew in American Life*; the mortician industry, "conspicuous waste" applied to the whole funeral ceremony, has got the better of American Jews, who are more American

[13] Based on investigations in Iowa, Greater Washington and Chicago. *Cf.* "Acculturation Without Assimilation? The Jewish Community of Chicago," *American Journal of Sociology*, November 1960; and in particular his summing up in the *American Jewish Yearbook*, 1963.

[14] "Emerging patterns and attitudes in American Jewish life," *American Journal of Sociology*, V, No. 1, June 1963, pp. 47-54.

than Jewish in this, since according to the Law and the Talmudic tradition funerals should be austere.

All this points to the American-Jewish community's being the source of few emigrants to Israel but of many visitors of all types, from the son of Senator Jacob Javits, who came from New York accompanied by his father to plant trees on the occasion of his *bar-mitzva*, to noisy small shopkeepers from the Bronx or Brooklyn and the young idealists who kneel on the ground at Lydda airport to touch the soil of the Promised Land for the first time. There are millionaires who write out a magnificent check for a worthy cause and never return again because, as the daughter of one of them explained to me, they then think they have done their duty. There are all those—and they are legion—who build synagogues and *yeshivot*, endow the Bar Ilan University and encourage an orthodoxy they have abandoned in their own country. What most of these otherwise so incongruous visitors have in common is a conformism that one should not be too quick to describe as hypocrisy, memories of and nostalgia for the "Jewish life" of their childhood, a clumsy and moving search for a dream that is often disappointed by reality.

Among the younger generations family ties with Israelis grow weaker, and personal memories of traditions grow dim. To the extent that American Jews lose their Jewish identity they will be less tempted to turn to (and help) Israel.

Since 1948, whatever their motives may have been, their contributions to most sectors of the economy and the cultural institutions of Israel have been enormous. Sometimes, considering this little state and the multiplicity of problems, conflicts and divisions in this (very limited) "gathering in of the exiles," I wonder what would have happened to it, in spite of the heroism of the pioneers, without the financial and political support of American Jewry, that amalgam of more than five million individuals, nearly all of whom are comfortably off and many of whom are rich and influential, still loosely attached to a Judaism that has many grades of meaning to them. Looked at from this point of view, certain current aspects of Israeli society seem to be projections of the loyalties, nostalgias, bad conscience and material success of the Jews of America. It is understandable that in their relations with the Israelis there should be plenty of occasions for friction and misunderstanding.

IS THERE A JEWISH PEOPLE?

The disappointment of Americans at the failure of their search for the people of the Bible brings us back to two questions that recur on many pages of this book: Are the so-called "Jewish" inhabitants of Israel still Jewish? Is there a "Jewish people" of which Israel is part?

These are questions on which everyone can contribute his own piece of valid testimony and claim the last word, and they can be discussed ad infinitum. Frequently they set emotion rather than reason to work. The thoughts that follow also arise out of personal experience and do not claim dogmatic truth.

All observers are struck by the diversities and contrasts of the Israeli population, which stems from one hundred and two different countries. The reaction of American students who arrive with a belief in the existence of a "Jewish people," which they lose in contact with the realities of Israel, is significant. They feel no sense of "unity" with a Jew from Cochin or Yemen, or even from Morocco. The "unity of the Jewish people" is a pragmatic concept that to some is part of a mystique deriving from a messianic vision and to others is a plank in a political platform for buttressing the state.

Deportations to Mesopotamia created a Jewish Diaspora as early as the eighth century B.C. At the beginning of the sixth century, the end of the Kingdom of Judah, following that of the Kingdom of Israel, led to the dispersion of the twelve tribes in the Caucasus, Armenia and particularly Babylonia. This began twenty-five centuries of tribulations, racial mixtures through the conversion of Gentiles and mixed marriages, and biological, social, psychological and cultural influences of all sorts, at the end of which one may well ask in the name of what criterion (race? religion? nationality?) it is possible to speak of the Jews' "unity" as a "people." We will return to the part played by pagan anti-Semitism, which was intermittent and unco-ordinated, and Christian anti-Semitism, which was systematic in degrading Jews, forcing them to turn inward and shut themselves in isolated communities, thus maintaining, reinforcing and even creating many of their religious traditions and cultural traits, whose importance I do not underestimate.

There were continually changing links of reciprocal causation between anti-Semitism and Jewish particularism (which was originally essentially religious).[15] The Jewish particularism that was the origin of and pretext for Christian anti-Semitism was for centuries reinforced and congealed by it in the ghettos. The progress of the Enlightenment, the development of democratic, industrial societies, led, broadly speaking, to a diminution of anti-Semitism and favored assimilation, which Zionist or religious partisans of Jewishness today regard as one of the gravest dangers that threaten it. The modern revivals of anti-Semitism, in particular the pogroms in Tsarist Russia and the European catastrophe perpetrated by the Nazis, should not be allowed to obscure the general trend.

The idea of a Jewish race has been demolished by the anthropologists. During my visits to Poland between the two wars, I remember my surprise at the frequency with which big, fair or red-haired men with blue eyes, their pale faces framed in ringlets, wearing long black coats like the throng of "little Jews" all around them, were to be seen in the alleyways of the Jewish quarters of Warsaw, Lodz, Czestochowa or Bialystok. Many Jews from Poland as well as Bessarabia and the Ukraine are descended from Slavs or Tatars, converted to Judaism under the military and political influence of the Khazars, who were masters of a great empire on the Dnieper from the sixth to the tenth centuries and embraced Judaism themselves. (Similar con-

[15] Jules Isaac has made a careful analysis of these links in *Genèse de l'antisémitisme*, Calmann-Lévy, Paris, 1956.

siderations apply to Jewish communities in China and India, which originated from the conversion of Chinese and Indians and not from the deportation of Jews from Palestine.) Centuries of inbreeding and of psychological and social segregation in the Polish ghettos gradually gave these offspring of converted Gentiles the cultural and often even the physical traits of the Jewish "race."[16] Their descendants, freed from all these determinisms, complexes and constraints, may be seen in the free society of Israel today. I defy an anti-Semite with the most highly

[16] Social, economic, linguistic and spiritual (religious) factors are so strong in combination that they can mask, change and sometimes totally obliterate the original ethnic factors properly so called. Hence the transformation of converted Slavs and Tatars into "typical" Polish or Ukrainian Jews. The age-long withdrawal into themselves of Jewish communities in the ghettos left its mark, both physically and morally. These multiple and profound effects were accentuated by inbreeding and natural selection (which, in the special circumstances of Jewish history, meant the elimination of the weak), the limited ways of earning a living open to Jews, their education and their dietary and religious traditions. Anthropologists have not yet studied the appearance of physical, psychological and social traits in the Jews of the ghetto and their sudden change among their children and grandchildren in the *yishuv* and now in the state of Israel. Work on immigrants by Israeli anthropologists, which is incidentally often very remarkable, for example, Elisabeth Goldschmidt's *The Genetics of Migrant and Isolated Populations*, Department of Zoology, The Hebrew University, 1963, has been devoted to the biochemical and genetic aspects of diseases. In the United States social anthropologists in a wider field have taken an interest in the changes observable among the descendants (second and third generation) of Jewish immigrants.

Léon Poliakov has made a solid and sensitive survey of these problems in the appendices to Vol. I of his *Histoire de l'antisémitisme*, Calmann-Lévy, Paris, 1955: Appendix A, "L'origine des juifs vue à la lumière de la sérologie groupale"; Appendix B, "La formation et la transmission des traits 'différentiels' juifs du point de vue de la biologie contemporaine," which includes the following finding (pp. 317–318) concerning physical traits: "It is absolutely impossible to track down a single one that occurs with sufficient frequency to be described as characteristic. The legend about the Jewish 'type' or 'look' is certainly very tenacious, and in its way it reflects an objective reality; but this reality corresponds to certain socially or vocationally determined psychological attitudes, ways of behavior, mimetics, if you like, the 'acquired' characteristic of which is indisputable."

Harry Shapiro, who studied the morphological characteristics of Jews in various countries, comes to similar conclusions (*The Jewish People, a Biological History*, UNESCO, Paris, 1960, pp. 66–82).

developed "flair" to recognize the "Jewish type" among the majority of young *sabras* of Polish origin on the campus of the Hebrew University in Jerusalem, or coming away from lectures at the Technion on the slopes of Mount Carmel, near Haifa. The "characteristics" of the "Jewish race" have evaporated in a few decades. The powerful tide of economic, social and cultural transformation has swept away pseudo-biological inevitabilities. A new people is being created every day in Israel; a young people that is neither an appendage nor the center of the now-legendary "Jewish people."

Can the Jewish people be described as a nation? The Jews have never constituted a national community in the usual sense of the term, and it is difficult to identify such a thing in their case. To the orthodox, "national survival" means the survival of Jewish particularism, which in the Diaspora is threatened with extinction—physical extinction in times of persecution and crisis in certain countries or, in other conditions, extinction by assim-ilation, "reformist" disintegration of the Mosaic and Talmudic tradition, and mixed marriage. Some acts of religious obser-vance—most notably the eating of *matza* at Passover—are also and above all demonstrations of belonging to a community, but not to a nation. Each ghetto was necessarily a polyvalent society that had to respond to all material and spiritual needs of its members. If the Jews had had the feeling that they constituted a nation, they would not have waited for Herzl and the end of the nineteenth century and the development of the Zionist move-ment to call for the creation of a Jewish state.

Toynbee notes in this connection "the contrast between the Diaspora's steady success in surviving—in spite of penalizations, persecutions and massacres—and the unsatisfactory character of all attempts since the Babylonian Captivity to re-establish a Jew-ish state on Palestinian soil."[17] It was anti-Semitism and politi-cal and economic insecurity, not the attraction of a community,

---

[17] Arnold Toynbee, A *Study of History*, Oxford University Press, 1961, Vol. XII, Ch. XV, p. 484, quoted by Raymond Aron in his penetrating article on "Les Juifs et l'État d'Israël," *Figaro littéraire*, February 24, 1962.

that led to the great waves of immigration to Palestine. This is why most of the Poles and Russians went there, and also the Germans of the fifth *aliya*, and, after 1948, the Egyptians, North Africans and other Jews from Muslim countries; the same applies to the small-scale emigration from South America today. Conversely, it is the lack of anti-Semitism and economic difficulties in the United States that explains why American Jews do not migrate to Israel. In the Soviet Union, the combination of persistent anti-Semitism and (in spite of some improvement) the poor standard of living of many Jews would induce a large number of them to go to Israel if they had the chance. The civil, cultural and moral integration of so many western Jews into their host countries—which is an indisputable fact—would have been impossible if a Jewish national consciousness had existed among them. That is why the double citizenship permitted by the state of Israel only delays the inevitable choice that faces immigrants from certain countries.[18]

The state of Israel is becoming a nation in the full sense of the term, with all a nation's characteristics, including, in the case of many *sabras*, nationalism. But it is not reasonable to conclude from this that the citizens of Israel are Jews "because they recognize themselves as a separate people which is creating its own history."[19] In fact the majority of them reject the principal cultural trait that for a long time held together the communities of the Diaspora, that is to say, religious observance, which was considered the whole basis of Jewish life. There is no Jewish nation. There is an Israeli nation. The state that came into existence as a result of Herzl's prophecies is not a "Jewish state." The Israeli state is creating an imperious national community that is conscious of itself, but does not include in that consciousness belonging to a "Jewish people."

[18] In accordance with the Nationality Law passed on April 1, 1952 as a corollary to the Law of the Return (May 15, 1949), Israel consents to the double citizenship of all immigrants of whatever origin. This is not granted by all the countries from which they come. Among those that accept it are France, the United Kingdom, Belgium, Switzerland and the United States (this list is not exhaustive).

[19] Saul Friedländer, reply to R. Aron, *Figaro littéraire*, March 10, 1962.

There seems to be a widening gap (among the extremist zealots it is an impassable abyss) between the part of the population that sees itself as essentially Israeli and the part, consisting of the orthodox, that regards itself as essentially Jewish.

Finally, without overstressing the point, there is the obvious impossibility of defining the "Jewish people" by religion. This is demonstrated by the divisions, dissensions and decline of religious Judaism, and the detachment from it of a large part of the population. Clericalist efforts to assure the survival of the "Jewish people" in Israel by confusing synagogue and state are doomed to failure.

In the Diaspora the Jewishness of the assimilated Jew is to a large extent (we will return to this later) ultimately maintained only by non-Jews who consider him a Jew. It is from them that his Jewishness derives all the increasingly fluid and disintegrating content and reality that it still possesses. Thus the part played by family names indicating Jewish origin is of capital importance; it is often his name alone that identifies and differentiates the Jew. Hence also the importance of the kind of "differentiation" of which he is the object. Between 1940 and 1945 this "differentiation" covered the whole gamut from the Nazi killing mania to the aid (a reaction inside Christianity against the anti-Semitism that it did so much to foster) charitably and fraternally and sometimes heroically given by Catholics and Protestants, priests and laymen, during the occupation and the resistance.

Any differentiation, whatever form it takes, tends to maintain the Jew in his difference, to prolong his Jewishness, slow down his progress to complete assimilation in the society of which he is a citizen. At the root of the "making" of the Jew lies anti-Semitism. "Since the Jewish religion has ceased to be a living reality to the Jew, the history of the Jews can no longer be the history of a religious movement but—the cultural message being a fiction—at most the history of a condition undergone by atomized, individual Jews. The history of the Jews becomes the history of those who make them Jews, the history of anti-

Semitism."[20] Assimilation can become total only when anti-Semitism ends, and with it the "making" of Jews. The basic and essential condition for that is a change in the attitude of the Christian churches (the beginnings of which are taking place before our eyes) and of hundreds of millions of men and women whom they fashioned from generation to generation and for century after century by an "education in contempt."[21] This has diminished, but deep traces of it survive. The Diaspora tends toward assimilation like an asymptote; it is impossible for it to be reached completely in the foreseeable future.

On the other hand, is the different and powerful effect of the Israeli crucible not producing rapid assimilation? Immigrants from the four corners of the earth are caught up in a new climate, a new society, a new world. They have rapidly to master a new language, undergo a period of military training that is a carefully devised instrument of simultaneous civic education and national integration. Many of them, particularly Ashkenazim, give up surnames that reveal their origin in the Diaspora and assume Hebrew or Biblical names that are typical of the young community. In the early editions of his famous little book Herzl advised the future Jewish state to permit a "federalism" of languages among its citizens, but he seems later to have changed his mind."[22] Nowadays the use of Hebrew is an essential condition of citizenship, of full recognition by the environment, of integration. The state pursues this policy methodically and exerts strong pressure toward Hebraization. Anyone who does not speak Hebrew is either a recent immigrant, a tourist or a temporary visitor. I very much doubt whether the government will encourage the French-speaking Jews from North Africa to

[20] *Ibid.* Friedländer, who is an Israeli, believes that the Jews form a "people." In his view, the solution to the dilemma of the Diaspora in a not-distant future will be for some total assimilation (which is an admission that for them the idea of the "Jewish people" is without content), while for others it will be "full acceptance of the fact of the Jewish nation," that is, emigration to Israel.

[21] To use a striking phrase coined by Jules Isaac, who used it as the title of his last book (Fasquelle, Paris, 1962).

[22] *Cf.* the evidence on the subject produced by his Hebrew translator, Berkowicz, *Zeitgenossen über Herzl*, Brünn, 1929.

preserve French as a language of culture. Most of the young Moroccans or Tunisians whom I met in Israel were being Hebraized at full speed. The influx of so many French-speaking immigrants has not led to proportionate reinforcement of French teaching in Israeli schools. On the contrary, during my visits to Israel I heard it argued in official circles that young North Africans "preferred learning English as a foreign language." The way things are going, it will not take more than two generations for families of Moroccan origin to have forgotten French totally in favor of Hebrew.

The "gathering in of the exiles" is also a vigorous remolding process, accompanied in many cases by detachment from religion. Hence the bitter feelings of orthodox Jews about a society that is too secular for their taste and that exercises many influences that, in their view, are destructive of Judaism. There is a great deal of truth in the caustic saying that in Israel the *olim* are more or less rapidly turned into Israeli patriots, "Hebrew-speaking Gentiles," about whom there is nothing Jewish except the memory of their origin. When the distinctions and prejudices against the "orientals" have been overcome, there will be nothing to prevent the assimilation of immigrants from becoming complete. Another saying current in certain circles is also intelligible in the light of this assimilation; the atheist *sabras* are described as *physically saved but spiritually lost:* saved by the Promised Land, delivered from hatred and persecution, but lost, or at any rate gone astray. That is what the orthodox think of all those Israelis who have ceased believing in the God of Abraham, Isaac and Jacob, and no longer follow His commandments.

ASSIMILATION AND DOUBLE ALLEGIANCE

Let us add to this rapid survey of great problems some reflections that may prevent misunderstandings.

Regarding "Jewishness" as the product of a sum-total of historical circumstances in which anti-Semitism plays a primary role, stating that reaction to anti-Semitism creates a feeling of (real or potential) interdependence among Jews, is not equivalent to reducing Jewishness to purely negative qualities. Interdependence prolongs the religious and social characteristics that distinguished Judaism at the time when its isolated communities were religiously observant and intensely alive. All religious Jews proclaim the existence and eternity of the "Jewish people," which are co-substantial with their faith. But in Israel there are also atheists and scientifically minded rationalists who proclaim their membership in a universal community. They are generally older men, *vatikim*, and in their case the feeling is a natural, spontaneous result of their sense of interdependence. Among the young, however, this sense has to be stimulated by education. "Jewish consciousness" has to be inculcated into them in the classroom, they have to be given lessons on the Jewish past, and it remains to be seen how successful these lessons will be. The relaxation of affective ties with the Diaspora among *sabras* is a fact of profound significance.

In the last resort, then, is it not the fate of the Jews of the present day to have to choose between two forms of assimilation? According to the leaders and theorists of Zionism, the greatest present threat to the "Jewish people" is neither anti-Semitism nor economic discrimination, but assimilation. "Assimilation has become the great danger since we left the ghettos and the *mellahs*," Nahum Goldmann told the leaders of the World Zionist Organization on March 16, 1963.[23] The Arab press hastened to draw the conclusion from this that "Dr. Goldmann regrets the ghettos."

---

[23] *Le Monde*, March 18, 1964. There is no doubt that assimilation is progressing. A solidly documented study by Moshe Davis, director of the Institute of Studies of Contemporary Judaism at the Hebrew University, of the three chief communities in the Western Hemisphere, those of the United States, Argentina and Canada, shows that the feeling of Jewish self-identification is on the whole continuously declining in them, particularly among the young. The probability of mixed marriage increases with acculturation ("Centers of Jewry in the Western Hemisphere; a Comparative Approach," *The Jewish Journal of Sociology*, June 1963).

In an article in the Lebanese newspaper *l'Orient* that appeared under the headline "Let Us Listen to Mr. Goldmann" its editor, René Aggiouri, wrote: "Which should one admire more, cynicism or ignorance? Mr. Goldmann calmly proclaims the danger of liberalism. The people of Israel were better off in the ghettos. Since the West has ceased to be anti-Semitic, the Jew is threatened; and Israel is his last refuge, his last ghetto. . . . Mr. Goldmann offers the Arabs the most decisive arguments against Zionism: the racist argument, the religious argument, the demographic argument. He gives them proof that the decision of the Church to revise its teaching on the Jews is in accordance with Arab interests, since it testifies to the liberalism that Mr. Goldmann denounces and hastens the assimilation that alarms him. Everything in the development of the western and Christian world is moving in favor of the Arabs and against Israel, provided the Arabs know how to make use of it: the end of anti-Semitism, the liberalism of the Church, the condemnation of racism. . . . Will the Arab governments understand this?" These intelligent comments suggest a new policy for the Arab governments. But under Nasser's influence there is little chance of their accepting it in the real context of their conflict with Israel.

It is true that in the course of centuries the ghettos "produced" Jews who lived a fully Jewish life, which itself excluded all danger of assimilation. I frequently noticed outside the *kibbutzim* that Ashkenazim, generally veterans, reacted positively to any piece of news indicating anti-Semitism anywhere in the world. They emphasized it, and tended to magnify its importance. The same individuals reacted negatively (and sometimes aggressively) to any piece of news indicating that Jews were living a normal life in any country of the Diaspora without being worried by anti-Semitism. These attitudes are much less marked among the Sephardim, and I never encountered them among *sabras*. No doubt there is a psychoanalytic explanation. Many *vatikim* of European origin preserve more or less conscious affective ties with their countries of origin, and *have* to justify their choice of Israel. But nowadays, if a Jew of the

Diaspora goes to Israel wishing to flee the assimilation that is undermining his Jewishness, is he not fleeing from Scylla to Charybdis? Many orthodox Jews in Israel proclaim that a new and mortal danger to the most sacred traditions of Judaism is now arising in the Promised Land, namely, the assimilation of Jews by the state of Israel, that is, "Israelization."

Obviously in these circumstances meetings between Israelis and Jews from the Diaspora often lead to talking at cross-purposes or degenerate into sharp disputes. Misunderstandings like those that arise between Israelis and American Jews who are summoned to Israel but do not listen to the call occurred, though on a smaller scale, in November 1963, on the occasion of a conference of French Jewry, another community threatened with "being completely engulfed by assimilation" in the course of the next two generations.[24] It is paradoxical that Israelis want to revive Jewishness among the Jews of the Diaspora at the same time that powerful, convergent influences are tending to destroy it in their own society. To be sure, Israelis consider the Diaspora the *galut*, "exile," and they believe that by immigrating to Israel, which puts an end to exile, Jews would rediscover their essential Judaism, the eternal Jewish homeland, the only one that can ever be fully theirs. But there can be no dialogue between the two kinds of assimilation, and attempting it actually involves the risk of laying bare profound differences. The interlocutors are never "on the same wave length," as the representatives of the Algerian Jews said after their conversation with Levi Eshkol when he expressed to the delegates of the Algerian community whom he received at the Israeli Embassy in Paris on July 2, 1964, the Israelis' bitter disappointment at their having chosen to settle in France instead of Israel.

Does double citizenship or "double allegiance" offer a way out of these difficulties? In the face of the danger of assimilation in the Diaspora, Zionist leaders have broadened their claims. Goldmann, their spokesman, has recently stated that the prin-

---

[24] *J.P.W.*, November 1, 1963. The conference was organized by the World Jewish Congress.

cipal struggle of the Jews henceforward is "not for equality—we have obtained that—but for the *right to be different*."[25] They must in his view struggle to acquire that right and resist the encroachments of national sovereignty that has taken brutal and intransigent forms. This is necessary, not only in the Soviet Union, where the Jews are an oppressed minority, but also in the countries of the free world, where many wrongly believe "that the state in which they live has the right to require their absolute loyalty." They too are faced with the problem of double allegiance, although "there are many who are unwilling to admit its existence and consider belonging to a world Jewish people unpatriotic."

Goldmann does not pause to consider the reality of this feeling of "belonging," or whether it is possible for a sovereign state to agree to some of its citizens' recognizing Israel as the center of their allegiance, or the insuperable juridical and moral difficulties created by the relations between "double allegiance" on the one hand and the "absolute loyalty" that the Israeli fatherland claims of its members on the other. He declares that no Jewish community will survive unless, over and above the "superficial" ties of capital investment and philanthropy, it attaches itself to Israel by cultural, religious, affective and moral ties, as well as others of a new kind still to be discovered. He goes so far as to quote as an example of excessive and unacceptable interference by a state with the rights of its own Jewish nationals the inquiry conducted by the United States Senate Foreign Relations Committee into the activities of the Jewish Agency[26]; and he claims that, if Jews do not accept the "cen-

---

[25] Speech to the Second World Congress of Jewish Youth, August 5, 1963. The italics are mine.

[26] Since the president of the World Zionist Organization made these statements, the State Department in Washington has clarified its position. In a letter addressed to the Council for American Jewry and published by the latter on May 7, 1964, it recognizes the state of Israel as a sovereign state and the citizenship in that state. It recognizes no other sovereignty or citizenship in this respect. It does not recognize any political or legal relations based on any religious identification of American citizens. It makes no discrimination between American citizens on the basis of religion. Consequently it should be clear that

trality" of Israel and abandon their right to double allegiance it will be equivalent to a consecration of "Jewish isolationism," which will be the "beginning of the end" for the Jewish communities of the world.

"Double allegiance" is merely an attempt at a compromise from which no practical solution can emerge. At heart its advocates believe it to be no more than a first step toward immigration to Israel. Many Israelis will never admit that it is sufficient for the Jews of the Diaspora to maintain "cultural, religious, affective and moral" ties with it. I have seen attempts at "double allegiance" made in Israel by French and American Jews whose sincerity and moral integrity are worthy of the highest respect. Their moral and professional situation is uncomfortable, however, and in the long run they will not be able to go on sitting between two stools.

In the last analysis the existence of the state of Israel seems to leave the Jews of our "second twentieth century" only two alternatives, not three, in the matter of national allegiance:

(1) Those who are "Israel-centered" must go there, become citizens of the young state, take an active part in its construction and devote themselves wholeheartedly to the success of the experiment.

(2) Those who are not Israel-centered and do not believe that the "Jewish people" constitute a national community must be citizens of the state in which they live, like any others, having only one allegiance and one country, however great their sympathy with and interest in Israel may be. They must, of course, enjoy full liberty to practice their religion. It is up to the Jewish religion, if it has the strength, to maintain intact among them loyalty to its great traditions.

the State Department does not consider the concept of the "Jewish people" as a concept in international law. This statement satisfied the Council for American Jewry, according to whom Judaism is a religion and implies no adherence to any national community.

9

The End of the Jewish People?

I

YAD VASHEM

On the way back from Jerusalem toward the mountains of Judaea, beyond the hills of Givat Ram and the flower-filled campus brimming with youth, of the Hebrew University and not far from Mount Herzl, where lie the remains of the prophet of the Jewish state, there stands at Yad Vashem, the monument to the martyrs and heros of the Holocaust. It is on a magnificent site with a view of the whole city as far as the Holy Places. To make it a tribute worthy of all that is recalled, to the heart and mind, by the sudden and brutal or slow and agonizing death between 1940 and 1945 of six million Jews, 1,800,000 of them children under fourteen, in prisons, ghettos, cattle trucks, forests, camps and gas chambers, was an almost superhuman task.

The builders of Har Hazikaron succeeded, however. On a rectangular site on a vast, paved terrace, they let stone and metal speak. Huge boulders from desert wadis were hewn to build the walls, and iron bars and barbed wire from the concentration camps were melted down to provide the jagged decoration of the great doors. The choice of materials, the pitiless rigor of the forms, the mass and bareness of the stonework surrounding the grotesquely shaped metal, resolve the violence and nightmare into an unforgettable act of testimony facing the pink hills under the blue sky. The interior is no less impressive. Once through the heavy door, in the semi-darkness of a hall

with the same stone walls, lit by a single torch, one sees the
great, irregularly placed paving stones, each of which, black on
white, bears the name, in Hebrew and in German, of a death
camp.

Close to this monument is a research center whose task is
to collect documents and all possible information about both
the massacre and Jewish resistance in Nazi-occupied Europe. According to the law that established it, Yad Vashem, frustrating
Hitler's purpose of wiping the "accursed race" from the face
of the earth (his "final solution of the Jewish question"), was
required to trace the name of every man, woman and child
who died during that period, "to record in the land of their
forefathers the memory of all the members of the Jewish people who perished . . . and perpetuate their memory." This is
an immense task that becomes more difficult with every day that
passes.[1]

Yad Vashem was a shock that caused me to think as never
before about the anti-Semitism with which I was first brought
face to face in the Polish ghettos between the wars.

Confronted as often as I was in Israel by reminders of the
catastrophe in the person of survivors from Nazi-occupied Europe, ex-members of the resistance and relatives of victims, I

---

[1] Arieh Kubovy, the chairman of the executive committee of the Yad Vashem
Foundation, in December 1962 (*Yad Vashem Bulletin*, No. 12) expressed his
fear that, in the absence of a vigorous campaign to rouse public opinion and
greatly increased funds, the objective might not be attainable. In June 1964,
during my second visit, a million and a half victims had been identified, but it
was not expected that it would be possible to go much beyond that, for the
following reasons: (1) from May 1944 onward the Nazis did not have time to
register the names of new arrivals at the death camps; at Auschwitz during
certain periods arrivals numbered from 10,000 to 15,000 a day; (2) a large
number of Jews died on the journey to the camps; (3) there was a large
number of very young children about whom it is impossible to trace details;
(4) a number of European Jewish communities (about 30,000) were totally
obliterated, leaving no survivors and no records. In spite of these difficulties, the
foundation has done an enormous amount of work, collecting millions of
documents, reproductions, microfilms, a library of 35,000 volumes on the history
of anti-Semitism, complete documentation of the Nuremberg trials, the Eichmann trial, etc.

am, of course, far from the only person to ask myself these questions: How was this methodical massacre, unique of its kind on this scale in the history of human society, possible in the twentieth century? How was the social and psychological environment in which it was perpetrated and tolerated produced? And I was brought back to the question of anti-Semitism by daily observation of the Israeli people, seeing (in spite of the reservations I have mentioned) what Jews have turned into in a few decades when, delivered from all the constraints of the ghetto, they are able to work, live and die in freedom.

THE DEICIDE PEOPLE

How, among peoples impregnated with the doctrines of Christianity for two thousand years, was it possible for a mentality, a sensibility, an intellectual and affective environment to exist that made possible the Jewish massacre during the Second World War? To those who, over and above all *raisons d'Etat* or *raisons d'Église*, are guided by a desire for truth, the answer is clear, and it is beginning to dawn on an increasing number of Christians, both Protestant and Catholic, even including certain dignitaries of the Roman hierarchy. Christianity worked indefatigably over the centuries to make the Jews odious by attributing to them collective responsibility for the death of Christ. In a Europe in which political and ecclesiastical power were closely linked, it inflicted on them the rigid and degrading rules of the ghetto which, particularly from the end of the eleventh century onward,[2] produced a pathological human con-

[2] M. Bernhard Blumenkranz, whose work on medieval Jewish history is authoritative, has demonstrated the importance of the "key date" of 1096, traditionally considered as having opened the period of the Crusades. From the twelfth century onward references to Jews in documents and literature are "the image of their new condition, of the greatest abjection." Henceforth they are characteristically referred to as *Iudei intoxicatores, Iudei cremati, Iudei occisi,* "Jewish poisoners, Jews burnt, Jews put to death." (*Juifs et chrétiens dans le monde occidental,* publications of the École Pratique des Hautes Études, Section 6, Sciences économiques et sociales, Mouton, Paris and The Hague, 1960, pp. 390–391).

dition deprived of the most elementary rights, primarily the right most essential for normal development of the personality, freedom of choice of work; and it made "education in contempt" and hatred systematic, official and consistent.

"The accusation of sole responsibility for the death of Christ, to the exclusion of the Roman soldiers and officials, who were completely exonerated, was worked out in the first centuries."[3] It is impossible, because of its sheer length, to draw up a list of authors who, from Leo the Great in the fifth century onward, reiterated that Pontius Pilate and the Roman soldiers acted in spite of themselves, in the course of their duties, while the instigators, those really responsible, were the Jews. From this was deduced the whole inexorable future history of the Jews, whose tears and suffering were just punishment for the crime committed. The doctrine of *felix culpa* formulated by St. Anselm served only to establish even more solidly the necessity of deicide in the divine economy of salvation. "The sin of the Jews," he wrote, "has enriched the world; for, if they had not crucified the Lord, the cross of Christ, the resurrection and the ascension would not have been preached throughout the world."

Jules Isaac's work on the origins of anti-Semitism could not fail to clash with Christian ways of thinking and feeling that had been preserved and transmitted for centuries and had entered into the Christian subconsciousness. It shocked the champions of "eternal anti-Semitism," to whom we will return. But although it has been criticized by theologians and specialists on secondary points and questions of method in the name of this or that school of contemporary history,[4] its basic conclusions have not been shaken: "Jesus had against him the leaders of Judaism, the high priesthood, the orthodox, the notables, a number of Pharisee doctors, and to the end he had for him the

---

[3] *Ibid.*, p. 269.

[4] Principally the *formgeschichtliche Schule* of K. L. Schmidt, Bultmann and Dibelius, to whom the "form" of a narrative makes it possible to discern the objective of the narrator, which was not historical but religious and was bound up with the life of the early Christians and their Church.

popular masses, at any rate in the limited field (Galilee and Judaea) in which he exercised his ministry. The majority of the Jewish people, which was already dispersed at the time, had never even heard of him. It is a challenge to truth to present the Jewish dispersion as 'providential punishment for the Crucifixion.'"[5]

It is another one to present the Jewish people as "deicides," although the allegation has been millions of times repeated since the beginnings of Christianity. Cardinal Bea, addressing the Vatican Council on November 19, 1963, after deploring an "ancient anti-Semitic tradition which is extremely strong in the Church," said: "Nazi propaganda has been effective, and has even insinuated itself among Christians. It has therefore been necessary to re-establish the truth. Let us not forget that the majority of the Jewish people did not agree to kill Jesus. Only a minority cried 'Crucify him!', and the princes of the Jews, in order to prevent a rising among the people, did not wish to put the Lord to death on the sabbath day. Thus the Jewish people is not a deicide, as certain Catholics claim."[6]

But it is true that the content of Christian teaching—spread (in spite of their differences) by both the reformed and the Roman Churches—was "the primary and permanent source of anti-Semitism, like a permanent, powerful stock-root on which all the other varieties of anti-Semitism grafted themselves."[7] Education in contempt, a weapon originally forged by the fathers of the Church in the sixth century and gradually perfected and popularized, was a theological creation, a combative reaction against the few handfuls of intransigent Jewish opponents who

[5] Jules Isaac, *Genèse de l'Antisémitisme, op. cit.*, p. 339.

[6] Henri Fesquet, report of the seventieth Congregation of the Ecumenical Council, *Le Monde*, November 21, 1963.

[7] J. Isaac, *op. cit.*, p. 338. The racial anti-Semitism of the Nazis, which was associated by them with a kind of neo-paganism but was also of economic and social origin, could not have been so successful among the German masses if the soil had not been prepared for it for centuries by Christian anti-Semitism, and the people had not been impregnated with conscious and unconscious anti-Jewish feeling.

engaged in "missionary competition"[8] with the young religion, which was already in a majority. These opponents claimed to be the only real "people of the Bible," the Bible on which Christians also took their stand. By the condition imposed on them they were turned into debased "witnesses" of the Passion of Christ and thus served as a powerful aid to the spreading, understanding and propagating of Christianity at a level within the compass of the masses.[9]

To throw light on the sources of anti-Semitism I suggest that a scientific team, trained in the methods of "content analysis" (which makes it possible to go a long way in the analysis of a text and the detection of the more or less secret and unconscious intentions behind it), should study representative samples of manuals used in seminaries, catechisms and sacred histories still published and issued by the ecclesiastical authorities in both town and country in France, paying special attention to accounts of the Passion and commentaries on it.[10] The same task could be done in Italy, as well as in Britain, where a Catholic writer, Barbara Ward Jackson, in an article entitled "Christians and Jews: Rooting Out the Fatal Myths," recently wrote: "Christian attitudes to the Jews are all too often fixed in childhood by a reading of the Gospels in almost primitive terms of 'goodies and baddies.' The Jews reject Jesus. Caiaphas cynically

---

[8] Blumenkranz, *op. cit.*, p. 337.

[9] [Rereading *Don Quixote* while working on this book, my attention was caught by the passage in which Sancho Panza pleads his cause with future historians: "It is true I am somewhat sly, and I have certain marks of the rogue, but it is all covered over with the great cloak of my simplicity, which is always natural and never artificial; and if I have no other virtue than that of believing, as I always have believed, firmly and truly in all that the holy Roman Catholic Church holds and believes, as well as that of being, as I am, a mortal enemy of the Jews, the historians ought to have mercy on me and treat me well in their writings"] (Part II, Ch. 8, Samuel Putnam's translation, Viking Press, New York, 1951). Is it not significant that Cervantes at the beginning of the seventeenth century should put these words into the mouth of an illiterate peasant?

[10] A first and courageous attempt to carry out this objective, using the methods of traditional scholarship and from a theological angle, is that of the Rev. Father Paul Démann, *La Catéchèse chrétienne et le peuple de la Bible*, with a preface by Cardinal Saliège, Cahiers sioniens, Paris, 1952.

hands Him over to the Roman power. Judas betrays Him for money. The crowd howls that His blood will be upon them and their children. These simple images of treachery and violence invade the childish mind with the force of myth. Unconsciously the Jew is seen as evil."[11]

There can be no denying that oceans of poison have been spread for centuries in millions of books and sermons bearing the ecclesiastical *nihil obstat*, from the most obscure manuals to the eloquent sermons of great preachers, from learned histories to essays by worldly and conformist men of letters, creating the anti-Jewish subconscious of the more or less Christian masses.

To illustrate this I think it not unuseful to quote three passages picked from a mass of others no less characteristic. They were written centuries apart, the first two by a famous preacher and the third by a contemporary essayist:

"It was the greatest of all crimes: a crime hitherto unheard of, that is, deicide, which was also the occasion for a vengeance the like of which the world had not yet seen." "The ruins of Jerusalem still smoking from the fire of the divine wrath. . . . O, the redoubtable wrath of God Who destroys all that He strikes! . . . It was not only the inhabitants of Jerusalem that You wished to punish, but all the Jews [when the Emperor Titus laid siege to the city the Jews had gathered there to celebrate the Passover]. . . . Certainly You remembered, O Lord, that it was at the time of the Passover that their fathers had dared to imprison the Saviour; You made them pay for it, O

[11] *The Observer*, London, August 18, 1963. Mrs. Jackson rightly draws attention to the importance and effectiveness of the myth of the "traitor people" in the affective dissemination of anti-Semitism among Christians. Education in contempt is based on two main pillars, the *deicide* people and the *traitor* people. The role of the "Judas myth" in the Dreyfus case is familiar. Here are two samples, chosen among many others equally significant: Maurice Barrès: "That Dreyfus was capable of treason I conclude from his race"; *Civltà Cattolica*, Roman organ of the Society of Jesus, February 5, 1898: "The Jews were created by a special decree of Providence so that traitors should never be lacking to noble causes." (*Cf.* Rabi, *Anatomie du judaïsme français*, Paris, 1962, pp. 74–75.)

Lord, and at this same time of the Passover You imprisoned
in their capital their children, the imitators of their stubbornness.
What words could depict their rage, fury and despair; and the
prodigious number of dead that lay in the streets without hope
of burial, their rotting bodies exhaling poison, pestilence and
death. . . . Divine justice needed an infinite number of victims;
it desired to see eleven hundred thousand men lying dead . . .
and after that again, pursuing the remainder of that disloyal
nation, He scattered them over the earth. And why? For the
same reason that judges, after having had malefactors broken
on the wheel, order their severed limbs to be exposed at various
places on the highways, to frighten other evil-doers. The comparison fills you with horror, but the Lord behaved more or less
in that way . . ."

"Because of this profound wisdom of God, the Jews still
survive in the midst of the nations, among whom they are
dispersed and captive. But they survive with reprobation upon
them, visibly fallen because of their infidelity to the promises
made to their fathers, banished from the Promised Land, having no land to cultivate, slaves wherever they are, without
honor, without liberty, with no status as a people. They fell
into that state thirty-eight years after they crucified Jesus
Christ."[12]

"God in His justice granted this last wish of the people whom
He had chosen ('May His blood be upon us and upon our
children'). Throughout the centuries, in all the lands in which
the Jewish race is scattered, their blood is upon them, and the
death cry uttered in Pilate's judgment hall covers a thousand
times repeated cry of distress. The face of persecuted Israel
fills history, but it cannot obliterate that other face, covered
with blood and spittle, for which the Jewish mob had no pity.
No doubt Israel could not be expected not to kill its God after
failing to recognize Him, but nor can Christian charity perhaps
be expected to feel that in the secret equilibrium of the

[12] Bossuet, *Sermon sur la bonté et la rigueur de Dieu* (preached at Metz in
1652), and *Discours sur l'Histoire universelle* (1679).

divine will the horror of the pogroms does not compensate for the insupportable horror of the crucifixion."[13]

The liturgy itself, particularly that for Easter, is full of anti-Jewish animosity, to which it has contributed. The celebrated Good Friday prayer, *Oremus et pro perfidis judaeis,* has led to a great deal of controversy about the meaning of *perfidia,* but the congregations who fill the churches are not Latinists, and the term "perfidy" is definitely pejorative in the context of their education. At all events, it was very ill chosen, and the abolition (since the eighth century) of the genuflection for this *oremus* alone accentuates its offensive character.[14] As for the Reproaches, the words of which are of great beauty and are sung on Good Friday after the prayers, they are still capable of instilling poison into people's hearts. In them Jesus reproaches the "Jewish people," as a collective entity, for its murderous ingratitude while attributing to Himself the sole merit for the blessings lavished on Israel by God, including the mission of Moses:

> I fed thee with manna through the desert: and thou didst smite me with blows and curses.
>
> I gave thee to drink wholesome water from the rock: and thou gavest me gall and vinegar.
>
> For thy sake I smote the kings of the Canaanites: and thou didst strike my head with a reed.
>
> I gave thee a royal scepter: and thou didst put a crown of thorns upon my head.
>
> I raised thee up with mighty power: and thou didst hang me upon the gibbet of the Cross.
>
> O thou my people . . .

[13] Daniel-Rops, *Histoire sainte, Jésus en son temps,* Paris, 1945, p. 526. The author modified this passage in later editions (1948, p. 534). The three above texts are quoted by J. Isaac, *Jésus et Israel,* Paris, 1948, pp. 369–370 and 382.

[14] In the liturgy for Holy Week introduced under the pontificate of John XXIII as the result of the latter's personal intervention, the word *perfidis* has been eliminated from the Good Friday service (March 27, 1959) and the *Oremus pro judaeis* was given the right of genuflection.

It is not surprising that anti-Jewish feeling should survive in the popular subconscious even in an age when religious practices are declining.[15] It provides political leaders with scapegoats on whom they can always fall back in times of difficulty. In Poland, where the Jewish population was reduced from two million in 1939 to about thirty thousand in 1945, there were still traces of virulent anti-Semitism fifteen years later among an ill-nourished and ill-clothed population controlled by an inefficient bureaucracy. In Warsaw in 1959 I heard the remark: "If things go wrong, it's because there are still too many Jews in the party and the government." In the Soviet Union the signs of anti-Semitism have been numerous in many fields: the obstacles put in the way of the principal observances (such as the use of *matza* at Passover); the publication of anti-Semitic pamphlets; the publicity given to and the severity of the sentences, even going as far as capital punishment, inflicted at trials for "economic crimes" (speculation, black marketeering, and embezzlement at the expense of the state, etc.).[16] Israeli statesmen, observing the fate of Jews in the Soviet Union, note that proletarian revolutions do not solve the "Jewish problem," an argument Ben-Gurion uses to press with redoubled vigor for the wholesale return of Jews to Israel. "Hatred of the Jews has not vanished and will not vanish so quickly—it will last until the day when the majority of our people are reunited in their liberated original home and its security is assured."[17]

[15] Its survival is favored by a number of expressions in the spoken or written language. In the provinces I heard a young country girl complaining that her brother—who, she said, had "pinched" her camera—was "very Jewish." From this point of view the English language is much richer, as is shown by Webster's Dictionary. The phrase "to jew somebody" is characteristic.

[16] A recent addition to a long series of anti-Semitic publications was an especially virulent pamphlet by T. Kichko, *The Naked Truth about Judaism*, illustrated with insulting caricatures, published at the beginning of 1964 under the aegis of the Kiev Academy of Sciences, which led to vigorous protests by western communist parties. The condition of the Jews in the Soviet Union is well documented in a periodical bulletin, *The Jews in Eastern Europe*, 31 Percy Street, London W1.

[17] Speech on the twentieth anniversary of the Warsaw ghetto uprising, April 21, 1963.

Use of the Jew as a political scapegoat has long since spread to the Arab world. Ben-Bella did not shrink from having recourse to it (a sad performance on his part for his friends of the French left). In April 1963, he announced the discovery, followed by about thirty arrests, of an "underground" in Kabylia, the outcome of a "plot" said to have been hatched by a highly incongruous mixture—Israel, the "imperialists," "certain Marxists" who happened to be of Jewish origin, and Boudiaf, who was vice-president of the Algerian provisional government in the war against the French.[18]

AGONIZING REAPPRAISAL?

Indoctrination in contempt and hatred continued for nearly two millenniums, and its effects cannot be wiped out in a few years. No one who during the occupation fought shoulder to shoulder with men and women of all types and conditions and origins can ever forget those admirable Christians, whether priest or lay, Catholic or Protestant, who at the peril of their lives practiced the recognition of man by man and remembered nothing of the Bible but the commandments of love and charity. They bore witness to (and many of them sacrificed their lives for) the necessity of an agonizing reappraisal. They proclaimed that the time had come to make a vigorous effort to eliminate the

[18] Press conference by the Minister of Information, Algiers, August 14, 1963. Partial historical studies of the Muslim attitude to Jews throughout the centuries show that there was no Arab anti-Semitism comparable to that of Christian origin. According to some orientalists (G. E. von Grunebaum, *Mediaeval Islam*, Chicago, 1946), tension between Muslims and Christians was for a long time greater than that between Muslims and Jews. L. Poliakov well describes the differences that from the first characterized the relations of Islam to the great monotheist religions from which it took its inspiration (*Histoire de l'antisémitisme*, op. cit., Vol. II, and in particular pp. 72–77). J. Madaule emphasizes the importance of the 1918 turning point in the development of the Arab world and its influence on the dramatic context out of which the state of Israel was born (*Les Juifs et le monde actuel*, Paris, 1963, pp. 130–131, and the chapter on "Jews and Muslims").

poisonous germs. They launched an appeal that will re-echo until it has been heard by the princes of the churches, who were (for the most part) mute during the sinister period when their voices would have made a tremendous impact. "I belong to the nations who persecuted the descendants of the prophets," a Protestant philosopher writes. "Even if I personally was not involved in the crime, I share the responsibility of the states, the Churches, the sociological Christianity, guilty of the massacres, deportations and tortures that have blazed the trail of Israel since its dispersion and are a decisive factor in its awareness of itself as a people exiled far from the real Land."[19]

Here is the voice of another writer, this time a Catholic,[20] faced with Jules Isaac's *Jésus et Israel*: "There is something so shattering in a first reading of the twenty-one propositions that make up this book that it is impossible to keep silent when Israel utters such a cry of anguish. The author is often right; it is actually shocking that he could be so right, and it would be just as shocking not to try to answer him, because many of his indictments of us are, I fear, the same as those that an infinitely more powerful Judge than he will one day pronounce against us. For it is useless to try to evade the fact that we Christians are nearly all responsible, in degrees that vary mysteriously between one soul and another, depending on their lights, and the torment of Jesus continues day and night in the world."

The Jewish tragedy of 1940–45 would not have been possible without the millenary policy of degradation and contempt, and in the eyes of a growing number of Christians this constitutes a stigma to be wiped out. In Europe under the Nazis brave deeds were done by Christians, both priests and lay, and also by some high dignitaries of the hierarchy.[21] But the Catholic Church has only very inadequately defended the silences of the Vicar of Christ in the face of the imminence and actual

---

[19] Paul Ricoeur, *Esprit*, June 1958.
[20] Julien Green, "Journal," in *Revue de Paris*, June 1949.
[21] Outstanding among those known to me personally was Mgr. Saliège, Archbishop of Toulouse, who comforted many hearts and awakened many consciences.

carrying out of the Nazi crimes. It is true that the documents
now available to historians make this an extremely difficult
task.[22]

In changing the Good Friday service, and above all in supporting the ecumenical movement which, among other things,
involves a change in the attitude of the Church toward the
Jews, John XXIII opened the floodgates and provided the impulse. Will the Secretariat for Christian Unity, of which
Cardinal Bea is the leading spirit, get the better of the resistances that at the end of the second session of the Ecumenical Council in November 1963 secured the removal of Sections
4 and 5 of the schema on ecumenism relating to the Jews and
religious liberty? Is this only a provisional retreat in the face of
political considerations dictated by the opposition of the Arab
countries whose bishops have become their spokesmen in the
council? Cardinal Bea emphasized in advance, when he distributed the documents and then presented them, that they were
strictly religious in character and that there was nothing either
"Zionist" or "anti-Zionist" about them. The second session of
the council set out on a path of temporization, *raison d'Église*
and compromises similar to those that motivated the silences
of Pius XII. Was Catholicism going to miss a striking opportunity of making the great reappraisal of its attitude toward
Judaism? Following the resistances we have mentioned, a new
version of the declaration on the Jews was presented at the
third session of the council and debated on September 28,
1964. It was drafted in vague terms, representing a substantial
retreat from the first version. It did not exonerate the "Jewish
people" from the crime of deicide (this term was no longer
used), but instead emphasized the Church's "unshakable hope"
of the conversion of the Jews; this deeply offended believers
in the Jewish religion. Finally yet another version, forming part
of Schema No. 8, "On the attitude of the Church toward non-
Christian religions," the inspiration of which recalls the first
version, was accepted by a large majority on November 20,

[22] See pp. 301–305 for a note on the "Silences of Pius XII."

1964. This was confirmed at the fourth and final session of the Council on October 15, 1965. The hesitations and haggling to which the declaration on the Jews led show the stubbornness of the obstacles encountered by the Church in its internal struggle with anti-Semitism. The necessary preliminary to winning this struggle is withdrawal of the charge of deicide and modification of Church teaching about Jesus and the Passion of Christ; it is "the beginning of everything," as Pastor Charles Westphal, president of the Protestant Federation of France, has well said.[23] But this, although necessary, is not enough; it constitutes only the negative aspect of the reappraisal. The relations between the two religions will have to be reconsidered in depth, their positive aspects disclosed, the minds of the young impregnated with the knowledge that Judaism was the source of Christianity, and all the consequences at all levels must be drawn from the celebrated saying of Pius XI that "spiritually we are all Semites."

Is it not true, as Barbara Ward Jackson said, that the catastrophe of 1940–45 imposed on all Christians of all denominations an examination of conscience carried out in all humility? According to what for a long time was official doctrine, the whole Jewish people was responsible for the crucifixion, and Pilate washed his hands of the crime. "Indeed the last tragedy in Europe is a crucifixion on such a scale that it should have burnt out forever any complacent confidence among Christians that, had they confronted the dilemma of a Caiaphas or a Pilate, they would have avoided their ignominy."[24] The second Vatican Council has confronted the Catholic Church and all its faithful with a dilemma. The future alone will show whether a millenary political prudence has yielded to the imperative of an opening to the world and the demands of truth.

[23] Cf. his statement after a visit to Israel, *Le Monde*, April 11, 1963.
[24] *The Observer*, London, August 18, 1963.

II

JEWS AS THE PRODUCT OF HISTORY

Since the beginnings of the Diaspora, the Jews progressively formed less and less of a "people," a reality based on ethnic and national characteristics and even (in our time) only on a common attachment to traditions, beliefs or religious practices.

Before the Diaspora, however, there was a Jewish people, whose origins and beginnings of sedentary life we can nowadays follow with a considerable degree of certainty, thanks to the progress of archaeology and biology and critical study of the Pentateuch (which was set in train with admirable clarity by Spinoza in his *Tractatus Theologico-Politicus*). It is possible to observe the development of its religious institutions and its legal code impregnated with health rules and moral principles.[25] In or about the eighteenth or seventeenth centuries B.C. nomadic Semitic tribes, whose long migration corresponds to the mission of Abraham, traveled from the region of Ur of the Chaldees to that of Aram-Naharaim, or "Syria of the two rivers," to the northwest, between the Euphrates and the Balykh, the religious center of which was Harran, where the moon-god was worshiped. One or two centuries later another migration of these tribes occurred, this time to the west of the Euphrates and then to the south, to the land of Canaan, where they took the name of Hebrews (Ivrim, "those from beyond" the Euphrates). They seem to have settled peacefully among the indigenous populations, whose language they spoke and at whose shrines they worshiped. Some of the Hebrews settled and remained in the land of Canaan.

One of the tribes, called the "Children of Israel" after one

[25] We owe a great deal to the fine edition of the Old Testament published by Edouard Dhorme (Gallimard, Paris, 2 Vols., 1962) and to his introduction, Vol. I, pp. xv–cxxvi.

of its ancestors, went down into Egypt in or about the fifteenth century, no doubt to seek pasture for its flocks. At first it enjoyed the favor of the Pharaohs (the story of Joseph) but then, under the nineteenth dynasty, was reduced to slavery. In the thirteenth century, before the time of Rameses II, the tribe began its exodus toward Sinai under the leadership of Moses. Moses gave the people the Law and the worship of Jehovah. According to the evidence of the stele of Pharaoh Menephtah,[26] their arrival in Transjordania and Canaan took place in approximately 1232–1225. They conquered the land of Canaan by force of arms, aided by tribesmen of the same origin as themselves who had been living among the indigenous population for several centuries,[27] and settled there under the leadership of Joshua and the Judges. The unified kingdom of the Hebrews lasted for barely a century (from about 1020 to 932), from Saul to the death of Solomon. It split into the kingdoms of Israel and Judah, of which the former collapsed in 721 with the capture of Samaria by the Assyrians, and the latter in 597 with the sack of Jerusalem by Nebuchadnezzar. The twelve tribes were deported to the Caucasus, Armenia and in particular Babylonia, and disappeared[28]; and with them the Jewish people in the plenitude of its existence as a simultaneously ethnic, national and religious community also disappeared forever.

Henceforth, even during the ephemeral restoration of the Kingdom of Judah under the Asmonean dynasty (from 168 B.C. onward) most Jews were dispersed in more or less developed communities far from the Holy Land; and from this time on-

[26] The reading of the hieroglyphic inscription "Israel" has, however, been disputed (cf. André Neher, Moïse et la vocation juive, Éditions du Seuil, Paris, 1956, p. 67).

[27] This coming together of various tribes of Hebrews in Canaan in or about the twelfth century is important. It explains in a rational and plausible manner how a united Jewish people arose out of human groups from very different cultural environments; some Jewish theologians regard this as an "enigma" or "miracle."

[28] Among the members of the second of these groups (descended from the tribes of Judah and Benjamin), were believers in Jehovah whom Cyrus permitted to return to Palestine, where they rebuilt the Temple of Jerusalem at the end of the sixth century.

ward the notion of a "Jewish people" is closely bound up with the reactions provoked by attachment to the Mosaic law of the communities of the Diaspora in Egypt, Alexandria and other big Greek cities, and later in the Roman Empire. The Jews practiced an essentially religious separatism deriving from the Torah and the observance of the commandments and their sacred ritual; hence the mistrust and hostility to which they gave rise. These lie at the roots of pre-Christian anti-Semitism. (In Egypt after the Hyksos tyranny it was nourished by a secular hatred of Asian invaders, who were generally Semites; in other words, by an "anti-Semitism" in the proper sense of the term, that is, far wider than merely anti-Jewish.) From the first century B.C. onward these reactions were reinforced by Jewish resistance to Hellenization at the religious level and by the success of Jewish proselytism. The manifestations of pagan anti-Semitism in Egypt, the Hellenist world and the Roman Empire appear at a date much later than that attributed to them by those who maintain that "anti-Semitism is eternal, as old as Judaism itself,"[29] and take a form that clearly marks them off from Christian anti-Semitism. "It was generally a spontaneous reaction, and was only exceptionally directed and organized," while the Christian variety kept alive by the Church was from the outset official, systematic, consistent and "pursued the very definite aim of making the Jews odious."[30]

I have no desire to underrate the importance that attachment to the Torah played for centuries in the Jewish communities of the Diaspora. As I have said, Jewish separatism was originally essentially religious. In historical reality actions and reactions intertwine, leading to a "spiraling" causality. The religious separatism of the Jews caused hostile reactions, which mingled with

[29] Christian and Jewish "extremists" join in maintaining theologically and often passionately the eternity of anti-Semitism; the former in order to exonerate Christianity more or less completely of its responsibilities, the latter to confirm their mystic belief in the "difference" of the Jewish people called on in spite of everything to await the fulfillment of the divine promises.

[30] Marcel Simon, Verus Israël. Étude sur les relations entre chrétiens et juifs dans l'Empire romain (134–425), Paris, 1948, p. 263.

those spread by the "education in contempt," nourishing and aggravating them. The latter, in turn, by setting up a wall of discrimination around the Jews (which extended to imprisoning them physically and morally in the ghetto) implanted in many of them a traditional loyalty rooted in these constraints. From many points of view the ghetto explains the religious history of Judaism, particularly certain characteristics of Hassidic mysticism. It was anti-Semitism, viewed as a whole, that encouraged fierce attachment to the Law, assured the survival of the Jewish consciousness, Jewish "difference," Jewish solidarity, which are the essential content of the idea of the "Jewish people" in the Diaspora. Without the persecutions, without the ghetto and its various forms and surrogates, the Jews, dispersed through the nations but taking part in the evolution toward political liberties and "enlightenment," would have been assimilated more rapidly and completely, as they have tended to be in the West since the end of the eighteenth century. Their separatism, fading with the weakening of its religious roots, would have ceased to make them "different," "alien" and suspect. Anti-Semitism produces Jewish feeling and is responsible for Jewish survival,[31] but Jewish separatism has helped it and (to the extent that it is prolonged by anti-Semitism) still helps it at the present day.[32]

Those of many schools of thought who, often from a theological viewpoint (whether Jewish or Christian), talk of the survival of the "Jewish people" in spite of its millenary trials

[31] A correlation has been observed among Jews between their experience of anti-Semitism, its intensity and duration on the one hand and on the other the feeling of Jewish solidarity and the rejection of assimilation (held to be impossible on the reality plane and objectionable on the moral plane). It is the Jews most directly affected by the catastrophe (by personal or family experience) who state: "Jews cannot live in the *galut*," or "Any self-respecting Jew must settle in Israel" (S. N. Herman, Y. Peres, E. Yuchtman, *op. cit.*, Table II).

[32] One of the principal points made by Sartre in his *Réflexions sur la question juive* (Gallimard, "Idées," 1962, pp. 83–84) is: "The Jew is a man whom other men hold to be a Jew; that is the simple truth that must be taken as the starting-point." In the light of study of the relationship between Jewish separatism and anti-Semitism and of the content of the idea of Jewishness and of the feeling of interdependence, this generalization seems to be penetrating but too simple in relation to the complexity of the facts.

and tribulations as a miracle have got things the wrong way about. It is not in spite of but because of anti-Semitism (or, from the point of view of Zionist mysticism or nationalism, thanks to it) that a Jewish specificity has to an extent survived in certain physical, cultural, psychological and even religious respects.[33] The non-existence of the phenomenon of anti-Semitism in Israel leads to the rapid ending of what was held to be an eternal Jewish specificity. To Jewish and Christian believers the idea of the "Jewish people" is a theological notion; to the leaders of Israel and the Zionist movement it is a political one, and to obdurate anti-Semites it is an emotional one.

As for Jews considered as individuals in the countries of the Diaspora of which they are citizens, they are the products of history, that is, of the conditions in which they and their forefathers lived; very varied products, since these conditions—economic, social and psychological—varied greatly, were more or less rigorous and formative in different countries and different times in different communities. Where anti-Semitism fades, Jewish specificity tends to disappear, as has been shown by studies.[34] Where it survives, it expresses itself and desires to express itself only in religious forms. The grandson of a Polish Jew who emigrated to the United States with the heavy, "specifically" Jewish, luggage inherited from the ghetto *may* become an American citizen professing the Jewish faith and practicing religion within the framework of the American way of life. In extreme cases one already meets in the democracies of Europe and America Jews, both men and women, who have no religious beliefs and are so

[33] *Cf.* the current behavior of rabbinical orthodoxy in Israel and its motivation (Chapter 8).

[34] In particular the studies of Jewish communities in the United States, Canada and Argentina commented on by Moshe Davis, *Jewish Journal of Sociology*, June 1963, pp. 14–19. The relaxation of ties with Judaism among Jewish students in Argentina is well analyzed in the report published by the "Primera Conferencia de Investigadores y Estudiosos Judeo-Argentinos en el campo de las Ciencias Sociales y la Historia," Buenos Aires, October 1961. This states (p. 6) that to the Argentinian student "anti-Semitism automatically becomes the mirror of his Judaism. Everything that diminishes or is likely to diminish anti-Semitism automatically affects his Judaism."

thoroughly assimilated to their environment that the only relic
of their Jewishness is their name.

ANTI-SEMITISM AND THE "JEWISH PERSONALITY"

The conditions in which Jews have lived since the distant times
when they really were a "people," the anti-Semitism of varying
degrees of acuteness they faced depending on the country and
the period, the amount of freedom they had to work in fields
of their choice and the degree of political liberty they enjoyed
determined the Jewish "basic personality," its varieties and transformations. What is there in common between the fierce war-
riors going from battle to battle, capable of the most appalling
cruelties, with which the Old Testament abounds, or the com-
panions of the Maccabees, or the indomitable rebels against
Rome who were slaughtered arms in hand by the legions of
Titus, and the somber, busy, anxious throng in long black coats
one saw in Pilsudski's Poland, keeping to the wall whenever they
ventured outside the Jewish quarter? Even then their condition
had greatly improved since the Middle Ages. The immense majority of European Jews are more or less closely descended from
men who lived in the ghetto, the perfection in discrimination
and polyvalent psycho-sociological molding of the individual. At
this point, let us reread a passage in which Bernhard Blumenkranz summarizes his conclusions: "When we think of the appalling situation of the Jews in the Middle Ages, it is the ghetto
that comes to mind, the distinctive badge, the exclusion from a
long list of trades and occupations, accusations of violation of the
Host, of ritual murder, poisoning wells, and the horrible series
of bloodthirsty persecutions that accompanies those accusations;
religious debates carefully organized with a verdict in favor of the
Christian prepared in advance, autos-da-fé of the Talmud, Jews
who were serfs of lords and princes, simple merchandise with no
will or rights of their own, bartered as advantageously as possible
or sold to the highest bidder, Jewish usurers forced into that

form of activity by an economy that closed all other outlets to them and hated and despised for it by all men of good will. They were a type of man whom society had put beyond the pale, exercising pressure for the greater profit of their prince or pressurized themselves at the prince's whim or pleasure, a mere form of currency exchanged among the great, an easy prey to hand over to the base instincts of an overexcited mob overstimulated by pious and bloodthirsty imagery and edifying and terrifying literature."[35]

On the one hand anti-Semitism fashioned the personality of the Jew who is alien to the society in which he lives[36] and is also a strange and evil creature; on the other hand its millenary influence fashioned the mass mentality from which were recruited in the twentieth century the organizers of the massacres and their innumerable followers who perpetrated them or accepted them without demur. Suspect, scorned, segregated, hampered in their working life, the Jews were forced to emphasize their peculiarities in every way. The laws of this complex determinism explain (1) the exaggeration of certain physical features, a bio-social phenomenon observable in isolated communities characterized by inbreeding; the conformity in mimicry, gestures and bearing of Polish and Ukrainian Jews descended from Slavs converted to Judasim is a phenomenon as remarkable as it is indisputable[37]; (2) the exaggeration of certain psychological features well described in the literature of the ghetto, including overdevelopment of the critical sense and of destructive analysis, escapism in dreams, an active imagination (which is peculiar to all minorities in a hostile environment, but among the Jews assumed special features), a cruel sense of humor, self-denigration and denigration of the community to which they belong[38]; (3) an intensification of cultural autarky,

[35] B. Blumenkranz, op. cit., p. 380.

[36] I recently asked a distinguished philosopher, a Jew driven from Germany by the Nazis who emigrated to the United States, what his definition of a Jew was. "A man who feels a stranger everywhere," he replied.

[37] Cf. Chapter 8.

[38] Rejection of members of their own community and hostility to them are characteristic of the internal relations of groups that are the object of dis-

in other words an attempt to find within the segregated community something with which to satisfy all needs, from the prescriptions of the dietary laws to food for the mind, the need for beauty, metaphysical truth, mystic communion with God.

The basic Jewish personality formed by the slow action of centuries does not totally vanish with a change in the environment in which it was born. As long as anti-Semitism and discrimination persist anywhere in the world the sense of interdependence prevents it from vanishing. But it survives most strongly among Jews who go on living "among themselves," prolonging their segregation by the force of inertia in countries in which they could rapidly disappear in the assimilating crucible. This phenomenon is observable in the United States, Canada, Britain and even in France among recent immigrants and the succeeding generation.[39]

If the "Jewish personality" was formed by conditions that breed anti-Semitism, it is bound to be profoundly affected by the disappearance of those conditions. That, as we have seen, is what is happening in Israel. Many young *sabras* already have little resemblance to their parents, and still less to their grandparents. Combatants in the Haganah and Palmah, soldiers in the Israeli army, victors in the Sinai campaign, they say that they feel very different from the Jews assembled in concentration camps by the Nazis and sent "like sheep" to the gas chamber. The phrase I quoted earlier—"they have lost the defects of their parents, but also their qualities"—is no doubt an oversimplification of a deep truth. The intellectual and affective traits that are the good side of Jewish anxiety (which is sometimes carried to the point of neurosis) are disappearing in Israel, together with Jewish separatism. The basic Jewish personality is a

---

crimination and prejudice (e.g. Negroes in the United States). The "anti-Semitism" of certain Jews, their attitude of exasperation about other Jews, has often been noted. The explanation is the internalization of prejudice and self-hatred subtly analyzed by G. H. Mead (*Mind, Self and Society*, Chicago, 1934).

[39] In the new "ghettos" of Canadian or American suburbia the physical togetherness of the Jews does not prevent cultural integration and the decline of Jewishness, as Moshe Davis has noted, *op. cit.*, p. 17.

complex product of the history of the Jewish communities in the Diaspora. In a different "history," in a different complex, a new personality is emerging.

The observer is struck by the speed of this development, which confirms the artificial character of the Jewish personality. It does not, of course, affect all Jewish immigrants to Israel, particularly the old, and when it does, the physical and moral effects are much less noticeable. But on the whole the impact of the experience is tremendous. In the land of Palestine, in a sum-total of geographic, climatic, social, cultural, political conditions profoundly different from those that formed it, the Jewish personality is disintegrating. The "Jewish people" is disappearing and giving place to the Israeli nation.

What a paradox. Israel, which to many practicing Jews foreshadows the fulfillment of the promises made by God to the chosen people, today demonstrates the chosen people's non-unity, non-uniqueness, non-eternity. The Israeli experiment is undermining the foundations of the Mosaic religion.

"Throughout the most diverse manifestations, whether in the case of Moses or Jeremiah, the Pharaohs or the Hassidim, Auschwitz or Tel Aviv, the Jewish testimony is always unique," André Neher writes. André Chouraqui, recalling the work of the historian S. W. Baron,[40] considers that the reunification into a single nation in the Holy Land of "human groups coming from different countries at different periods constitutes one of the great enigmas of history." To Rabbi Zaoui religious faith and collective prayer are "the secret of the duration of Israel, the people of the Bible that has survived all the tribulations of the centuries because of the synagogue and thanks to its prayers."[41]

Belief in the uniqueness and eternal specificity of the Jewish people and its messianic vocation is an article of faith, the basis of a religious attitude. Seeing the Jewish people as a group

---

[40] A *Social and Religious History of the Jews*, French trans. Paris, 5 vols. 1956–64.

[41] André Neher, *Esprit*, February 1958, p. 116; André Chouraqui, *Tiers-Monde*, October–December 1962, *op. cit.*, p. 665; André Zaoui, *Revue de la Pensée Juive*, October 1950, p. 132.

progressively built up out of Semitic nomadic tribes that gradually became sedentary and settled in Palestine, originated monotheism and created the Bible, and then from the eighth century onward was dispersed and subjected to repeated deportations, persecutions, massacres and severe social and psychological conditioning; believing there was nothing "miraculous" in the group's reactions of stubborn resistance and accentuated separatism and nothing eternal in the resulting physical and moral characteristics, especially when these are compared with the results of successful assimilation in modern democratic societies and in the Israeli community—all this is a positivist, agnostic attitude, shocking, I fear, to men such as I have just quoted whose faith I respect and whose courage and noble-mindedness I admire.

But what remains today of the "unity" of the Jewish people? The Jews of the *gola* and those of Israel preserve a link to the extent that anti-Semitism survives, in other words to the extent that their destinies are interdependent, or may be interdependent. The interdependence between a shoemaker in Kiev, an Iraqi worker in the Timna mines, an Argentinian *kibbutznik* in Galilee, a banker in Paris and a doctor in Brooklyn may seem very slender. Nevertheless it exists, actually or potentially, and it was strongly felt at the time of the European catastrophe. Nazi anti-Semitism revived the hazards and the tragedy of Jewish life.

In the twentieth-century Diaspora Jewishness is buttressed mainly by the sense of interdependence. It is because of that sense and the name I bear that I, a citizen of France, who recognize no homeland but France, accept and will to the end of my days continue to accept my Jewishness as a fact of my life, without pride or provocation but also without the slightest embarrassment or shame. It is also because of that sense that in Israel I do not feel a total stranger to a Kurdish patriarch who entertains me at his *moshav* at Nes Harim or a Moroccan barber whose complaints I listen to in a *shikun* at Katamon. So it will be as long as Jews anywhere in the world are considered guilty members of the "deicide people," suspected and decried by some, feared by others, useful scapegoats to many. Changing one's name (which in Israel is done with a view to Hebraization and national unification over and above the different ethnic groups) can in the Diaspora be a powerful catalytic agent of assimilation. To him who chooses this as a final solution of his personal problems or those of his children, to him who has only a minimal sense of interdependence and can ignore it without anxiety or a bad conscience, a change of name is justified. The decision whether or not to have recourse to it depends on him alone.

The expression "Jewish people," when used in connection with the realities of the present day, refers, in an often confused way, to the Jewish community in Israel and the sum-total of all the Jews in the Diaspora. I have stated all the reservations I have about the term. Let us nevertheless use it, attributing to it the various meanings attached to it by religious Jews, Zionists and the leaders of the state of Israel, and ask what are the principal dangers that today and in the immediate future threaten the survival of this "Jewish people."

They are of two kinds, having causes either outside or inside Israel.

III

ARAB THREATS: THE PALESTINIAN PROBLEM

The most obvious of the former is the Arab threat. The Arab states consider themselves in a state of war with Israel, and since 1948 have not ceased to proclaim their desire to throw the Israelis into the sea and wipe their state from the map of the Near East. The agreement proclaimed in Cairo on April 17, 1963, between Egypt, Syria and Iraq on the constitutional basis of a future Arab federation was accompanied by renewed threats to "settle the Palestinian problem" by the destruction of Israel. But Arab unity is fragile, and is liable to frequent and brutal shocks in various countries. Revolutions and bloodthirsty *coups d'état* have taken place, particularly in Iraq and Syria. Never-theless, in spite of divergencies and mistrust, dissensions and even conflicts between political regimes (e.g. between Bou-medienne's Algeria, Nasser's Egypt, Hassan's Morocco, Saud's Arabia and al-Salal's Yemen), Arab unity is making progress, its principal objective and cementing factor being the setting up of a huge anti-Israel front. In this sense the "summit" conference of thirteen Arab heads of state in Cairo (January 13–17, 1964) reinforced it. Only Arab solidarity, the final communiqué de-clared, could serve "the just cause of the Palestinian Arab people aspiring to self-determination and liberation from the imperialist Zionist grip." The first "national Palestinian congress," held in the Jordan sector of Jersualem from May 29 to June 2, 1964, to which all the sovereigns and heads of Arab states (except the Emir Faisal Saud) sent their representatives, proclaimed that the "Palestinian problem will never be resolved except in Palestine and by the force of arms," called on all the Arab chiefs of state to establish military training camps, rejected "all at-tempts to consider the Palestinian problem to be that of the refugees"—that is to say, rejected any solution that would set-tle the Palestinian refugees elsewhere than in their "homeland" and decreed that they should no longer be called "refugees," but "those who will return." A national assembly of the "Organiza-tion of Palestinian Liberation" was to be elected and begin work in 1966.

It is not my intention to estimate the risks of armed con-flict between Israel and the Arab world or to consider their relative military strengths. I mention the Arab threat because of the important part it plays in the background of the country's economic and political life and the daily life of its citizens. Also the official views on the matter that one hears and reads in Israel call for some reservations and criticisms.

It is impossible to stay in Israel without becoming aware of the security problem. The government, the press, the radio, continually remind the country of the permanent threat under which it lives. Israel, it must not be forgotten, is half the size of Switzerland; it has 590 miles of frontier, of which 330 are with Jordan, from which Tel Aviv is only twelve miles distant. The political parties do not all approach the security question in the same way; the Mapam has for a long time criticized the Mapai, and Ben-Gurion, in particular, for making an obsession of it without having fully explored the possibilities of negotiation with the only "possible interlocutor," that is, Nasser. On the occasion of the celebrations of the fifteenth anniversary of the foundation of the state in May 1963, Ben-Gurion and Moshe Dayan, now a legendary military figure, solemnly warned the Israeli people that grave testing times, graver even than those of the war of independence or the Sinai operation, lay ahead.

Israel's political leaders remained astonishingly calm at the manifestation of Arab hostility represented by the proclamation of April 17, 1963, as well as the Cairo conference and the Palestinian national conference. They declared their willingness, in spite of all threats, to work the Jordan waters scheme and maintain the allocations within the limits foreseen by the Johnson plan. They did not seem to regard the prospect of hostilities as close, but made it clear that they would intervene if Jordan (where King Hussein's regime does not fill them with immediate apprehension) came down on Nasser's side. On that point everyone in Israel, over and above all their differences, seemed to agree; Israeli forces would immediately have to occupy the whole area west of the Jordan, and Nasser would have given Israel an excellent opportunity and excuse for increasing its territory, resources and power—and perhaps also of thus ensuring its survival. No doubt that is one of the chief reasons why he has never tried the experiment.

But Israeli statesmen—the veterans as well as the "young"— do not nurse any illusions. A negotiated settlement of the chronic Arab-Israeli conflict presupposes two things: (1) an Arab leader strong enough to be able to impose such a settlement without being accused of treason by a public whose hatred has been fanned for fifteen years; and (2) the "technical" possibility of absorbing the Palestinian Arab refugees who, including those in Egypt, Jordan, Syria and Lebanon, number about 800,000.[42] An Arab federation under Nasser's leadership might theoretically meet these two conditions, but in practice, assuming that Arab unity were achieved under his aegis, when the choice came between peace and war to solve the Palestinian problem, he would be compelled to choose war, for the fragile solidarity of the Arab states is based on a nationalism whose principal cementing factor is aggressiveness against Israel. In the last resort the only thing that can dissuade him from having recourse to arms is the strength of the Israeli deterrent. Hence the necessity of not being outdistanced by him militarily. The slogan for the indefinite future must be *si vis pacem, para bellum*. At least these are the conclusions of an important article published immediately after the Cairo agreements by Moshe Dayan in an Israeli military journal and reprinted in *J.P.W.* (May 3, 1963) on "Arab unity and the Palestine question."

This realistic attitude is the more deeply rooted since the Israelis believe that in the hour of crisis they will be able to count only on themselves. No doubt they will benefit from the sympathy of individuals and discreetly receive moderate amounts of material aid. But the Jews were left to their fate by the leaders of the free world during the Second World War (Churchill and Roosevelt are still often and severely criticized), and again during the war of independence and the Sinai operation; and Israeli leaders have no illusions about the future. The two great powers, drawn closer by the Moscow agreements, will not risk a nuclear war to save the tiny state of Israel.

Is its existence likely to be threatened by the Arabs during the next decade? The present margin of superiority in favor of Israel is, in the view of experts, primarily based on organization, technique and abundance of gray matter.[43] But the relation of

[42] These figures are very controversial, and accuracy is hard to come by. So far as Jordan is concerned, see A. M. Goichon, *Esprit*, July 1964, pp. 168–170.

[43] Israel needs technicians; at present they are in short supply, both in quality and in quantity. The major effort to fill the gap required by economic growth and the integration of the "second" Israel is also essential for the country's security.

forces depends on the international situation, and in particular
on the aid that Egypt receives from the Soviet Union and other
countries; and it will be profoundly affected when the Arab states
have been modernized by industrial development and economic
growth. The time this will take is hard to predict, but the process
is inevitable. If the population of Israel, and its productive capacity, have not greatly increased in the meantime, if it fails
to maintain its scientific and technical advantage and its superior
organizing ability and skill in the use of the latest equipment,
it runs the risk of destruction. The Jews who sought to escape
their persecutors by taking refuge in the Promised Land would
fight to the death, but they would be at the mercy of enemies
who encircle and by their numbers could crush them and they
would be caught like rats in a trap.

Such, in brief, are some of the reactions to the Arab threat
that I observed among the Israeli public and political leaders,
in academic circles, and among militants of the Histadrut.

According to the official Israeli view, responsibility for the
problem of the Palestinian refugees is that of the Arab states
alone, since they gave the Arab population orders to leave in the
first months of 1948. But in spite of the repeated statements
to this effect by Israeli delegates to United Nations commissions,
the assertion seems to be unproved.[44]

Several phases can be distinguished in the war of independence. From November 30, 1947 to the end of March 1948,
fighting on the Jewish side was done by the Haganah, the Irgun
Zvei Leumi and the Stern gang. During the second phase, up
to mid-May 1948, the Haganah, which had become a national
army in embryo, clashed with Arab forces organized under the
leadership of regional military leaders. During the third phase,
from May 14, 1948, and the date of the establishment of the
state, the Israeli army fought the regular armies of Egypt, Jordan,
Syria, Iraq and Lebanon. Broadcasts from Arab countries re-

---

[44] See the solidly documented articles by A. M. Goichon in *Le Monde*,
December 27, 1963 and *Esprit*, July and August 1964.

corded by the BBC and reports of the special political commission and other United Nations documents mention no order of evacuation given by the Arab states or local Arab authorities. On the contrary, it seems that from the second phrase onward the principal Zionist leaders, both political and military, considered a massive Arab exodus to be desirable from the point of view of the future state. The dynamiting of the small Arab village of Deir Yassin, near Jerusalem, on April 9–10, 1948, and the massacre of the whole population (carried out by the Irgun and the Stern gang as a reprisal for the violation of ten Jewish women), was a tragedy that shocked the Arab population. There were other "operations" of this kind at Khissas and Sassa in Upper Galilee. The Israelis can argue that they responded to violence with violence, but in that case, whether religious or not, they forfeit any claim to be a "chosen" people or, more modestly, one "different from others."

Another official Israeli claim is the full equality of its Arab citizens—in social status, political and economic life, educational and vocational training opportunities and benefits of membership of the Histadrut. It seemed clear to me that this full equality neither had been achieved nor was achievable in existing circumstances. It is probably true that the Arab minorities in Israel are "privileged in relation to their fellows in the neighboring countries and in the whole of the Near East."[45] But it is impossible to deny that the Arabs in Israel do not fully share in the building up of the state. As one travels from place to place, one can see (as I did in the Afuleh and Nazareth region) that their land is rarely irrigated. In 1959–60 one-fifth of the arable land (4070 square kilometers) was cultivated by peasants belonging to "national minorities" (Arabs, Christians, Druses), but only one-forty-seventh of the irrigated land (28 out of 1340 square kilometers). In the present situation how many of the 220,000 Arabs in Israel can be expected not to admire the shining figure of Nasser and not to consider him their natural leader? The problem of the Arab minority in Israel can

---

[45] Rezak Abdel-Kader, *Le Conflit judéo-arabe*, Maspero, Paris, 1961, p. 304.

be solved only as part of the Arab-Israeli conflict as a whole. That is no reason why Israel should not do more to turn its Arabs into true citizens of the state. That is one of the principal criticisms of the government made by the Brit Shalom ("Alliance for Peace") group, with which Martin Buber was associated, as well as a number of distinguished scholars of the Hebrew University of Jerusalem.

Does this mean that a return of the Palestinian refugees to Israel could now be envisaged? This has been skillfully advocated in various quarters, in particualr by an Israeli journalist and now a member of the Knesset, Uri Avnery (*Le Monde*, May 9 and 10–11, 1964), and with arguments that at first sight are appealing. But, things being as they are and will remain in the foreseeable future, the proposal breaks down on two points.

It is totally unrealistic to expect the Israelis to admit to their territory a million, or even only a half million, Arab refugees who for fifteen years have been systematically indoctrinated with hatred of Israel. It is also impossible to forecast how many would choose to return, and whether their choice would be free. And even if Israel agreed to this idealistic and humanitarian solution and opened its gates, would Nasser and his "allies" really abandon the project of destroying Israel, which is the mainspring of Arab nationalism? Is the proposal not equivalent to asking the Israelis to commit suicide? Those who would re-admit the refugees are reduced to banking on a "change of heart in the refugee camps as well as in the Arab world as a whole" and relying on the Israeli security services to carry out the formidable, impossible task of "discovering the spies and saboteurs who will try to infiltrate into Israel"[46] during a re-patriation operation in which the numbers involved would certainly reach a quarter and might well reach half of the present Jewish population of Israel. How could the Israelis not be alarmed at such a prospect? With their country under-mined from within by a huge fifth column (a rapidly increas-

[46] Uri Avnery, *op. cit.*

ing one because of the Arab population explosion), how long could its unity and independence be expected to last?

The other rock on which the proposal founders is that it is not desired by the Arab leaders. They want it no more than they want to see the refugees established in their own Arab countries, granted compensation and integrated into a productive life within the framework of an Arab society and culture, which, according to Senator Humphrey's report (1957), is the only realistic way of solving the problem. To the Arab chiefs of state the refugees are an irreplaceable trump card. That is why the question of establishing the historic responsibility for the exodus of the Palestinian refugees is in the present circumstances a question of moral but not of political interest. Alfred Coste-Floret rightly points out that "so long as the Arab leaders aspire, not to a solution of the refugee problem, but to a dissolution of the state of Israel, the settlement of this tragic business is not in sight."[47]

There is no lack of problems nowadays on our planet. The conflict between these two peoples has older and deeper roots than many others. At the "summit" conference in Cairo the Arabs proclaimed "the natural right of the Palestinian people to reconstitute their country" and declared that Israel had no right to exist. The Israeli reply is that the Jews preceded the Arabs in the land of the Bible, that since the sack of Jerusalem by Titus remnants of the Jewish people have always remained there, that, as shown by the Bar Kochba rebellion and the successive flare-ups of the messianic spirit of which that of Sabbatai Zevi is only the most famous, they always aspired to the Return, which was begun more than a hundred years ago by Sir Moses Montefiore's settlements and developed by the successive *aliyot* of the twentieth century. How often in Israel one is brought up against the ebb and flow of history. Nowhere was I more conscious of this than at the Church of the Holy Saviour near Abu Gosh, where on the Biblical site of Kiryat Ye'arim, which for twenty years sheltered the Ark of the Cove-

[47] *Le Monde*, May 31–June 1, 1964.

nant, there is a spring that was used by the Hebrews to water
their flocks, and was then used by Roman legionaries and Arab
herdsmen. The crusaders built their admirable arches there, and
later Mamelukes and Turks and then Arabs again occupied the
site, and now, among the *kibbutzim* and *moshavim* scattered
in the mountains of Judaea, Lazarist priests grow their fruit
trees in the shadow of the French flag.[48] Two peoples of the
same Semitic origin, whose brotherhood extends over three thousand years, now bitterly dispute this land. When will their
confrontation cease? Israel may one day be crushed by the
united, industrialized Arab masses. But also—and this is the
surest hope—modernization among the Arabs may be accompanied by an internal revolution that will make obsolete their
present anti-Israeli fanaticism, which is now a political necessity. "It is only when conditions have been established for the
setting up of real popular regimes in the Arab countries, opening the way to the setting up of such a regime in Israel, that
peace between Jews and Arabs will be achieved and the Jewish-Arab conflict will be finally buried with the last relics of
imperialism in the Near East."[49] But it will also be necessary
for Israel's present mentality toward the Arabs to become obsolete, thus making possible a real integration of the Arab
minority into Israeli society without depersonalizing them. "This
internal revolution in the Arab world, when it occurs, will constitute such a leap forward that the people of Israel will be
bound to complete its own revolution," wrote Rabi in *Esprit* for
April 1962, commenting on Abdel-Kader's book.

But all that, alas, lies in the future. Meanwhile let us admit
that the Jewish-Arab conflict does not involve only disadvan-
tages to Israel. A people relapsing into forgetfulness, tempted
by normalization and the discovery of the "good life," particularly in the urban areas, is constantly reminded of the Arab
threat, and this far-from-imaginary specter puts a brake on
idleness, selfishness and apathy, favors survival of the pioneer-

---

[48] The crusaders' church, with its dependencies, was offered to Napoleon III
after the Crimean War and forms a small French enclave.

[49] A. R. Abdel-Kader, *op. cit.*

ing virtues and fortifies civic solidarity. Paradoxically, in the present situation, it helps the *halutzic* spirit and thus certain essential values of Jewish idealism.

On the other hand, the Arab threat (felt to be more imminent, or less, depending on the situation) forces the government to spend vast sums on defense and also, in order to break its isolation, on costly technical aid projects in various Asian, South American and in particular Black African countries. This weakens the collective sector, encourages compromises with private capital on the economic level and favors the "N.E.P." In domestic politics it also imposes other compromises on the government to ensure its stability and preserve national unity; that is to say, with rabbinical orthodoxy and its clericalist claims.

I have already mentioned the importance of another external danger now proclaimed by the Zionists, namely, the decline of anti-Semitism, which favors assimilation in the Diaspora, the decline of religious practices, and mixed marriage, all of which threaten the Jewish personality at its source. If Israel in the years ahead is to resist aggression by the united, modernized Arab states, it must, in the opinion of its leaders, have about five million inhabitants. But how can that aim be achieved if fewer and fewer Jews throughout the world are attracted to Israel, and fewer and fewer feel even a sense of interdependence and preserve at any rate some traces of their Jewishness?

ISRAELI THREATS: ASSIMILATION AND AFFLUENCE

As for the dangers that threaten the Jewish people with extinction inside Israel itself, we have already met them and need only recapitulate them briefly.

In the first place, the Israeli crucible tends to bring about profound changes in immigrants' Jewishness, disintegrating the traditions of each ethnic group and fusing them into a new complex corresponding to a new nationality. It must be admitted that from their own viewpoint the criticisms of the orthodox are not unfounded. In the Diaspora, assimilation, mixed marriage and the decline of religious practices are the gravest dangers that threaten the "Jewish people" with extinction; and, parallel with this, economic and social development in Israel constitutes a new kind of assimilation liable to produce "generations of Hebrew-speaking Gentiles," Israelis who are Europeans in Asia, no more and no less.

These views, which I heard expressed a number of times in religious circles, call to mind another internal danger—adaptation to the typical attitudes and ways of behavior of a society on the way to affluence, tending toward hedonism on the western and more particularly the North American pattern, precipitating the decline and oblivion of *halutzic* values. There is no doubt that in the towns of Israel we are confronted with ever-increasing psychological and sociological traits characteristic of a technical civilization. Israel seems ready to accept this; many young men in responsible positions in administration and business actually regard the process as desirable without seeing its dangers. In their pleasures and entertainments and style of life a substantial proportion of young people have already been won over by the "models" of the industrialized societies of the west.

In Israel I was often reminded of dangers to which we have been alerted by certain humanist critics of our technological societies. The greatest works of human genius, Homer, Dante, Shakespeare, which have come down to us after surviving centuries of wars, revolutions and dark periods of history might (these moralists say) not survive the transpositions, manipulations, "digests" to which they are liable at the hands of a triumphant and universal mass culture (*Cf.* Norman Jacobs [editor], *Culture for the Millions?* Van Nostrand, Princeton, 1961). Similarly, the people of the Bible, after three thousand years of tribulations and persecutions, may contribute to their own destruction in their recovered home by surrendering to an imperious and undiscriminating mass culture. This is a danger Israel shares with other young nations whose economic growth coincides with a wholesale and (let me add, to avoid any misunderstanding) *necessary* spread of mass communications.

In his address to the second World Congress of Jewish Youth in Jerusalem Nahum Goldmann made an urgent plea for non-conformism, directed in particular to the Jews of the Diaspora. The exhortation might with equal or perhaps even more reason have been addressed to the Jews of Israel, to put them on their guard against their conformism to western mass culture. If the younger generations become deeply impregnated with this during the decades ahead, where will they find the strength necessary for the social advancement of their country, the development and extension of its pioneering institutions, its spiritual influence, the dangerous adventure of its mere existence and survival?

In the eyes of the religious, Judaism has been undergoing a miraculous renascence since returning to its sources. But dangers threaten it. The tribulations of Israel are not yet over. A proportion of its children, putting an end to their exile, have by heroic efforts acquired and built up a place of refuge for themselves. Two million Jews have gathered in Palestine, exposing themselves to new trials and new dangers—not only Arab hatred, but also the new industrial environment that many of them ardently desire and help forward with their own hands, although this may be like pouring water on the fire of the needs of social justice and the prophetic spirit.

Most of the Israeli leaders, whether political or religious, veteran *halutzim* or young *sabras*, over and above all their differences unite in their harsh judgment of the Jews of the Diaspora, whose only future role, in their view, is to serve Israel as the center and spiritual home of Judaism. Perhaps, in view of the preceding observations, they should be more circumspect. The "Jewish people" and the "Jewish spirit" are exposed to grave perils in Israel. Let me quote, for what it is worth, this sally by a young Canaanite intellectual: "The Jewish Agency ought in future to help Jews, not to leave the Diaspora, but to remain in it"—a cruel remark which offers food for thought.

10

Restlessness and Happiness

It is often said that anxiety constitutes both the essence of and
the ferment necessary to Jewish spirituality, that it is thanks
to it that the Jews have made their most important contributions in science, art, mysticism, action, and that there is no
Judaism without it. "Judaism is essentially a self-assumed tragedy"[1] admirably sums up this view of Jewish history. To others,
who do not believe in the eternal characteristics of a chosen
people or the inheritance of characteristics passed on from generation to generation (leading to the differentiation of a "race"),
but only in an age-long molding process by a sum-total of
material and moral living conditions inseparable from anti-
Semitism, and in the transmission and accentuation of certain mental characteristics, anxiety, restlessness, the "Jewish
tragedy," while losing nothing of their positive and creative
aspects, are susceptible of purely rational explanation. But
the rationalist attitude, too, leads to a dilemma: Which should
the Jews choose, restlessness or happiness?

I

RESTLESSNESS?

Understandably, frequent anxiety is expressed in Jewish circles
nowadays about the drying up of anxiety, that precious "poison

[1] Rabi, *Esprit*, June 1958.

injected by history."[2] There are some in Israel who take the opposite view to that of their leaders and hope the Diaspora will not be reduced to the role of handmaiden to the recovered Jewish national home; they want it to remain a fertile and irreplaceable "reservoir of anxiety," having a spiritual value in itself by virtue of its Judaism. Among Israeli poets, at any rate those of European origin, there are signs of fear that, "together with the anxious tension that still animates the most 'modern' Israeli poems,"[3] some of the permanent values of Judaism will weaken or disappear among the *sabras*. One of these poets, David Shimonovitz, suggests,

> Perhaps these children born in the freedom of the Revival
> Have poorer and less lofty souls than the
> Mortally harassed children of the Diaspora.

> ("Drops of Dew in the Night")

It is true that "consciousness of the precariousness of the life" today constitutes the "essential dignity of the Jews."[4] "Paradoxically, when Jews have abandoned everything, their faith and their religion, they still remember the outrage of history. It forms part of their instinctive, collective memory, permanently maintaining an inevitable sense of anxiety, which even the marginal or peripheral Jew receives his share of."[5] Regarded from this angle, anti-Semitism is a kind of involuntary gift made to the Jews by their enemies. We humiliate you, they seem to say, we persecute you, we make you live dangerously, we kill you, but we make you this gift of anxiety, the seeds of which will continue to be sown among your children from generation to generation. They, or at any rate those strong enough to make their anxiety fertile, will thus derive an advantage from their Jewish birth. They will be more likely than others able to stand up to the pressure of their environment, to avoid being

---

[2] Jacques Borel, "La poésie israélienne contemporaine," *Critique*, May 1963, p. 421. *Cf. Poètes israéliens d'aujord'hui*, Albin Michel, Paris, 1960.

[3] Jacques Borel, *op. cit.*

[4] V. Jankélévitch, *Évidences*, December 1950.

[5] Rabi, *Anatomie du judaïsme français, op. cit.*, p. 181.

swallowed up by it, to resist subjection of their minds to external causes (and yet, the skeptical observer remarks, how many Jews today permit their minds to be thus "subjected"?).

Jewish anxiety is a psychological, ethical, social fact, expressed differently according to the spatial and temporal context in which it arises, increases or diminishes. Its manifestations may range all the way from weak and intermittent to typical forms of anxiety and neurosis. A study of the basic personality characteristic of the "Jewish spirit" in the ghettos of Poland or Hungary could, I think, have been successfully undertaken, and such a study might still be undertaken today in the last "closed" Hassidic or orthodox communities, using, with the necessary adjustments, of course, the hypotheses of Kardiner and Linton.[6]

According to these, the frustrations to which the individual is subjected by the physical and social environment in which he lives produce anxieties in him. He attempts to respond to them by security systems consisting of institutions that form one of the principal elements in his basic personality. These are the "institutionalized defenses" that the ghetto offers numerous examples of: its ethico-religious prescriptions, its bans and taboos and strict interpretation of the *halacha*. The deeper and more stubborn the anxiety, the stricter the rules that serve as defense against it.

A plea for anxiety must emphasize that it feeds on dissatisfaction with present reality and seeks something different and better; it is essentially the spirit of wishing for higher things. I know a number of Jews who were criticized for their restlessness at the age of twenty, which was regarded as a fault; but such worthwhile things as they have done in the course of their lives were entirely the result of it. In a civilization in which economic abundance, multiplicity of technical means and dispersion of activity militate against solitude and reflection and extend the "facilities" of material life to moral life, anxiety has a more important function than ever. That is no doubt why

---

[6] A. Kardiner and R. Linton, *The Individual and his Society*, Columbia University Press, 1939; R. Linton, *Culture and Mental Disorders*, Springfield, 1956.

current Christian teaching has exalted it as the "eighth virtue," which "conditions the rest."[7]

Israeli society has made huge strides since the establishment of the state; in spite of all internal and external difficulties, it has entered a period of economic growth and accelerated industrialization. The Jews, Edmond Fleg tells us, are characterized by concern with the terrestrial world, some being attached to life in order to ennoble it, others to exploit it.[8] In Israel the trend toward the ennoblement of life (the idealism of the pioneers, the *kibbutz* movement, Israeli socialism) is now in danger of being submerged by other trends—the desire for "normal" life, the thirst for abundance and happiness. But Jewish anxiety is not dead in Israel. I have heard the situation stated, particularly in Ashkenazi circles, in more or less these terms: In the past sixteen years our work of construction has been rapid and satisfactory in many ways. On the material plane we have undoubtedly made progress. Spiritually we have not kept pace. We bask in complacency at our successes; we try to convince ourselves and others that the thirst for social justice is assuaged by universal access to the goods of a technical civilization, and that the cries of the prophets resounded in the Promised Land to bring us the American way of life.

Israel is on the borders of affluence. And now what? And why? These are the questions asked by Yizhar Smilansky, with other members of his generation. Smilansky is a member of the Knesset, one of the leaders of the "young group" in the Mapai, and author of *Sippurei Mishor* (Histories of the Plain)

---

[7] Cf. the *Bulletin des Conférences de Saint-Vincent de Paul*, May 1963, "The Eighth Virtue, Anxiety," in which the following passage occurs: "There are, as everyone knows, three theological virtues, called faith, hope and charity. Also there are four cardinal virtues, which are strength, justice, prudence and moderation. I do not know to what extent we practice all these virtues. But I fear greatly that there is another in which we are deplorably lacking, and that is the virtue of anxiety. . . . Being anxious means realizing that life is a continuous process of creation, not stubbornly adhering to outworn survivals. Without a certain anxiety it is not possible to believe, hope or love. The eighth virtue conditions the others; it is to be hoped that it will be very strong among Christians of the present day."

[8] *Pourquoi je suis juif*, Les Éditions de France, Paris, 1928, p. 30.

in which he criticizes surrender to the values of security and comfort in the name of creative anxiety. All the answers they have been given so far are, in his opinion, more or less disguised forms of escapism. Should Israelis seek refuge in buying themselves "a good time" and in various forms of "distraction"? And then what? Neither the haven of a quiet corner (or job), nor orthodox religion, which is no longer a religion that *seeks*, nor the religious *kibbutz*, which has not withdrawn into its shell, nor the solidly established *kibbutzim*, offer solutions to the problems common to all "satisfied" societies. "The crisis of our generation is not one of material needs but of the spirit."[9] These questions must be faced, and stupid self-satisfaction fought. "Every man has to take stock of himself, know the truth about himself." How can the questions be answered without a purpose for which one is ready to sacrifice comfort and material benefits? Every man must rediscover such a purpose for himself. This is a spiritual matter. Perhaps in mass society the answers may come from small groups of men, as in the past they came from the mountains of Judaea and the Greek islands. Is tackling this problem an endless task, like Sisyphus pushing the rock uphill? "But one thing is clear, and that is we cannot flee from the question. We can only postpone the time when it catches up with us. Conventional wisdom is not enough for our generation."

So there are still cases of living anxiety in Israel. But how much longer will they last?

II

HAPPINESS?

An apologia for Jewish anxiety cannot be justified unless it is backed by the belief that the sufferings of the Jewish people are, as it were, an essential attribute, demonstrating their eternal

[9] The quotes and summary of Smilansky's views are taken from his statements in *J.P.W.*, November 8, 1963.

vocation and inseparable from the spirituality that characterizes them. The believing Jew is convinced, or wishes to convince himself, of the eternal nature of anti-Semitism, whose absence would mean the relentless advance of assimilation and the end of the Jewish people and the Jewish spirit. The dilemma is clearly expressed by spiritually minded Jews: "Anti-Semitism is a part of ourselves, of our being and our life."[10] This Jewish belief in the eternity and necessity of the Jewish tragedy has its counterpart on the Christian side in the (Augustinian) theological doctrine of the eternal necessity of the Jews as the punished, debased witnesses of the Passion of Christ.

Thus the defense of the Jewish tragedy is conducted more or less consciously and openly. Among those who adopt this attitude and carry it to its logical conclusions are many men deserving the highest respect, who accept and embrace the tragic situation of the Jew for themselves and their families, with all its present and future implications. In other words, they volunteer for their role in the tragedy. But, having paid them this tribute, how can we blind ourselves to how weak and, in the eyes of some, how shocking, this plea for Jewish anxiety is? Against it speak the facts of our time—above all the European catastrophe of 1940–45 and the people of Israel's own experience. Is it not heartless (even if there is a mystique behind it) to want to preserve the poisonous source of Jewish anxiety, that is, anti-Semitism, forever? Is it an acceptable price to pay for the presence among some Jews of spiritual ferments that are alleged to be irreplaceable and unreproduceable by other means? The lesson of the apocalypses of the twentieth century is that in the evil exploitation of technical progress the worst is always possible, and the revival of scientific and technical terrorism like the Nazis' is always to be feared. How can one desire the prolongation of "anxiety" if it involves such terrifying risks? If there were one chance in a thousand that preservation of the Jewish condition in the Diaspora as a self-assumed and desired tragedy might one day lead to another catastrophe, should one

---

[10] Rabi, *Anatomie du judaïsme français, op. cit.,* p. 230.

not do away with the condition as rapidly and effectively as possible, whatever the spiritual "loss" might be?[11]

Similarly, even if (as is by no means certain yet) assimilation into the state of Israel led to the destruction of the traditional values of Judaism and the "Jewish spirit," it would be unreasonable to condemn the Israeli experiment in the name of those values without giving it credit for a tremendous contribution that is by no means inconsistent with them. The state of Israel has rescued hundreds of thousands of men and women, freed them from complexes and anxieties, enabled them to forget appalling memories in action and often in the joy of creation. It has set a whole generation of young people, children or grandchildren of anxiety, on the path of liberty and full personal development. Are the permanent values of Judaism able to flourish only on tragedy? Mosaic religion is not, like certain trends in Christianity, oriented toward unhappy, suffering man— homo patiens (to use a phrase dear to Leibnitz), obliged to suffer physical, metaphysical or moral pain—comforted by Divine Providence in his worst ordeals: each hair of his head is counted "in the best of all possible worlds."

Continuing this line of argument, the defenders of the Jewish tragedy might be taken to task for displaying an excessive contempt for the realities of the modern world. The men of the industrialized societies of the twentieth century, exploiting advances in medicine that prolong human life, in education that informs and qualifies, in techniques that multiply and distribute consumer goods, are being drawn toward the satisfaction of more and more varied material and cultural needs and a conception of happiness whose models are generalized by

[11] A friend, a distinguished biologist of Jewish origin, reminds me in this connection that an historian of science quoted by Robert Oppenheimer has calculated that in the past two centuries the number of scientists in the world has exactly doubled every ten years; in other words, 90 per cent of all the scientists who have ever lived are living now. My friend added: "In any case, in the scientific field the argument that a contribution by the 'Jewish spirit' is indispensable is very weak. It can be dispensed with, and will be increasingly dispensed with in the future."

mass communication. The humanist enclosed in the traditions of a higher culture, the moralist, the mystic, may, each from his own viewpoint, criticize the forms taken by the race to happiness, the gratifications that it seeks, the psychological and moral characteristics that accompany it. Efforts can be made to control the trend, to channel it "upward." But to ignore it is to condemn oneself to empty speculation and vain illusion. Israel, at the present stage of its development, is necessarily affected by the great phenomenon of our time. To the realists, the *sabras* who are technicians and often even more or less technocrats, it seems perfectly normal (and satisfactory) that Israel try to become an economically prosperous society like other prosperous western societies, offering its citizens the same amenities as they. Thus, if the primary aim is the ending of the Jewish tragedy, the paths are already traced. And they are also the paths taken by history since 1945.

On the one hand, we see in the Diaspora the assimilation of an increasing number of Jews, to their country of birth or host country, a phenomenon linked with the decline—whether temporary or lasting—of anti-Semitism.[12] Their exclusive allegiance to their homeland is accompanied by a decline in their religious traditions which are felt and practiced by them in very varied ways.

On the other hand, there is Israel. Those drawn to it by feelings of "interdependence," or motivations of a religious, intellectual, affective, national or economic nature, or often a mixture of them all, those who are "Israel-centered" and regard it as the land and hope of the "Jewish people," will choose to emigrate to it. The state of Israel is the truth to those who consider it a spiritual home and for those who seek a haven. It is the truth to those motivated by faith and those drawn by the urge for survival and the legitimate call of happiness. To these people Israel is the logical and reasonable answer, free of ambiguities and conflicts. Double nationality, double allegiance,

---

12 Except of course in the Soviet Union.

are bastards, provisional solutions, doomed to failure. They also provide food for anti-Semitism by prolonging the particularism of the Jewish condition. Thus there exists in the Diaspora a marginal field for recruiting by Zionist organizations anxious to increase the number of the Israel-centered Jews by education and carefully devised propaganda have a marginal field for recruiting in the Diaspora. But the field is restricted by the fact that there is no obligation of any kind—national, moral or religious—for the Jews of the Diaspora to become citizens of the state of Israel. Immigration to Israel is not a categorical imperative hanging over their heads, like a Kantian law in the starry sky. Those who feel the necessity will themselves have formed and nursed it in the secret places of their minds and hearts.

III

DIALOGUE

So you, too, end by admitting that Israel, caught up in the relentless stream of technical progress, is becoming an industrial society "like the rest." You agree that Jews in the Promised Land, transformed into Israelis and absorbed in the pursuit and possession of physical comforts and mechanized prosperity, and the products of universal mass culture, are losing the best part of themselves and even the memory of their millenary restlessness.

But why not admit that the "realistic" sabras of whom you speak go too far? If their views triumph, it means, I am convinced, the end of everything precious and irreplaceable in Judaism. Fortunately technocrats do not yet prevail in Israel and even if they came to, all would not be lost. Thanks to the conditioning that made them, there have always been good "detectives" of spiritual problems among the Jews. In Israel itself there are already those who feel that the prosperity and affluence toward which people are hurrying, this technical progress that fascinates them, are not ends, but means. But means to what end?

The young state is faced with happiness. There is less and less worry about men's material destiny. The kibbutzim are becoming increasingly comfortable, places of withdrawal if not of retreat. The Histadrut will soon be offering everyone the security of the welfare state from the cradle to the grave. Worry is concerned with the settlement and integration of new immigrants. It is relative, provisional.

Those who hoped that, having shaken off the anxieties of the Diaspora, the Israelis would become idealists, missionaries, "artisans and guardians of the universal doctrine of justice, charity and peace,"[13] *have, alas, been sadly disappointed. Others who seek the answer to the spiritual crisis of Israel in standarized prosperity and mass culture are blind. The affluent society will kill the spirit of Judaism as surely as a new idolatrous cult. It will be the death of all that is fertile and vital in the Jewish spirit. Communities of "happy," satisfied people, fashioned, in Israel and the Diaspora, by the environment of a technical civilization and conditioned by it, having lost all prophetic impulse and messianic inspiration, will represent no more than the corpse of Judaism. A Jew surrounded by abundance and press-button amenities, dozing in the daily monotony of prosperity, is no longer a Jew.*

This is not the fact. We have not got to that stage. Travel through Israel and look at its factories, its new towns growing in the desert, its Herculean labors to irrigate the Negev, the *shikunim* packed with orientals, the hard and dangerous daily work done in the new *kibbutzim* and *moshavim* on the frontiers. Israel is not yet dying of abundance. There is still a struggle to satisfy the elementary needs of recent waves of immigrants and to push the frontiers of the Third World back beyond those of Israel. Moreover, you yourself saw signs of a new restlessness among certain Israelis that force you to admit that the race to happiness has not entirely stifled what you call the "Jewish

[13] André Zaoui, *Le Figaro Littéraire*, March 10, 1962.

spirit." Above all, you are overlooking a latent anxiety, more or less under control and repressed, that fills Israel today, from Dan to Eilat—the Arab threat. Every day hatred of the state of Israel is instilled into millions of men, and the Arab leaders proclaim their intention of wiping it from the map and annihilating the Jews in a struggle which the latter (again abandoned to themselves) will one day have to fight at odds of ten to one, perhaps twenty to one. Israel without anxiety? What a bitter absurdity.

Also I deny your assumption. The Jews, while accepting technical progress and its material benefits, cannot renounce the better part of themselves. Perhaps Judaism in history has been a self-assumed tragedy. But I will never admit that henceforth it can survive only as a tragedy desired by its victims. There are many currents in the rich stream of Judaism: Pharisaism, which has been so unfairly treated; Hassidism, which communicates with God in joy; and the Davidian tradition, that symphonic opening to happiness, life seized and enjoyed in all its splendor of the senses and the spirit. Sadness and self-withdrawal are products of the Jewish condition imposed by history.

Even if you accept and secretly desire a precarious life, a "tragic" situation for yourself and your children, take care not to underrate the need for happiness felt by thousands of other Jewish children, sons and daughters of survivors of the castastrophe, grandchildren of the ghetto, those who have escaped from the Jewish condition. In spite of your honesty and your commitment, in the face of the realities of our time you run the risk of making yourself look like an aesthete of anxiety. Man, after all, was made to develop his body and soul. Have the Law and its doctors ever denied that? If the sacred books contain attacks on certain gross forms of pleasure, they must be placed in their historic and prophetic context.

Your "happiness" stifles all ambition among the young except personal and family interests or the demands of the new nationalism—which in our eyes is vain, anachronistic and contrary to universal values. It stifles the spirit of self-sacrifice. You de-

plore the withdrawal of Judaism into its shell, but it is you who consent to it and organize it in the selfishness of the affluent society. Judaism will survive only by permanently rediscovering its messianic ardors.

You are asking too much. Can the young state of Israel live and propagate a universal ideal while conducting a bitter daily struggle to feed, clothe, house, educate and integrate its immigrants, exploit its resources, ensure its security and build up a society in which consumer goods are fairly distributed? Some of the best minds in Judaism have admitted the necessity of restraining the messianic spirit for a few generations to enable Israel to concentrate on its work of construction.[14]

In other words, desiring the end of the Jewish tragedy does not mean desiring the end of the "Jewish spirit." It seems inconceivable to me that everything possible should not be done to avoid another Auschwitz. Judaism is an historical accident, whose spiritual fruits have for the past twenty-five centuries been paid for at a high price—an infinity of sadness, misery, suffering and bloodshed. To me that price seems exorbitant and monstrous, whatever your arguments may be and at whatever level you may place them, and I reject it as vigorously as I reject your assumption. Happiness does not necessarily destroy what is precious and irreplaceable in the "Jewish spirit."

We do not speak the same language. To me your conception of Judaism as an "historical accident" seems cheap and revolting. That "accident" was also the 3000-year history of a religion, a faith that remained unconquerable in spite of everything and everybody, a multiform spiritual quest at the highest level of man.

Throw away your cold analyses, cast off your sociologist's clothing and I do not know what else besides. Look into your heart, Jew, since that is what you still claim to be. Are you capable of watching without a qualm the disappearance from the world scene of an "accident" whose uniqueness and vicissitudes

[14] Gershom Scholem, *Sabbatai Zevi and Sabbatianism*, Jerusalem, 1957 (in Hebrew).

*have in the course of the centuries produced men who have
left imperishable traces in the fields of thought, religion, science,
philosophy and social idealism? There is no need to quote
names. You know as well as I do that without the Jews
(though they have been periodically decimated and thus deprived of potential geniuses whose number will never be known)
humanism and its highest hopes would not be what they are
today.*

*Judaism is not an accident, but a metaphysical attribute essen-
tial to the history of mankind. In spite of all superficial variations, the reactions to it will be the same to the end of time.
The Jews, sublimating what is best in themselves, must remain
faithful to the mission assigned to them on Mount Sinai—to
be a people of priests and righteous men in the service of all
others. In the age of the nuclear bomb, electronics, supersonic
aircraft and interstellar ballistics, everything possible must be
done to preserve them biologically and protect them spiritually.*

*Let your lonely crowds—including those in Israel, if you in-
sist—hurry toward what you call "happiness," let them lose
themselves in it, let them wander astray in the world-wide fairground of this fin de siècle, let them go to pieces in the crazy
pace of "normal" life. But keep a small place for our anxiety
and our tragedy. Keep some oases of Jewish anxiety, at any rate
in the Diaspora, just as in the natural world reserves are kept for
the protection of plant or animal life, gifts of the Creator, that
are threatened by man's stupid killings and the poison of his
towns; keep some reserves of salutary, fertile anxiety that may
produce the prophetic outbursts of which this technical world,
in bondage to new idols, has such need.*

You are right, we do not speak the same language. You have
not understood me. You have not noticed that this whole book
is riddled with anxiety.

Supplementary Notes

THE *MOSHAVIM*

In current Israeli usage the term *moshav* generally refers to a *moshav ovdim* (*moshavei ovdim*[1]), a co-operative village of small farmers run on the principles of equality and mutual aid. The Jewish National Fund grants each family a farm on a lease that is automatically renewable provided that the family works the farm itself without the aid of paid labor. Sale of the produce and purchases necessary for the running of the farm take place through a central co-operative. Some agricultural machinery is the property of the *moshav*. Authority is in the hands of a general meeting of the members, which elects a village council; the latter decides on the sale of farms and the admission of new members.

Similar to the *moshav ovdim* is the *moshav* (*moshavim*), often referred to as the "middle-class" village, in which the collective ideology is greatly relaxed. Villages of this type are largely inhabited by recent "oriental" immigrants who have been directed into farming, and they are consequently often known as *moshavei olim*, or "immigrant villages."

There is also the *moshava* (*moshavot*), or village of individual farmers, generally situated in the coastal region (cultivation of citrus fruits), whose status is similar to that of small peasant proprietors in France.

Finally, the *moshav shitufi* (*moshavim shitufim*) is based on joint ownership of land, like a *kibbutz*. But each family owns its own house and is responsible for its own domestic arrangements and for bringing up its children, as in a *moshav ovdim*, and can make free use of its share of the profits. This intermediate pattern between the *kibbutz* and the *moshav* is rare.

The Jewish agricultural population was in 1961 distributed as follows:

[1] The plural form is given in parentheses.

	Per cent
Moshava	29
Moshav ovdim or *moshav olim*	40
Moshav shitufi	1
Kibbutz	26
Transitional or training centers	4
	100

Like the *kibbutzim*, the *moshavim* are organized in federations, the chief of which, the Tnuat Hamoshavim, affiliated to the Histadrut, in 1964 included more than 300 co-operative villages, with a total population of about 100,000.

I have noted the important role that the *moshavim*, thanks to their modern methods and the progressive education of the younger generations, already play and will increasingly play in integrating into Israeli society a large proportion of "oriental" immigrants and solving the problems of the "second" Israel.

In 1964 the *moshav* movement was confronted with a serious crisis. A bill governing their status and the relations between their members aroused lively controversy among them, as well as in political and trade-union circles. Hitherto these matters had been governed by general consent on principles derived from the pioneers of the second *aliya*, which were closely related to the idealism of the founders of the *kibbutzim*, and subject to the free agreement of their members.[2] The only legal basis was the regulations applicable to co-operative societies promulgated under the British mandate more than thirty years before.

New legislation was made necessary by the economic and demographic changes that the *moshavim* had undergone and the crisis of pioneering values that was felt in them, as elsewhere. In the case of serious offenses (such as sale of co-operative produce on the private market or neglect of a farm) the bill proposed that repeated offenders who failed to yield to persuasion should be subject to a maximum penalty of exclusion from the *moshav* by the village council, with a right of appeal to an ordinary court. The promoters of the bill intended it as a measure to preserve the collectivist character

---

[2] The first *moshav ovdim* was established in 1920 at Nahalal by dissidents from Degania.

of the *moshav* movement in the new conditions of Israeli society. The bill in its original form was submitted to a committee of the Mapai presided over by the Minister of Justice, and was greatly amended. This is one of the areas in which "realists" and the left wing clash, and the fate of Israeli socialism depends on the issue.

THE ORGANIZATION OF THE HISTADRUT

In 1964 the Histadrut had 872,000 members, including wives, who have the same rights as members. Including families, 1,400,000 persons, that is to say, nearly two-thirds of the Jewish population, plus 50,000 Arabs, enjoy the benefits of membership. The three other trade-union federations seem very modest in comparison, and two of them are in practice affiliated with the Histadrut, which means that it has under its wing about nine-tenths of the Israeli working population. The Mizrahi movement, associated with the National Religious Party, the Hapoel Hamizrahi, has about 70,000 members, who subscribe to the Kupat Holim and are represented on its council. The same applies to the 27,000 members of the Poalei Agudat Israel, which is associated with the most conservative religious party. Only the National Federation of Labor (Histadrut Ha'ovdim Haleumit), founded in 1934 by the revisionist organization and having about 70,000 members, has an independent system of social services and mutual aid.

Ultimate authority in the Histadrut is theoretically in the hands of the convention, which is supposed to meet on an average of every four years. The number of delegates to the last convention (February 1960) was fixed at 801. Thanks to a carefully considered voting system and secrecy of the ballot, all the economic activities and shades of opinion of its members, it is claimed, are represented. The Mapai obtained a 55.4 per cent majority, represented by 444 delegates, and it holds most of the chief positions in the organization.

The convention elects a council of 322 members, in which the parties are represented in the same proportions, and the council in turn elects from among its members an executive council of 105 members. This council elects a central bureau of seventeen members for the day-to-day conduct of affairs. One of them is the general secretary of the Histadrut, who is one of the most important personages in the country. At present the post is held by Aaron Becker.

Each member of the central bureau is responsible for one or more departments, of which the principal are:

Trade-union affairs, including productivity, workers' health and an economic research and statistical office
Organization (co-ordination of local activities)
Employment
Integration of immigrants
Technical training
Mutual aid (co-ordination of social services)
The liberal professions
Arab affairs
Education and culture
International relations (with trade unions abroad)
Labor legislation
Finance

In spite of the spirit of co-ordination implicit in the program of these departments working on a national scale, the overcentralized organization of the Histadrut weighs heavily on its local organizations. The crisis through which it is now going, some aspects of which we have studied, indicates the necessity of structural changes.

THE LAVON GROUP AND THE LAVON AFFAIR

I have several times mentioned the Lavon group (Min Hayesod, "of the base"), formed round Pinhas Lavon, who during the early years of the state was one of the most influential leaders of the Mapai after Ben-Gurion, its famous and authoritarian leader.

The origin and *raison d'être* of the group was the "Lavon affair," which poisoned Israeli political life like a malignant tumor for more than ten years.

The "affair," as it is generally called in Israel, arose out of a shady and fantastic-sounding secret-service story dating from 1954. A series of sabotage operations intended, among other things, to blow up an American cultural center in Cairo and some movie houses showing Hollywood films (the blame for these outrages was to be attributed to the Egyptians) ended in a lamentable fiasco, and Lavon, then Defense Minister, was held responsible by Ben-Gurion. I shall make no attempt to describe the political and judicial repercussions, a detailed account of which would easily fill a fat volume, but will leave the task to some future historian. Who "gave the order"? The Minister or the head of the secret service? A number of parliamentary committees successively exonerated Lavon, and finally in 1960 a committee of seven ministers did the same, but nevertheless in 1961 Lavon, under pressure from Ben-Gurion and his friends, had to resign from his post as general secretary of the Histadrut and all his offices in the Mapai. The most important recent developments have been the decision of Levi Eshkol, defying the grand old man's opposition, to put an end to Lavon's quarantine; the reopening of the affair at the end of October 1964 by Ben-Gurion, who emerged from his *kibbutz* in the Negev to go to Jerusalem and submit to the Minister of Justice a dossier which he claimed was supported by new facts; the immediate secession from the Mapai of the Lavon group (November 7) in reply to this, and its formation of a new labor party (the fourth in Israel), the Min Hayesod; and the resignation of Eshkol, who was opposed to the reopening of the "affair," and his prompt return to power (December 23, 1964), which was a grave setback to Ben-Gurion.

Lavon, now sixty-three is a brilliant speaker and a strong and controversial personality, and he has succeeded in attracting some distinguished men, among them the philosopher Professor Nathan Rotenstreich of the Hebrew University of Jerusalem. The group has established a political platform and acquired an audience among some intellectuals and *kibbutznikim*. It was involved in interminable Byzantine negotiations between the three socialist parties concerned with the possibility of unification. The 1965 elections, however, far from bringing this about, confirmed the split in the Mapai and led to the birth of a fifth party of the left, Ben-Gurion's Rafi; Ben-Gurion took Shimon Peres with him. These squabbles have been inflamed by the stubbornness of the old Mapai leader, to whom the "affair" is a question of justice and morality involving the very foundations of the state. They were condemned by personalities coming from very different environments for wasting ministers' time and constituting an unpardonable luxury in a country that ought to be devoting all its vital energies to its economic growth and security.

THE "SILENCES" OF PIUS XII

Having come across the problem of the "silences" of Pius XII in connection with the great massacre, let me content myself with a few remarks here. Rolf Hochhuth's play *Der Stellvertreter* ("The Deputy"), which must be read in full if it is to be judged fairly, created a sensation throughout the world; and rightly, because Hochhuth had the courage to remind those who were only too happy to forget it of the Jewish tragedy of 1940–45. With the aid of solid research he resuscitated the chief individuals who planned it and carried it out under orders from the Nazi leaders, and he forced the Catholic Church to ask itself questions that it ought to have faced in broad daylight nearly twenty years earlier.

The young German dramatist's play is not a masterpiece. Its principal weakness is the picture it gives of Pius XII, which is oversimplified to the point of caricature; it would have been better not to have put him on the stage at all. Nevertheless it is based on an assemblage of facts whose historical correctness has not been impugned, either by learned discussions, protests or indignant or contemptuous comments. During the Second World War six million Jews were massacred in Christian countries, and the Supreme Pontiff did not publicly protest against this crime. I have read many opinions expressed by Christians of various denominations, including those by the Rev. Father Riquet who, although he was himself deported by the Nazis, contents himself in the face of this complex and highly intricate problem with stigmatizing Hochhuth's "imposture," rejecting "sneers at Catholicism," and using arguments and excuses that bypass or circle the point at issue without ever touching on it.[3] If one grants Father Riquet that "he [Hochhuth] has failed above all to understand the solidarity that in the Church of Christ unites the members to the head and causes an affront to the latter to be felt by all," how can one hope for a free and independent opinion on a Pope's behavior from any member of the Church, whether priest or lay? "Papolatry is a popular cult, but is it really a Catholic one?"[4]

On the Church side the most significant answer, implying all the others, was the letter addressed to the British Catholic weekly *The Tablet* by Cardinal Montini on the eve of his election to the Holy See. The future Pope Paul VI expressed himself in terms that were very vigorous and sometimes actually lacking in serenity; they created the impression that, having been the colleague of Cardinal Pacelli

[3] *Le Figaro*, December 17, 1964; lecture at the Cercle Interallic, April 10, 1964 (*Le Monde*, April 12–13).

[4] J.F., *Le Monde*, December 17, 1963.

(the Secretary of State and future Pope), he felt himself to be personally involved. In the last resort the only argument that he put forward was that of the lesser evil:[5]

Let us suppose that Pius XII had done what Hochhuth blames him for not doing. His action would have led to such reprisals and devastations that Hochhuth himself, the war being over and he now possessed of a bitter historical, political and moral judgment, would have been able to write another play, far more realistic and far more interesting than the one that he has in fact so cleverly but also so ineptly put together: a play, that is, about the *Stellvertreter* who, through political exhibitionism or psychological myopia, would have been guilty of unleashing on the already tormented world still greater calamities involving innumerable innocent victims, let alone himself.

It would be as well if the creative imagination of playwrights insufficiently endowed with historical discernment (and possibly, though please God it is not so, with ordinary human integrity) would forbear from trifling with subjects of this kind and with historical personages whom some of us have known.

The letter (though in full it runs to a considerable length) presents no facts in reply to the questions raised by the dramatist, but puts forward a defense of Pius XII based (apart from an emotional eulogy of his character and a discreet hint of his saintliness) primarily on the categorical claim that his silence was the lesser evil. A careful reading makes it seem very doubtful whether the cardinal had read the play. He indignantly condemned a sacrilegious onslaught his only knowledge of which seems to have been based on press reports and articles.

The future Paul VI, who is more "Pacellian" than "Roncallian," (to quote Pastor Pierre Bourguet's striking expression in connection with the encyclical *Ecclesiam suam*), appeared to maintain that a Supreme Pontiff who ran the risk of denouncing Nazi crimes to the whole Christian world would have been guilty of "political exhibitionism" or "psychological myopia." It is a harsh judgment. But what is it based on? "What do we know"[6] after all? What does Paul

---

[5] *The Tablet,* June 29, 1963. Cardinal Montini's starting point was a previous article in that journal on "Pius XII and the Jews" (May 11, 1963).

[6] Title of an article by Rémy Roure, *Le Figaro,* December 30, 1963.

VI know himself? He has produced no evidence and can produce none. No historical precedent can be produced either way. But can it not be maintained that no compromise between the two camps, no political calculation, no *"raison d'Église"*[7] ought in these exceptional circumstances to have prevented the "successor of Peter," the "Vicar of Christ," from raising his voice in protest? That, underlying the harrowing controversies aroused by *The Deputy*, was the deep feeling of many Christians, in whose eyes the Church in its 2000-year-old history has had the honor of not always having so stubbornly rejected the call of conscience and the way of martyrdom.

The publication of diplomatic archives, in particular German and American reports and the notes of the Papal Secretariat of State,[8] will make possible a more sober and dispassionate judgment of this painful process. What role was played in the temporizing attitude of Pius XII by his obsessive fear of Europe's, and particularly Italy's, being overrun by Communism, his experience of Hitler's reactions during the years when he was Nuncio in Berlin, combined with a certain admiration for and sympathy with Germany? The documents published by Saul Friedländer (who very creditably completely effaced himself behind them) contribute some solidly-based evidence on these matters.[9] According to von Bergen, the German ambassador, the information about the extermination of Polish Jews submitted to the Vatican by the allies and the Jewish Agency was regarded by Pius XII as "exaggerated," though its reliability was confirmed by German Jesuits in his entourage. The State Department has published a telegram dated January 5, 1943, addressed to Cordell Hull, the Secretary of State, by Harrison, his minister in Berne. The letter reported a dispatch from Harold Tittmann, assistant to Myron Taylor, President Roosevelt's personal representative at the Vatican. On the eve of delivering his 1942 Christmas message, Pius XII received Mr. Tittmann, who reported their conversation as follows:[10]

> With regard to his Christmas message, the Pope gave me the impression that he was sincere in believing that he had spoken therein clearly enough to satisfy all those who had been insisting

[7] J. M. Domenach, *Esprit*, February 1964.

[8] The Vatican has so far refused to open its archives for reasons indicated by Jacques Nobécourt (*Le Monde*, November 21, 1964).

[9] *Pie XII et le IIIième Reich*, Éditions du Seuil, Paris, 1964. (English translation *Pius XII and the Third Reich*, Knopf, New York, 1966.)

[10] *Ibid.* (English trans.), p. 133.

in the past that he utter some word of condemnation of the Nazi atrocities, and he seemed surprised when I told him that I thought there were some who did not share his belief.

He said that he thought it was plain to everyone that he was referring to the Poles, Jews and hostages when he declared that hundreds of thousands of persons had been killed or tortured through no fault of their own, sometimes only because of their race or nationality.

He explained that when talking of atrocities he could not name the Nazis without at the same time mentioning the Bolsheviks and this he thought might not be wholly pleasing to the allies. He stated that he "feared" that there was foundation for the atrocity reports of the allies but led me to believe that there had been some exaggeration for purposes of propaganda.

As Jacques Nobécourt wrote when publishing an extract from this document, "The Pope obviously wished to put a full stop to allied representations aimed at inducing him openly to condemn the Hitler regime and its crimes against the Jews."[11]

[11] Le Monde, June 14–15, 1964.

SHORT GLOSSARY OF HEBREW TERMS

*Plurals of masculine nouns end in *im*, feminine in *ot*.

Aliya ("Ascent") Wave of immigration to Israel.

Bar-mitzva Boy aged at least thirteen called on to practice religious observances like an adult; by extension, the synagogue service that consecrates him in this state.

Galut The Exile.

Garinim (from *garin*, "nucleus") Members aged about twenty of a youth movement that prepares them for *kibbutz* life.

Gola The dispersion or Diaspora.

Haganah ("Defense") The principal Jewish armed force under the mandate.

Halacha (in the religious sense) Basic religious doctrine having the force of law.

Halutz ("Pioneer") Founder of agricultural communities before the creation of the state of Israel.

Hanoar Ha'oved Vehalomed ("Student and Working Youth") Histadrut youth movement.

Hashomer Hatzair ("Young Guardian") Zionist youth movement that founded the Artzi *kibbutz* in 1927.

Haver ("Member") Indicates primarily membership of an agricultural community, *kibbutz* or *moshav*.

Hevrat Ovdim ("Workers' association") Organized by the Histadrut.

Ihud Hakvutzot Vehakibbutzim "Unification of *kvutzot* and *kibbutzim*," one of the three principal federations of *kibbutzim*.

Kashrut Total of dietary laws under the Mosaic law.

Kipah Ritual skullcap.

Knesset ("Place of assembly") The Israeli parliament.

Kolel (plural *kolalim*) Scholar devoted for an unlimited period to the speculative study of the Torah and the Talmud.

Kupat Holim ("Sick Fund") Organized by the Histadrut.

Kvutza ("Group") Refers to the earliest pioneers of agricultural communities; often used as a synonym for *kibbutz*.

Ma'abara ("Place of passage") Transit camp for new immigrants.

Matza Unleavened bread eaten at Passover.

Min Hayesod ("Of the base")   Pinhas Lavon's group.

Mitzva In the religious sense "observance"; in the moral sense "good deed."

Nahal (initials of the Hebrew words for "Combatant Pioneering Youth")   For the role of this organization in the Israeli army see pp. 26–28.

Olim (plural of *olè*)   "Those who ascend" to Israel, immigrants.

Palmah (initials of the Hebrew words for "Assault troops")   Commandos of the Haganah.

Shalom ("Peace")   A greeting.

Shehita Ritual slaughter.

Sheirut ("Service")   Collective taxicab service.

Shikun Dwelling house.

Shofar Ram's horn used in important Jewish services.

Taref Not in conformity with the *kashrut*.

Tnuva ("Harvest")   Organization that collects and sells agricultural products in the socialist sector.

Treifa (noun of *taref*)   Non-kosher food.

Ulpan School giving intensive instruction in Hebrew.

Vatik ("Old")   A veteran in relation to a newcomer.

Yeshiva Religious high school.

Yishuv The Jewish community in Palestine under the mandate.

Zaddik ("The righteous")   Title given by his congregation to an especially venerated rabbi.